Carry On Regardless

Carry On Regardless

Getting to the Bottom of Britain's Favourite Comedy Films

Caroline Frost

WHITE OWL
AN IMPRINT OF PEN & SWORD BOOKS LTD.
YORKSHIRE – PHILADELPHIA

First published in Great Britain in 2022 by
White Owl
An imprint of
Pen & Sword Books Ltd
Yorkshire – Philadelphia

Copyright © Caroline Frost 2022

ISBN 978 1 52677 478 1

Printed and bound in the UK by CPI Group (UK) Ltd,
Croydon, CR0 4YY.

Pen & Sword Books Limited incorporates the imprints of Atlas,
Archaeology, Aviation, Discovery, Family History, Fiction, History,
Maritime, Military, Military Classics, Politics, Select, Transport,
True Crime, Air World, Frontline Publishing, Leo Cooper, Remember
When, Seaforth Publishing, The Praetorian Press, Wharncliffe
Local History, Wharncliffe Transport, Wharncliffe True Crime
and White Owl.

For a complete list of Pen & Sword titles please contact

PEN & SWORD BOOKS LIMITED
47 Church Street, Barnsley, South Yorkshire, S70 2AS, England
E-mail: enquiries@pen-and-sword.co.uk
Website: www.pen-and-sword.co.uk

Or

PEN AND SWORD BOOKS
1950 Lawrence Rd, Havertown, PA 19083, USA
E-mail: Uspen-and-sword@casematepublishers.com
Website: www.penandswordbooks.com

Contents

Introduction

The sight of a handsome young man inexplicably attached to a rogue trolley careering down a hospital staircase and out through the swinging doors, the sound of a scantily-clad young lady's squeals as she bolts into the bushes to spare her blushes, the glint of Charles Hawtrey's round glasses always the same style whatever the era, Kenneth Williams's indignant, crisp tones and of course, the conspiratorial chuckle of Sid James...

These are just a few of the elements that instantly identify one of the British public's great viewing pleasures – escaping for ninety light-hearted minutes into a world of very British nonsense, deceptively straightforward storylines, familiar faces, mayhem-inducing misfits, vanquished snobberies, rescued romances, a myriad of misunderstandings and frequently foiled capers – in short, the world of Carry On. For many, it's a world that's never lost its comfort, charm and appeal, whatever more modern critics might have to say. And it's a world that, four decades after the gates at Pinewood Studios closed for the final time on cast and crew (let's draw a veil over the 1992 reboot, for a while at least), deserves a fresh look – if only because, however easy they all made it appear, the team's extraordinary success has in all those years never been repeated.

This isn't a book of facts and figures, nor any attempt at a film-by-film compendium, although, to be sure, the franchise statistics remain impressive. To this day, there still haven't yet been as many Bond films as Carry Ons, and 007 does not enjoy anything like the same profit-per-pound ratio. Nor will this attempt to cover the wealth of extra-curricular material, whether that be TV compilations, Christmas specials, plays, novels or even cartoons, that have all kept the flame burning in the many years since the film cameras stopped rolling. Nor am I even going to delve into the mechanics of *That's Carry On!* with its Greatest Hits-style compendium of all the other titles up to that point. There are already plenty of those fact-filled tomes, thanks to the tireless efforts of Robert Ross, Morris Bright and co, containing more than enough to keep a firm fan quiet on a rainy Sunday afternoon, plus a whole bunch of devoted aficionados competing for the title of ultimate expert in the field.

Instead, what this offers is a celebration of a big screen phenomenon, a golden moment in cinema when cast and crew, stars and writers, came together at the right time and place, to create something unique – not just in the history of British film, but across our broader culture.

I'll be asking, what was it about the Carry On films that captured the hearts of their audiences, and held onto them across thirty films and two decades? Was it the scripts, that effortlessly moved between the muddy earthiness of a camping site in post-war Britain to the wobbly grandeur of ancient Egypt, from a suburban London police station to a frankly unconvincing Revolutionary-era France, all these locations united by the potential on every page for our collective sense of the ridiculous? Or was it the cast, whose deceptively easy chemistry belied the professionalism of a versatile troupe honed by years of treading the boards and the disciplinary demands of repertory theatre, radio and blossoming TV?

Or were audiences just hungry for something on screen that held a magnifying glass up to some of our most revered institutions and figures – the NHS, James Bond, the military, Henry VIII, the police, Cleopatra – and then warmly tipped a wink and cocked a snook, wringing gags, giggles and groans from the unlikeliest of places?

If the series' golden age in the late 1960s saw its list of locations broaden, from the Khyber to the Kasbah, the Sahara desert to the high seas, its humour remained entirely British in both sensibility and silliness, bridging two distinctive eras of homegrown comedy. The first Carry On film in 1958 hoped to entertain audiences brought up on highly visual gags, slapstick and farce. By the time it finished two decades later, the series was known for its more risqué elements, with its constant use of double entendre and general leaning on far saucier seaside-postcard ribaldry.

That increasing ripeness through the years is one of the reasons these films – often grouped as one entity, despite the nuances of this gradual evolution – fall down in the eyes of many modern critics. They cite their lack of political correctness, and worse, abundance of cliché and implicit laziness of everyone involved.

Another complaint is the lack of representation on screen. The hospital titles throughout the series enjoyed many jokes at the expense of the blossoming NHS, while overlooking the huge contribution made by nurses from all over the Commonwealth. It wasn't until 1970 that popular entertainer Kenny Lynch appeared, and then only fleetingly, as a bus conductor in *Carry On Loving*. A full three years later, stunning actress Pauline Peart's role in *Carry On Girls* was even smaller.

The Carry Ons were as limited in this respect as almost every other British film of the era. When the central premise of much mainstream comedy was the belief that anybody deemed 'foreign' was somehow worthy of mockery, the series was a product of its time. Like so many other titles of the period, these films would no doubt be cast very differently were they to be made today. Audiences and attitudes rightly change, and so do filmmakers.

But some of the criticisms of outrageous sexism, unacceptable racism and other casual bigotries directed specifically at the Carry On series don't stand up to proper inspection. As we will discover, many of the films' storylines see displays of sexism, racism, class snobbery and other old-fashioned prejudices utterly undone in the telling. While the films are tireless champions of mayhem and innocent mischief, any really serious campaigns of ill intent, whether romantic, criminal or just mean-spirited, are invariably foiled. And no one ever, ever gets the better of Hattie Jacques.

As for cliché, it's easy to see why a modern viewer might think that. We've seen variations of the Carry On gags and set-ups a million times since, but what we have to remember is that Carry On did them first. These people were pioneers, breaking the mould of comedy, influencing their contemporaries as well as all who followed. But if they've been much imitated, when it comes to timing, delivery and memorable punchlines, they've never been bettered. Their legacy is secure.

If you still need persuading, well, I'll have fun in the trying. So with thirty films to get through, we'd better begin to carry on...

Chapter 1

How It All Began

'The Bull Boys'

It's a chilly but sunny Friday morning in August 2020, and I'm driving to Pinewood Studios, which means turning off the A40 just before it becomes a motorway. I'm coming from Ealing, and as I enjoy the trees and fields on either side of me, I revel in the fact that I'm retracing the route Sid James must have taken to work so many times when he lived in a house two streets away from mine, his front wall marked these days with a blue historic plaque.

The site of Pinewood Studios is enormous; a military-like compound with tight security and precise instructions as to where to park and who to meet. I look around and see huge buildings, fleets of service vehicles and teams of people milling about, all there to play their unique role in the British film industry. I've been given a map and realise that, quite without knowing it, I'm already standing on Peter Rogers Way.

A couple of turns and I'm standing in front of the main doors of Heatherden Hall. Although this Victorian country house is dwarfed by so many of the buildings around it, it's clear that it remains the beating heart of Pinewood Studios, and it's gratifying to see that the plaques lining its huge porch belong to Gerald Thomas, his brother Ralph, Peter Rogers and his wife Betty, and that this talented quartet has never been forgotten.

On the other side of the road is a long hallway leading to more buildings instantly familiar to Carry On fans, whether as a hospital corridor, a school hall or whatever use the always canny Peter could find for it.

It is in this hallway that the Carry On stars are celebrated – Sid's plaque sits above Hattie's, Kenneth is naturally paired with Charles, Kenneth Connor is with Peter Butterworth, while Terry Scott shares a wall with Bernard Bresslaw. Joan Sims is there too, for the moment by herself. Although the films are remembered elsewhere in one of Heatherden Hall's many galleries, this is a light, airy space, with lots of sunlight pouring through the windows, and it delights me to see these names, as familiar as cousins, sitting so prominently in one of Pinewood's central thoroughfares.

They stay with me while I wander through the mansion's back garden, its immaculate lawn recognisable from dozens of Carry On films, as well as James Bond, *Doctor in the House*, even the more recent Elton John biopic *Rocketman*, and then through some of the enormous sound stages that have ensured the studios' enduring reputation as the place where every director in the world wants to work. I make my way as far as the space where the grass was painted green for *Carry On Camping* over half a century ago and wonder, not for the first time: how would the series and its stars fare in the Pinewood of today?

'The past is a foreign country. They do things differently there' – at least according to anybody who reaches for LP Hartley's words to describe an era of British life and its collective way of thinking and behaving, now seemingly forever lost.

Well, to this, I throw down the gauntlet and say, do they really? Because it seems to me that for every facet or foible that seems unique to its era, there is an equally timeless counterpoint, capacity or sensibility that would appear to defy restrictions to this or any age.

Specifically, was 1958, the year of the first ever Carry On film, really so different from today? For sure, we may no longer have the stomach to poke fun at our national institutions – many would argue we no longer need fictional filmmakers to point out their many absurdities, they're doing a fine job of that all by themselves – but to this day, and I hope evermore, we retain the capacity, social duty even, to laugh at each other, with each other and, most importantly, at ourselves.

Carry On, more than any other series in history, took on the task of providing a big screen framework for Britain's official national pastime, namely taking the mickey. The longer the series ran, the bigger the task became of tweaking the creative funny bone in accordance with real life's social revolutions and evolutions. To see how far the series had to travel, we have to go back to discover just how foreign was that country when the Carry On films made their arrival more than six decades ago.

Universally, the Space Race was on, as the start of the year saw Explorer 1, America's first successful satellite, launched into orbit, less than a month after its Soviet rival Sputnik 1 fell to Earth.

Down on our planet, Nikita Kruschev became Premier of the Soviet Union, while his US counterpart, President Dwight D. Eisenhower, became the first American elected official to be broadcast on colour television.

The European Economic Community was properly formed, but the British would find their membership blocked by French president Charles de Gaulle, who won his national election the same year with 78 per cent of the vote.

In America, a prodigious 14-year-old schoolboy named Bobby Fischer won the US Chess Championship; Pizza Hut opened its doors for the first time in Wichita, Kansas; Muppet Man Jim Henson created his own entertainment company; and Elvis Presley joined the Army.

The winners of that year's football world cup were Brazil, and Pope Pius XII declared Saint Clare the patron saint of television.

Back at home, football fans everywhere grieved for Manchester United after the Munich Air Disaster killed eight of the team and injured their manager Matt Busby.

The Queen gave her eldest son Charles the title of Prince of Wales, while her husband the Duke of Edinburgh opened the London Planetarium. The last debutantes were presented to royalty, before the ceremony was abolished. Far away from court, Bertrand Russell launched the Campaign for Nuclear Disarmament.

The Prime Minister Harold McMillan opened Britain's first motorway, the Preston Bypass – later to become part of the M6 and M55 – and the first parking meters were also installed in the UK.

The BBC created the Radiophonic Workshop and in October, two long-running TV shows made their broadcast debut, *Grandstand* for sports fans and *Blue Peter* for the rest of us.

Cliff Richard's debut single 'Move It' reached number two in the charts, while a a little-known Liverpool band called The Quarrymen paid 17 shillings and six pence to record their first tracks – a cover of Buddy Holly's 'That'll Be The Day', as well as 'In Spite of All the Danger', an original song written by two of their line-up, Paul and George.

For us Brits, there was a lot to sing about. Economic growth was steady throughout the decade, although not as speedy as on the Continent. The long-time Conservative government continued the welfare state policies set out by Clement Attlee's Labour government of the late 1940s, which saw the number of private and council housing estates increasing and slum dwellings diminishing.

The average British weekly wage for manual jobs was £12 13s 6d, and unemployment was relatively low, at around 2 per cent over the course of the 1950s.

For most, the standard of living remained consistently on the up as prosperity slowly returned. In 1958, four years after the end of wartime rationing and with hire-purchase controls relaxed at the same time, holidays and hobbies became accessible to many for the first time.

Increasing numbers of us jumped into new cars for family adventures, often spent in newly popular holiday camps, while at home we saved up for life-enhancing inventions like washing machines, vacuum cleaners and electric fires. The Queen's Coronation in 1953 inspired millions to splash out on a television set for the first time, and most homes already had the wireless and the gramophone to spin our burgeoning collections of 78rpm records.

Only a year before, Harold McMillan had told his 50 million citizens, 'You've never had it so good,' and with the brand new invention of fish fingers on our plates, it would be difficult to disagree with him.

For the young and fancy-free, there were plenty of ways to spend their new-found spare cash. It was the era of jive, skiffle and rock and roll, which meant that dance halls and other stomping venues were bustling wall to wall with the decade's other great invention, the teenager. And, if you couldn't squeeze in there, well, there was always a trip to the pictures.

The two most popular types of film at the time were the British military epic championing the valour of our wartime homegrown heroes, and the comedy revelling in more attainable but eccentric daydreams.

1950s audiences had already watched the triumphant stories of Guy Gibson and Douglas Bader, told in the unashamedly patriotic *The Dam Busters* and *Reach for the Sky*.

In 1957, David Lean's *The Bridge on the River Kwai* became UK cinema's biggest international success of the decade, proving the appetite for a nostalgic wallow in British former greatness wasn't limited to our shores.

Greatness of a much less heroic type was on offer by our comedic stars of the same period, including Norman Wisdom, Peter Sellers and Alec Guinness. With enduring titles including *The Lavender Hill Mob*, *The Ladykillers* and *Kind Hearts and Coronets*, Ealing Studios carried the baton for the nation's funniest films, at least until 1955 when the BBC moved in. Three years later, British comedy would carry on(!) in its new, more enduring home, thirteen miles up the Western Avenue at Pinewood.

Admittedly, we lost some of our biggest names to the American studios during this era, both in front of the camera and behind. Directors including Carol Reed, Alberto Cavalcanti and Robert Hamer all decamped to make their fortunes in Hollywood, while the faces of some of our finest stars such as James Mason, Deborah Kerr, Stewart Granger and Jean Simmons soon graced the billboards above Sunset Boulevard.

But we kept many more. Big names like Michael Redgrave, Laurence Olivier and Dirk Bogarde joined those of Jack Hawkins, Richard Todd and Kenneth More above the bill, while Diana Dors proved America didn't have a monopoly on the blonde femme fatale.

Most significantly for this book, huge audiences during the 1950s ensured successful return business for both romantic comedies like *Doctor in the House*, and for the thrills provided by Peter Cushing, Christopher Lee and their fellow residents of the Hammer House of Horror. Whether we were laughing loudly along in the cinema, or pinned to our seats with fear, it seems we couldn't resist the return to the screen of increasingly famous, familiar faces – fangs optional.

It was against this background that the acorn of an idea was first sown, one that nobody could have any idea would grow and blossom into Britain's largest ever film franchise, and run with barely a blip for the next two decades. Twenty-five years later, in 1983, William Goldman brought every aspiring filmmaker some kind of bleak reassurance when he wrote in his industry bible *Adventures in the Screen Trade*, 'Nobody knows anything... Not one person in the entire motion picture field knows for a certainty what's going to work. Every time out it's a guess and, if you're lucky, an educated one.'

Despite this almost certainly true maxim, if anybody could claim to know exactly what he was doing, it must be Peter Rogers, the man who brought the first Carry On film into being and ruled over his ensuing franchise like a benevolent dictator. He always said that no one person was above the bill, 'Carry On itself is the star,' but if it is anybody's theoretical baby, it is surely his. What on earth inspired him to do it, how did he manage it, and what was unique about him that meant he succeeded in pulling off something almost unimaginable?

An initial dip into Peter Rogers's background, with his comfortable, conventional childhood in Rochester, Kent, would appear to give little to indicate what a colossus of the British film industry he would become, although his first show of professional rebellion might give us a clue.

Having grown up with two brothers who followed their father Claude into his licensing business, Peter was expected to do the same. At first, he did try to toe the family line but his more creative passions soon trumped the wishes of his father, who reluctantly agreed to support him while he turned his hand to writing plays. His mother Alice was far more encouraging, despite Peter receiving constant rejection letters for his efforts, but she died in 1944 and he found himself ejected from the family home when his father remarried.

Perhaps this lack of family support early on explains Peter's tireless creative drive in the years that followed, but the time he spent desperately unwell in his mid-twenties surely had even more to do with it. He had expected to follow his brothers into wartime service, but instead, aged just 26, he was struck down by cerebral spinal meningitis, a debilitating illness which he was extremely lucky to survive. As it was, he was confined to a hospital bed for nearly a year. When he finally recovered, his biographers report, 'Peter, who was not a religious man, blessed whoever had looked down on him and saved him. He was determined more than ever now to make a success of his life.'

And succeed he did. Post-war, his resumed playwriting found an audience, on BBC radio at least. Having previously worked as a journalist, he was given the job of scriptwriter at the religious film company of J. Arthur Rank, a man as devout a Christian as he was pioneering in the British film industry. As Peter later reflected, 'There was Methodism in his madness!' This unit was soon closed, but this was an era when fortune favoured a young man prepared to work hard in London, and Peter was clearly no slouch. He got a new job with the *World Press News*, where his assignments included editing the film page. This meant attending screenings and other functions in the West End, which is where he met his future wife, Betty Box.

If there is one element of luck to counter all of the ambition, effort and talent in Peter Rogers's story, it must be his first encounter with Betty and the social circle that he happily joined as a result, and at such a formative moment in his career. Betty was already an established name in the British film industry, along with her older brother Sydney, who had a scriptwriting Oscar to his name for *The Seventh Veil*. By the time Peter met the talented pair, Sydney had been drafted by J. Arthur Rank to run Gainsborough Studios. By virtue of his quickly blossoming relationship with Betty, Peter became one of the Box inner ring, alongside Betty, plus Sydney and his wife Muriel, a group united by their great love of film. Peter became quick to offer Sydney script ideas, and before long Sydney offered him a full-time scriptwriting contract at his new Studio. After all those years hopelessly sending off script after script from his home in Kent, Peter was finally in the room with people who could bring his ideas to life, and it wasn't an opportunity he would squander.

For financial reasons, Gainsborough was soon forced to shut its doors. By the early 1950s, the team were based instead at Pinewood Studios, a semi-rural retreat deep in Buckinghamshire's bosom of Iver Heath, a leafy location whose surroundings would become deeply familiar to Carry On audiences in the decades that followed.

For now, Peter was hard at work trying to make commercial successes out of his catalogue of ideas, and making the transition from scriptwriter to producer. In this he was advised and inspired by the success of his wife Betty – the couple had married in 1948 – who operated out of an office next to his. She spent her time making box office triumphs for the Rank Organisation, including *The Clouded Yellow*, starring Trevor Howard. Significantly for us, this was her first time collaborating with director Ralph Thomas (remember that name!), who had previously worked for her brother Sydney. Betty and Ralph would go on to enjoy a working partnership that lasted more than thirty years and included such big screen hits as *Appointment with Venus* (1951), *A Day to Remember* (1953) and the incredibly successful *Doctor in the House* (1954) and all its sequels.

Meanwhile, Peter battled with various projects such as *You Know What Sailors Are!* and *To Dorothy a Son*, stars including a delightful Kenneth More and a slightly more demanding Shelley Winters, and other industry executives. Prior to Carry On, his biggest success was the TV series *Ivanhoe*, which starred Roger Moore and whose most memorable element is probably its catchy theme tune.

If the ambitious producer was struggling, being part of a supportive creative circle meant he knew where to look for help. Inspired by his wife's success with her director Ralph Thomas, he asked her if he could create the same kind of partnership with her then editor, Ralph's younger brother Gerald.

In the story of Carry On, the only person who could argue for equal top billing with Peter Rogers is Gerald Thomas, the cool-as-a-cucumber director of every single one of the titles in the series.

Originally from Hull, in the then East Riding of Yorkshire, Gerald had originally set his heart on a career in medicine, before his studies and aspirations were interrupted by wartime duties. Following service for the Royal Sussex Regiment in Germany, France and the Middle East, he returned home and changed direction to film, initially working in the post-production rooms at Denham Studios.

He was quickly able to build up an impressive CV as an assistant editor, cutting Laurence Olivier in *Hamlet*, John Mills in *The October Man* and Margaret Lockwood in *Madness of the Heart*. He was even courted by Disney to edit *The Sword and the Rose*. By the time he returned to Pinewood to work on his brother's romantic comedy *Doctor in the House*, he was regarded as one of the country's finest editors.

He was unproven as a director, however, until Peter Rogers gave him his break. Peter and Gerald made their collaborative debut with a children's film called *Circus Friends*, and then with an adaptation of Arthur Hailey's *Time Lock*. Given only a tiny budget to play with, Peter brought all his creative skills to bear in making the production look more luxurious than it was, while Gerald succeeded in bringing the film in on time and on budget, a feat he would repeat with astonishing consistency in the decades to follow. *Time Lock* was a hit, and the pair's combined efforts would serve as the rock-solid template for all their future work together, not least the Carry Ons.

Peter had also written the script for *Time Lock*, but what he really wanted was a full-time contracted writer to complete his line-up for future projects. Norman Hudis was his man.

Born in Stepney, East London, Norman always credited a film for his first ideas to be a writer, or at least a journalist. The film was *This Man is News*, a comedy mystery about a reporter who has to solve a crime for which he himself is suspected. It was one of Britain's box office hits of 1938 and starred Barry K. Barnes and Valerie Hobson. Thus inspired,

Norman began his career aged 16 as a newspaperman on his local title, the *Hampstead and Highgate Express*.

Like Gerald, Norman found his first professional ideas thwarted by the war. He joined the RAF on his 18th birthday and spent most of the next five years as a telephone operator in England and the Middle East. In Egypt, he began writing for the *Air Force News* from their main office in Cairo, and also started coming across real-life personalities that would later turn up in his Carry On scripts. It was in the RAF that Norman encountered buffoonish characters of authority, men he called 'gruff grandpas' – figures we would see springing up frequently in his later work.

Back in Britain after the war, Norman joined the publicity department of J. Arthur Rank. His job – championing British films across the world by getting their pictures in magazines – took him from Rank's London office to studios in Islington, Denham and finally, Pinewood.

By Norman's admission, he stayed in this role for 'too long', seven years in fact, before he felt inclined to pen his own work. His play *Here is the News*, all about a press room operating in a country under dictatorship, was finally performed in repertory and enjoyed enough critical acclaim to bring him to the attention of Rank's executive producer Earl St John, who had funnily enough produced *This Man is News*, Norman's original professional inspiration.

Earl St John was sufficiently impressed to offer Norman a job as a trainee scriptwriter, but not sufficiently impressed to put any of his words into production. After two years of throwing ideas up in the air, Norman went freelance where he became a prolific writer of 'B' features.

This was an efficient production business model whereby American producers paid for cast and script, and got the rights to the whole Western Hemisphere. British companies made the film in three weeks or less and cleared a tidy profit. Before television came along, this was a lucrative, efficient exercise. Once television arrived, it all but disappeared.

Fortunately, before that happened, Norman found he had a proper hit on his hands, *The Tommy Steele Story*, made at Beaconsfield Studios in 1957. Once this low-budget no-brainer became a multi-million pound box office success, Peter Rogers, long convinced of Norman's talent, took a much safer bet on his screenwriting power and offered him a full-time seven-year contract. Norman's first task? To write another film for Tommy Steele, this time a musical called *The Duke Wore Jeans*. In better news, this would be Norman's first film to be directed by Gerald Thomas. The pair worked well together, and the great success of the film augured well for future projects.

There they were then, the complete creative trio, suited, booted and ready for work. All they needed was a project, and that presented itself in 1957, when an unsolicited script arrived on Peter's desk.

The title was *The Bull Boys*, the story of a couple of ballet dancers conscripted into army service. In writer R.F. Delderfield's hands, it was a straight romantic drama with little to distinguish it from hundreds of other scripts, and nobody seemed to want a bar of it. Even when French film star Leslie Caron's name was waved around in relation to possible casting for the lead, Sydney Box who had owned the rights originally, couldn't raise anybody's interest, which is why he passed it Peter's way.

Peter thought it might work better as a comedy, but he had equally bad luck trying to get the big writers of the time to look at it, with Ray Galton, Alan Simpson, Eric Sykes and Spike Milligan all turning him down. The producer turned to another funnyman, John Antrobus, who accordingly came up with some jaunty enough separate scenes, but Peter was after a more logical complete narrative. He told his biographers, 'Rightly or wrongly, I have always felt that audiences like to believe in their comedy.'

Instead, he turned to somebody already on his books, Norman Hudis, with one simple instruction: make it into a proper comedy.

Norman sat down with Peter and Gerald Thomas and between them they sketched out something that sounds so obvious in hindsight, so simple and yet universally appealing, it seems strange it took anyone so long to come up with what would become a magic formula for not just this initial effort, but the first few Carry On titles.

It was Norman who devised a whole new landscape for that first film, to include an irascible but secretly warm-hearted person of authority, tasked with supervising a bunch of well-intentioned but cheeky, often clumsy incompetents, who test everybody's patience, initially set out on a course of disaster before somehow coming good just in time for the credits.

To think, in a parallel universe where the meeting of these three talented men didn't take place, there might have been produced a long-forgotten drama about two ballet dancers dealing with conscription, possibly (but probably not) starring Leslie Caron, now tucked away somewhere on a high, dusty shelf in the archives of the British Film Institute.

But that meeting did happen and all three set to work for the newly shaped film, under the aegis of Anglo-Amalgamated Pictures and its executives, Nat Cohen and Stuart Levy. It was Stuart Levy whom Peter Rogers credited for originally coming up with the new title, *Carry On Sergeant.*

Looking back, could anyone else have pulled off what was to become such a unique jewel in British entertainment's crown? Could anyone else have offered anything to match Gerald Thomas's capacity for swift, slapstick direction and his unique comedic eye, Norman Hudis's talent for painting a humorous but humane landscape with his words, and Peter Roger's knack for overcoming all obstacles in bringing his vision to the screen?

Of course, we'll never know, but it is abundantly clear that each of them had distinctive and complementary skills that were to give the project its best possible fair wind from the very first day of production. And just like that, they were off.

Chapter 2

Reporting For Duty

*'I'll tell you, mate – two of everything that you
should have two of, and you're in!'*

Kenneth Connor in *Carry On Sergeant*

Despite his great talent, Norman Hudis was always a humble man. In his memoir, he took the liberty of sharing some advice for other screenwriters, but even here he played down his own great gift, suggesting, 'You should find out how to do it reasonably right by doing it dead wrong first and hacking your own path through the jungle of art, technique and commerce.'

There was clearly more to Norman's skill than this, but the phrase that jumps out for me here is 'hacking your own path'. Because what Norman, and other great writers of his era had that today's writers far more often have to do without, is a wealth of personal life experience, relatively speaking. After years of wartime service, facing a deadly enemy, finding comradeship in peril, setting up home and office overseas, missing loved ones back home, returning to Britain and building another life, Norman and his peers had a treasure chest of memories, stories, personalities, anecdotes into which to delve – a personal hinterland on which to draw creative inspiration. For his very first Carry On script, despite being placed in the most English of settings, Norman looked to his experiences of RAF service in the Middle East during the war, and his realisation that 'as every fair-minded serviceman, of whatever rank knows, it is the Army and RAF sergeants, and their Royal Naval and Royal Marine counterparts, who really, day to day, run the armed forces'.

His memoir fondly recounts the actions of his Unit, RAF's no.55 Repair and Salvage Unit, who remained, in his words, 'delayed and deprived but, because of the innate, gruff spirit of the time, not demoralised'. That affection and respect for his own group of challenged but ultimately triumphant fellows shines through on the page of not just *Sergeant*, but his entire canon of Carry On titles and is key, I believe, to the fondness in which they are held.

From the barest bones of *The Bull Boys* script, Norman fashioned a story of unlikely triumph, threaded through with sentiment and romance.

> *'Out of 24 men, I'm lumbered with one hypochondriac, one natural-born candidate for the glass house, a rock and roller, a shadow of a man haunted by lord knows what, a poppy-chasing layabout and some lethal idiot who gets himself locked in you know where.'*

His central narrative concerns a deceptively blustering sergeant set to retire, who makes a bet on his final conscripts becoming his very first star platoon. The bunch of hapless misfits he encounters does not make this a likely prospect, until they overcome their own inadequacies to make his dream come true.

Meanwhile, a newly married couple find their plans for their wedding day – and night – disrupted when the groom receives his conscription papers only minutes after leaving the church. Determined that love will conquer all, his bride follows him to his barracks where they conspire to be together.

Finally, another hypochondriac, angst-riddled recruit does his best to sabotage himself, professionally and romantically, before being saved by a kindly medical officer and the love of a good woman.

And that was it. While not exactly the most demanding, complicated or epic tale, Norman's script contained enough comic caper, slapstick humour, banana-skin mishaps and shiny-eyed sentiment to appeal to audiences, and Peter Rogers knew it.

As soon as the script was polished enough, the producer approached the film company Anglo-Amalgamated, the same people who had just financed his two Tommy Steele hits. It was run by Nat Cohen and Stuart Levy, and it was they who requested the title become *Carry On Sergeant*. Later, Peter always credited Stuart Levy in particular for this impactful idea.

Despite their enthusiasm for the project, these bean counters made it clear that no meat would be allowed on this experimental bone for Peter and Gerald, but producer and director somehow made it work, preparing a backbreaking schedule that would achieve three minutes of film going in the can per day. To avoid spending extra money on locations and props, Peter enlisted the cooperation of the military's top brass, making such an outlandish list of 'essential requirements' that eventually his liaison, Major Michael Forbes, suggested he might like to continue his correspondence with theatrical agencies instead, but somehow all came good. In answer to my question earlier of just what was unique about Peter Rogers that meant he was able to create Carry On, every story about him hints at ingenuity and, above all, tirelessness when it came to overcoming obstacles.

The only luxury he permitted himself when it came to filming was his choice of studio, and what a luxury it was.

When Barbara Windsor made her first trip to Pinewood, she remembered, 'It's how I imagined Hollywood to be.'

Sure enough, this 90-acre site, tucked into a quiet leafy corner of Buckinghamshire, twenty miles from London and surrounded by fields and trees, was, even then, the jewel in the crown of the British film industry.

Heatherden Hall, the large Victorian country house at the centre of the estate, was previously a country retreat and discreet meeting place for politicians and diplomats to relax and confer. It was transformed in 1935 when building tycoon Charles Boot and millionaire industrialist J. Arthur Rank teamed up to turn it into a film studio. In his rich history of the place, Morris Bright explains how they wanted it to have an American studio feel, with a name to match. One day, Charles Boot looked out at the garden, covered in pine trees, and came up with Pinewood. The initial days of construction included five separate stages and a water tank that could hold 300,000 litres of water. At the centre of the estate remained the stately pile, and at the studios' opening, one toff was reportedly overheard complaining, 'It's as if a millionaire with a beautiful house has allowed movie making to go on in the back garden.'

That's exactly what it was, and Heatherden Hall has gone on to become one of the most filmed country houses in the UK, with every bit of its corridors and cornices appearing on screen over the last seventy-five years. Before the Carry Ons moved in, its beautiful manicured lawn was where Norman Wisdom came a cropper with a lawn mower, and later Odd Job's hat smoothly beheaded a statue in *Goldfinger*. Fans of films from *Bugsy Malone* to *Chitty Chitty Bang Bang* and *The Prime of Miss Jean*

Brodie, plus TV shows from *One Foot in the Grave* to *Midsomer Murders*, will all recognise its elegant façade, and of course the producers of both Carry On and James Bond have long taken copious advantage of such a telegenic landscape on their doorstep.

By the time Peter Rogers was scouting for space, Pinewood had long laid claim to being our country's answer to Hollywood. Screen idols to have passed through its doors included a young Richard Attenborough, Anna Neagle, John Mills, Moira Shearer, Deborah Kerr, Jean Simmons and Dirk Bogarde. Aspiring starlets also crossed its threshold, through J. Arthur Rank's own Charm School, or Company of Youth, to give it its official name. Future Carry On star Shirley Eaton was one of the glittering alumni, alongside Joan Collins, Claire Bloom, Diana Dors and Petula Clark. Pete Murray, Donald Sinden and Patrick McGoohan all added to the mix, and it was even where Christopher Lee learned his winning ways.

This heady cocktail of visiting superstars and local British folk is captured nowhere more romantically than in the 2011 film *My Week with Marilyn*, depicting the unlikely but true tale of the friendship between Ms Monroe and a young production assistant, Colin Clark, when she arrived at Pinewood to appear in *The Prince and the Showgirl*. Eddie Redmayne played the star-struck Clark, and I was lucky enough to interview him before he became, well, Eddie Redmayne. I was moved to hear that they had filmed on the very same set previously graced by Marilyn herself, and just how entranced Eddie was to be gazing in Clark-like devotion at his co-stars Michelle Williams and Dame Judi Dench. It seems the power of Pinewood endures.

Back in 1958, this glittering roll-call and the peerless production values and technical expertise on offer meant that the price for filming in these hallowed studios was upgraded accordingly. But for Peter, who'd previously worked at Pinewood alongside his wife and knew lots of familiar faces, there was nowhere else he wanted to be, much to the chagrin of his coin-counting bosses at Anglo-Amalgamated.

His distributors were very keen on him going instead to Elstree, where they had a business partnership with ABC Studios, but Peter had never worked there before. He was familiar with Beaconsfield Studios, having made the TV series *Ivanhoe*, but this meant he was able to make the strong argument that Beaconsfield's sets were all full up – presumably with great piles of swords, shields and brigandines!

Still, how to keep the prices down at Pinewood to figures that he could get past his people at Anglo-Amalgamated? Well, anybody who's ever visited a film set will know that, to the uneducated eye, it seems like an awful lot of people are standing around, waiting for an hour to move a cable. While these are actually all highly-skilled technicians with a specific job to do, during this particular era, studios did also fill the decks with salaried staff who, if they were honest, they could have done without. Peter knew exactly who he needed and whittled the crew sheet down to a much smaller workforce. Of course, persuading their bosses of the rightness of this exercise was a different matter, and here Peter's familiarity with the studio helped him out once again.

For everyone in the film industry, the end of production 'wrap party' had become one of the set-in-stone traditions, where the entire cast and crew had the chance to unwind with a drink and let loose, often after weeks of backbreaking work. So it was with huge groans that the crews of Pinewood received the news that the Rank Organisation were pulling the plug on such hedonistic jamborees, because of J. Arthur Rank's strong religious beliefs. Because Peter was coming in as an independent producer, he was able to steer his own ship when it came to such events, and he swiftly promised to reinstate the much-missed ritual. Needless to say, the staff of Pinewood were equally swiftly reconciled to his plans for a reduced workforce and demanding shooting schedule. Looked like the crew were going to earn their knees-up!

To put into context just how much meat Peter had carved off the bone with his budget for *Sergeant*, five years earlier his wife Betty Box had made *Doctor in the House* for £125,000, and now here was her husband, presenting a bottom line of less than £80,000. Nobody except Peter believed it could be done. Years later, he marvelled at how straightforward the negotiations were considering how much money he was looking to save, remembering, 'It was the most expensive studio in the country and there was I trying to come in with a modest budget. I said, "This is all I have to spend." It happened to be a time when Rank had banned end-of-picture parties, so they said, "If you give us a party, we'll meet your figure." So that's how we got in.' This budgetary background helps explain why he needed all the help he could get with props and locations from the Army, and why his list of requests was so surprisingly long when it reached Major Forbes. The cast of Carry On has long complained about tiny pay packets but, at the beginning of the series anyway, there really was hardly any money to pay for anything. But the reward for all this parsimony was having the good fortune to film in the best studio in the land. Peter always said there was no one star of Carry On except the title itself, but there is surely a case to be made for best supporting role, and that would go to Pinewood.

In the absence of luxurious external locations, casting was as crucial as script. With one eye no doubt on his bank balance, Peter made no attempt to sign up any big screen star, instead, in what became his model for the next twenty years, he spread his riches between a number of jobbing B-listers and created an extremely effective ensemble. Key to the success of the film was the central role of the beleaguered Sergeant Grimshawe, and William Hartnell had plenty of form in donning military apparel for the screen, with previous roles in Carol Reed's *The Way Ahead*, the Boulting brothers' film *Private's Progress* and the lead role in TV's *The Army Game*. His fellow recruits from that particular show included Norman Rossington and Charles Hawtrey, and Charles reflected later that it was definitely being seen on the small screen playing an army man that got him the role in *Sergeant*.

The same similarity was one of the reasons Peter Rogers hadn't employed *The Army Game* writer John Antrobus for the script, lest his ideas accidentally leak from one to the other, and Norman Hudis equally wondered why anybody would pay to go to the cinema to see the same faces they could watch for free on TV. By his own admission, though, he was equally certain years later that nobody would want to pay to watch a ship sink in the Atlantic! Perhaps, after all, the opposite was true and the similarity between the two projects did them both a favour. It certainly helped Norman Rossington, who was not only asked to return to *The Army Game* following his appearance in *Sergeant*, but also secured a pay rise.

If there is a star turn to be spotted in *Sergeant*, it is one of Carry On's great anomalies, and that is the casting of Bob Monkhouse as newly wedded Charlie, the juvenile lead. The former gag writer was by then a face known to millions, with his own ITV show plus a BBC sitcom to his name. I should admit at this point I am Bob's biggest ever fan. He was tagged the 'British Bob Hope', but to me he was a lot more than that. He didn't need to rely on an autocue or a stable of other writers, instead he had an encyclopaedic armoury of jokes, the memory of a chess champion and nobody ever worked harder in the whole of show business. It gratifies me enormously that his talent has been reassessed and recognised in recent years. However, despite his effortless charm as Charlie, I would have to agree with those who say he was never quite right for Carry On. He was a naturally charismatic attention-grabber whenever he appeared, but he wasn't the everyman comedic actor that the films required and he would have unbalanced their narrative had he become a regular. Peter Rogers clearly recognised this. Bob recorded in his memoir how the producer gave with one hand, then stole with the other, when Bob encountered him fresh from watching the rushes of *Sergeant*. "'I'm more than delighted with you, my lad," he said, slapping me on the back. "You're going to be my golden boy." He never hired me again.' Never mind. As a huge fan of both, I'm quietly glad this happened, as Carry On didn't need Bob, and Bob didn't need Carry On.

Other familiar faces and radio voices belonged to Gerald Campion, Terence Longdon, Kenneth Williams, Hattie Jacques and Kenneth Connor – who were cast in ways that summed up the entirety of British male-dom, the oafish Gerald (as Andy Galloway), intellectual snob Kenneth Williams (as James Bailey), the whining, snivelling Kenneth Connor (as Horace Strong), the seductive Terence (Miles Heywood), to join the knock-kneed Charles Hawtrey (Peter Golightly), all under the doubtful scrutiny of Hartnell's Sergeant Grimshaw. Shirley Eaton played Charlie's new bride Mary with wide-eyed coolness, while Dora Bryan appeared as romantic enthusiast Norah, a woman with Horace Strong firmly in her sights.

It was a very busy professional period for Kenneth Williams. In contrast to his notorious contempt for his own appearances in the later films, his diaries included only a professional-sounding aside in his very first mention of what was to play such a huge part in his life, writing on Wednesday 2 April 1958: 'Out to Pinewood to do practice drilling with a CSM of the Queen's for the film *Carry on Sergeant*.'

In real life, the conscripts would have been aged between 18 and 21. On screen, they all looked at least 30 – Charles Hawtrey was actually in his early forties! – but the cast's intrinsic appeal and skill with Norman Hudis's lines meant nobody who watched them ever complained.

Filming began on 24 March 1958, mostly on Stage B at Pinewood, but with exteriors shot at the Queen's Barracks in Stoughton, near Guildford in Surrey, and none of Peter Rogers's scrimping ever showed on screen. After all, it wasn't an ambitious, alien planet they were creating, but a small, intimate world, perfectly formed.

The casting and the script were all, and the film's success was far less about the central romantic triumph of Charlie and his bride Mary than the unlikely comradeship of James Bailey, Peter Golightly and Horace.

As Horace, Kenneth Connor really stole the show, particularly with his elastic eyebrows that were in turn fearful, anxious, weary and genuflecting in the face of authority. Kenneth Williams was able to channel his own sense of being an intellectual outsider into the role of James Bailey, not remotely eager to please but instead knowing his own mind.

'Your rank?'
'That's a matter of opinion.'

Kenneth later wrote of his glee in muttering a spontaneous 'Charming' as a beret was plonked on his head. Gerald Thomas told him off for being on the edge of the frame as he spoke, but he allowed the line to stay in, the first of many gestures of what Kenneth would call 'indulgent direction' that made Gerald enduringly popular with all the actors. He never failed to create an amiable atmosphere around him on set, while remaining at all times very much in charge.

Some of *Sergeant*'s lines don't stand up to modern scrutiny. Horace Strong screams just because his medical officer turns out to be a woman, and the campness of Kenneth Williams and Charles Hawtrey is meant to create a laugh, just because it jars against the traditional military setting. Plus, of course, it's a very male environment, with little room for women. The all-female brass band in action at the end might look like some sort of feminist statement by the filmmakers, but in fact they were the only band Peter Rogers could recruit on the day when his original plan fell through – I suppose that's equality. But, considering the setting, it's remarkable that there is no real bullying, abuse nor singling anyone out for humiliation, as we've seen in so many other military films. This one is instead a mess-room sigh to collective ineptitude, and salutes and cheers all round when it is overcome.

If Peter, Gerald and Norman had been concerned that fans of *The Army Game* wouldn't bother to make a trip to the pictures for more conscription fodder, they needn't have worried. *Carry On Sergeant* clearly touched the hearts of a nation for whom National Service was still the norm. It wouldn't be abolished completely for another two years. The challenge of a thwarted wedding night, the ripe material created by different classes and intellects thrown together, the antics that taxed the furrowed brows of those nominally in command, plus the comradeship and romance that succeeded against the odds, all combined for wholesome, accessible fun to which cinema audiences flocked.

Carry On Sergeant, made in the end for just £78,000, ended up taking half a million pounds at the British box office. Following its premiere on 1 August 1958, it became one of the most successful films of the year, coming in third behind *Dunkirk* and *Bridge on the River Kwai*, proving the enduring national appetite for military fare, whether of the heroic type, or the distinctly more down-to-earth, boy-next-door variety.

Chapter 3

Star Spotlight – Charles Hawtrey

'Oh hello!'

Picture the scene. The interior of a department store, with both Charles Hawtrey and Kenneth Williams scrambling for space in a women's dressing room, before they emerge, resplendent, in the finest coats and hats. Comfortably dressed in drag, they make surprisingly pretty women. It is *Carry On Constable*, and both of them are on duty, about to arrest a shoplifter. But, oh, the dresses… Hawtrey bursts out, 'Do you know I haven't done this since I was in the army, at a camp concert.'

Williams puts him right, 'This is no laughing matter.'

There, in a nutshell, is what these two actors brought to the Carry On franchise – Hawtrey's unashamed delight in playing up to his effete personality, and Williams's more complicated relationship with both his sexuality and his more cerebral leanings. The simplicity of the scene, bonkers though it is, belies two far more complex characters, even as they offer a level of campness previously unseen by British audiences.

For Charles Hawtrey, perhaps the acorns for such Carry On antics were sown with his forays into revue, where he was often required to dress up as a lady. This wasn't just unbecoming, pantomime dame garb either, but properly genteel hats, taffetas and furs, and he reportedly revelled in it. On one occasion, on stage in 1939, so convincing was he that audiences departed the theatre believing they had been watching an actress called Charlotte Tree. But such skill was only one of many strings to the actor's bow. By the time he joined the Carry On crew for its first outing in 1958's *Sergeant*, Charles could already boast an entertainment career lasting more than three decades, and an impressively diverse one at that.

A natural-born performer, he was treading the boards from his teenage years, while he trained at the Italia Conti Academy of Theatre Arts in London – an impressive list of fellow alumni includes Noel Coward, Clive

Dunn, Anthony Newley, Gertrude Lawrence and fellow Carry On-ners William Hartnell, Leslie Phillips and Wendy Richard.

Charles soon became one of showbusiness's early 'triple threats', skilled in acting, dancing and music. As a soprano-singing student, he even secured a recording deal, which brought him the tag 'the angel-faced choirboy'. His first record for the Columbia and Regal label was called 'I Don't Want To Play in Your Yard', a title that wouldn't appear to encourage a High C, and yet more recordings followed.

School was also where he picked up his distinctive Received Pronunciation tones, which could have led the passing fan to assume he came from higher social echelons. In fact, Charles's roots lay in a working-class family in suburban Hounslow, where he was born George Frederick Joffre Hartree in November 1914. While relations with his father and brothers were reportedly strained, Charles's bond with his mother Alice was much deeper, and would prove to be the most significant connection of his life.

His provenance has previously led to some confusion, with many believing him to be the son of the revered theatrical knight Sir Charles Hawtrey, a false notion our Charlie seemed quite happy to let pass uncorrected for much of his career, sometimes even referring to himself as 'Charles Hawtrey Jr'.

His own path was not empty of dramatic luminaries, however. No sooner had he graduated from school than he was appearing on stage, in London's West End and further afield. His co-stars from this period included such legends as Charles Laughton and Vivien Leigh.

The big screen beckoned too, where Charles's eternally childlike appearance and comedic timing made him an effective foil for one of British cinema's greatest stars of the era, Will Hay. In preparation for all the mischievous but inept groups of people he would later meet in Carry On, Hawtrey joined in with Hay's capers of benign confusion through a series of films. Just as Hay's consistent portrayals of incompetent authority helped pave the way for the success of Carry On, so traces of Hay's talent for visual comedy can be glimpsed in Hawtrey's later performances – the flick of his eyes, the telling turn of the head. For his own part, he remained forever proud of his association with such a popular entertainment figure, often citing it as evidence of his own professional pedigree.

Other highlights include a piano-playing scene in the great *Passport to Pimlico*, a musical moment he later somehow self-credited as 'writing the music for the film', and even a cameo role in the London-shot *Sabotage*, so he could always more truthfully claim to have been directed by Alfred Hitchcock.

By 1940, Charles had almost thirty films to his name, plus a handful he had directed. Only a few years later, he was also a regular voice on radio, teaming up with Patricia Hayes for the Children's Hour hit *Norman and Henry Bones, the Boy Detectives*, and providing the voice of Hubert Lane, the snooty nemesis of *Just William*. By the end of the war, it's easy to agree with Carry On historian Robert Ross's assessment of Charles Hawtrey as 'an icon of British comedy'.

And yet, he knew rejection. Somehow, everything folded for him shortly after the war and, despite all those strings to his bow and his impressively broad portfolio, he couldn't seem to get a gig. Dave Ainsworth wrote the award-winning play *Oh Hello!* about Hawtrey's life, and he still sounds surprised when he tells me, 'He lost it all completely. It was just a blank. It seems inexplicable.'

Roger Lewis, in his fond but wry biography of Hawtrey, speculates that the actor got caught in that middle ground, of finally growing out of his childlike demeanour but failing to become anything more interesting. He wonders too, if the actor's homosexuality, still twenty years from being publicly legal, may have helped bring his career to a sudden stop. He speculates, 'Perhaps there was only room for one licensed queer, and that was Frankie Howerd … scowling, beaming, lip-smacking, rambling and full of sauce.'

Whatever the cause, the catalogue of beseeching letters from Charles to the BBC makes for pitiful reading, begging to be cast, listing his achievements, offering to take a pay cut, the works. Fortunately, for him and the reader, a relatively short time passed before he was cast in *The Army Game*, ITV's very first sitcom, following the exploits of Hut 29, a dysfunctional group of soldiers during their conscription for National Service – sound familiar?

Charles's role of Private 'Professor' Hatchett brought him to the attention of producer Peter Rogers, who was musing on the possibility of some sort of big screen version. Thus did Charles appear in 1958's *Carry On Sergeant*, and went on to appear in twenty-three films of the series.

'He was an immediately engaging character,' is how Ainsworth explains his appeal. 'He didn't used to appear at the beginning of the films, but then he turned up, you heard "Oh hello!" and immediately you're there with him.'

'I belong to this rambling club and once a week we do like to go as far as we can.'

The playwright credits those formative years with Will Hay for much of the actor's skill in getting the Carry On audience onside while doing very little. 'He had that apprenticeship with a master, not just in variety but also in sometimes silent comedy, so the facial features, the mannerisms were very important. He could play visually so well, he didn't need to speak to be funny. As with someone like Tommy Cooper, Charles Hawtrey didn't have to open his mouth to reach us.'

Of course, a lot of this was down to his extraordinary appearance. Never mind what aesthetic the stylists on each separate Carry On film might have been after, Charles presented them a challenge too far, with his distinctive cherubic features and wafer-thin figure. Clothes that might have looked wrong on anyone else somehow got absorbed into his own eccentricity – whether it was his ballooning trench coat in *Spying*, or his defiantly unexotic Trilby and almost cosmonautical brown sunglasses for the beach in *Abroad*.

Lewis makes an acute point in his biography of Hawtrey that the actor's very angular personal dimensions weren't ones he sought to downplay. They may have disqualified him from leading-man status, but they were an integral part of his appeal, and instead of diminishing them, he instead added to them with what the author beautifully terms 'insect grace'.

Lewis writes, 'He's always wearing peaked caps or plumed hats. He'll carry a rapier cocked at a gallant angle. His movements are full of sharp gestures. He's abrupt and angular and you'll find yourself watching him.'

He could have added that, even without a hat, Charles seldom went unadorned. His pottery disguise in *Cleo* was a case in point, tucking himself into an urn when he sought to spy on the Egyptian queen and her lover Marc Anthony. And, of course, whatever the historical setting or role he was playing, without fail, his little round glasses were as constant as his pudding bowl of black hair and his clipped RP tones, often accompanied by over-exaggerated moans and groans.

Throughout the series, Charles's performance and style are equally consistent. Somehow, he remains knock-kneed but elegant, eager to please but never taken real advantage of. He is the eternal innocent child, with an adolescent glint we spot in his eye even before we hear 'Oh hello!' And he appears to have a remarkable lack of vanity, with a series of string vests, bobble hats and sou'westers doing little to flatter his emaciated form. When he strips off for *Cleo* and invites a nubile young maid to join him in the tub, he looks about as seductive as a plucked chicken.

'Camp' offers the easiest catch-all term for much of this. Before learning about Charles's personal demons, we can glimpse, possibly with the benefit of hindsight, his knowing vulnerability, his underlying sense of personal tragedy protected by an ironic defiance and, above all, wit.

By only the second film in the series, *Nurse*, we find the actor in a dress, and it's only the first of several forays into drag. By his seventeenth outing, in *Carry on Again Doctor*, he goes full Dame Edna in his guise as Lady Puddleton, prettied up and sent to infiltrate his rival doctor's clinic. Here, Charles gives Jack Lemmon's Daphne, the double bassist in *Some Like It Hot*, a run for her money, in all Puddleton's delicacy and finery – no pantomime dame garb here, instead the full *Tootsie*-like confident glamour of fur-collared nightie and sequinned specs.

The frocks aside, Charles invariably plays effeminate, physically weedy characters. The effect on screen is of a meek mummy's boy who never got to play in the sun with the other boys, but can suddenly be called upon to erupt into unpredictable, chaotic behaviour. His characters are often bumbling, accident-prone and the victim of physical mishaps and narrative misunderstandings.

The first few Carry Ons – *Sergeant, Nurse, Teacher, Constable* – all entrench this idea. Whether training on a military base or patrolling the local beat, Charles is always hamming it up, eager to please while unable to follow basic instructions, game if not able, but never without dignity.

'I couldn't leave home without bringing something bright and gay for the poor indisposed constables.'

The later films find him increasingly cast as someone in authority, undoubtedly to be duped by the underlings around him – such a position seeing the boot on the other foot from his days opposite the more senior Will Hay.

I don't believe the hospital titles make adequate use of Charles's talents. He is barely heard in *Nurse*, for the most part confined to bed listening to the radio, while the first *Doctor* film finds him only suffering labour pains in sympathy with his pregnant wife. As Surgeon Ernest Stoppidge, he gets one of the best lines in the second *Doctor* title – 'I do not object to jiggery but I do take exception to pokery' – while in *Matron*, his best scene alludes to what he is not up to. We are invited to assume from the sounds that he and Matron Hattie Jacques have embraced, only to discover that in fact they're curled up happily together, watching a television soap opera. We hear the same teasing sounds with his landlady in *Loving*. This time, they turn out to be playing cards. With Charles and the ladies on screen, there is always a lot of ooh-ing and aah-ing, but never any action.

The period romps of Carry On's golden age give the actor a far bigger chance to shine. He appears more equipped physically to hold his own in such challenges as the glorious sword fight finale of *Don't Lose Your Head*, where he stands haughty but ridiculous in a topplesome periwig as the Duke de Pommefrite, elegantly prepared to meet his guillotine maker, even when a messenger arrives with a note.

'Drop it in the basket, I'll read it later.'

Khyber finds him crucially guarding the mountainous path, even if his most celebrated character, Private Widdle, does end up surrendering his woollen underpants and endangering the British Empire, after complaining of the cold and 'the way the wind whistles up the Pass'.

These celebrated spoofs also find him cast gloriously against type. As Antony's father-in-law Seneca in *Cleo*, he lusts after women in almost Sid James-esque style and even disappears into an urn to spy on the lead couple's promised lovemaking. In *Cowboy*, he is the puny Native Indian, Big Heap, whom we are invited to believe has somehow begotten his screen son, Bernard Bresslaw. The mother could presumably have shed some light on this unlikely instance, but she is never seen.

In *Jungle*, he is 'Tonka the Great, King of Lovers, Father of Countless' – the mind boggles – a powerful king of his tribe, but also weak in the face of his wife played by Joan Sims, while *Henry* finds him cast, quite unpredictably, as the Queen's companion of the bed chamber, and an enthusiastic one at that. 'As the King's taster, I have to try everything before he does.'

In *Spying*, Hawtrey even acknowledges the nonsense of him being a special agent as soon as he's asked his name.

> 'Bind.'
> 'James?'
> 'No, Charlie.'
> 'Number?'
> 'Double O O.'
> 'O what?'
> 'Nothing. They just took one look at me and said, 'Oh! Oh! Oh!...'

With such casting, with his mere presence in such masculine roles, Charles helps poke fun at the nonsense of traditionally macho stereotypes, and in that sense, he's very much ahead of his time. We see this most outrageously in *Camping*, when he emerges from a tent, in a shop, where he's been entwined, obviously, with a pretty young lady. 'Splendid girl, and so helpful – do you know, she's been showing me how to stick the pole up!' As if.

Director Gerald Thomas knew how to play on this, explaining in a 1966 interview, 'Apart from the comedy value of the unlikely role he plays, I'm careful to arrange the right timing for his actual appearance, so that the two factors combined surprise the audience into instant risibility.'

We see this from the early days of *Constable*, when he enters late but with a flourish. Years later in *Camping*, he is given a solitary part clearly written purely to keep him in the picture, and he rewards the creators' efforts with the perfect delivery of a schoolboy remark when his tent is blown off by explosives.

'I knew I shouldn't have eaten those radishes'.

The surprising but rich contribution made by Charles to the series was brought into sharp focus after he was replaced in the cast for *Cruising* in 1962. One critic took sad note of this, saying of the film, 'It may be the first one in colour, but in being the first one without Charles Hawtrey, some of the colour is lost.'

Four years later, Charles was only added to the cast of *Screaming* after the American distributors demanded it. Peter Rogers had cast someone else, before critic C.H.B. Williamson complained in *Cinema Today*, saying he hoped the decision wouldn't affect the film's box office return. Peter was forced to reassure his bosses at Anglo, and Charles took the part of lavatory attendant Dan Dann, a showy supporting role.

He was certainly an integral part of the team, both on screen and off, where he sat smoking his Woodbines between takes, playing cards with Sid James and everyone else. One observer described him as 'a Sherpa, helping the others up the mountain to dizzy heights while he himself failed to get due credit'.

Sure enough, it was his desire for acknowledgement, and his perceived lack thereof, that finally brought his Carry On work to a sad and abrupt end – that, and of course, the drink.

Charles's dependence on the bottle was well known by both cast and crew, and writer Talbot Rothwell even referred to it obliquely in *Carry On Abroad*, where Hawtrey's Eustace Tuttle is a drunken, bowler-hatted mummy's boy, not a character who would normally be found sunning himself on a foreign beach. In the film, he happily drinks his own suntan lotion before passing out on the sand.

However, while they made fun of it on screen, Charles's constantly inebriated state tested all those around him. Kenneth noted in his diary, 'It's not the eccentricity, or the grotesquerie, or the homosexuality that puts one off Charles; it's the excruciating boredom.'

A poignant example comes from the memoir of Barbara Windsor, who recounts filming with Charles on a conveyor belt for *Spying*, and her shock at seeing him topple over. She wrote that she feared he'd fainted from fright during the dramatic scene. In fact, he'd passed out from drink.

Jamie Rees, a child actor who returned to stage with a tour de force performance as Charles in Ainsworth's *Oh Hello!* tells me:

I can't imagine how difficult it must have been growing up in the 1930s, then living through the 1940s and 50s as a gay man. I think I'd have been very angry myself, possibly hit the bottle. It must have been a tough life. I feel very sympathetic towards him.

Today society is a fairer place and there are support groups for every faction or affliction you can think of. This wasn't the case in Hawtrey's day and it would be all too easy to paint a picture of a flawed and foolish failing actor – an architect of his own downfall – but he was brought down by external events. Where else was there for him to go? His lifestyle was illegal, frowned upon and meant to be hidden away. It must have been horrible, but he did his best to live it. I think he was very brave.

Charles's drinking grew noticeably worse after his mother died in 1965. The pair, always close, lived together before her death and, though she suffered from dementia, the actor loyally brought her to set where he'd have to lock her in his dressing room for her own safety.

In his memoir, Kenneth recounted an incident in the canteen during the filming of *Carry On Teacher*, when Charles's mother dropped her cigarette ash into her handbag, which promptly caught fire, while her son was telling a story. Joan Sims cried out to Charles, who swiftly poured a cup of tea into the bag and snapped the handbag shut before carrying on with his anecdote. Kenneth called him 'a true eccentric' who, like any actor, hated to be interrupted.

Dave Ainsworth comments, 'He really turned a bad corner after his mother died in 1965. And his life descended as his career descended.'

Producer Aubrey Philips recounts Charles's acute loneliness after losing the one person he felt close to. He says, 'I didn't know him when his mother was still alive, but he missed her a great deal, and when he'd had a few drinks, if you were sharing digs with him, you're hear him at night talking to his mother.'

In drink and in grief, the actor became increasingly obsessed with the recognition he felt was owed to him, and things came to a head in 1972, when he withdrew from the *Carry On Christmas* TV special, after an argument over billing. Losing his battle to be named above Hattie Jacques, the fading star withdrew from the production at unseemly short notice. In the play *Oh Hello!* Jamie Rees has him say, 'You can carry on without me,' and that's exactly what they did. Charles would never again appear in a Carry On production.

The postscript to those heady years wasn't a glamorous one. Relying on his Carry On fame, he made ends meet with work in pantomime and theatre, where audiences would greet him delightedly with applause, only for it to wilt away as he forgot his lines and bumped around the stage. His last ever professional appearance came in a 1987 episode of children's TV programme *Supergran*, a whimpering end to a career that had begun with such promise over sixty years before.

By then, Charles had retired to Deal on the Kent coastline, where he became notorious for his excursions along the seafront, dressed extravagantly, keeping his eye out for prospective encounters with other men, refusing requests for autographs and invariably making his way to a local pub. One neighbour told his biographer Roger Lewis, 'People wanted him to be like he was in the Carry On films, but on his own he became his true self – and so often he was just a sad little man.'

When he did make the headlines, it was for all the wrong reasons, such as in August 1984, when his house caught fire after he went to bed and left a cigarette burning. Photos show a distressed, frail Charles being carried to safety by a fireman, an incident that twenty years earlier would have been treated with hilarity on the set of Carry On, but now could only add to the sense of a tragic demise.

Four years later he collapsed in a local hotel doorway and was diagnosed with peripheral vascular disease, brought on by years of heavy smoking. When he was told he would have to lose his legs to save his life, he refused – according to Barbara Windsor, he said he wanted to go out 'with his boots on' and, very soon after, he did.

It was a tragic end for an actor who had shared the stage and screen with so many greats, but hankered constantly for his own leading-man status. That was never going to happen because of how he looked and sounded, but what I find far sadder is that this disappointment deprived him of any lasting satisfaction in what he did achieve – giving us so many perfect comedic moments.

Chapter 4

First Cabs Off the Rank

'Ding dong! Carry on!'

Leslie Phillips (who else?) in *Carry On Teacher*

In October 1973, Peter Rogers appeared as Roy Plomley's guest on *Desert Island Discs*. Before he named his favourite book and solitary item – a bound volume of *Punch* from the 1960s and *Elégie* by Jules Massenet respectively – he was asked by his host about the box office success of *Carry On Sergeant*. 'It made a bomb,' he replied. Plomley moved smoothly onto the subject of its successors, asking genially, 'You made some more?' Peter chuckled, before explaining, 'I didn't. I made the same one again.'

There, in a nutshell, was the creative formula for, if not all the Carry On films, at least the first half-dozen brought to life by the pen of Norman Hudis. There had been no thought of turning the Carry On tag into a series until the success of *Sergeant* naturally brought the creative team back to the table. Norman was by now fielding all sorts of flattering offers from rival producers, but he decided to stick with Peter, a loyal act for which he was rewarded with an improved contract.

Peter said, 'In my opinion, Norman could write anything, but we began with a comedy which was so successful that it seemed a pity not to continue.'

And off they went, making five more films over the next four years – *Nurse, Teacher, Constable, Regardless* and finally *Cruising*.

While the narrative concerned the customary bunch of misfits doing their feeble best through a series of misunderstandings and mishaps, physical challenges and romantic pursuits, Norman also exploited the low-hanging fruit of comic potential presented by such noble towering institutions as the National Health Service, the education system and the police force. Behind the main thrust of personal comic capers and pitfalls, he pointed out many of the established but unquestioned processes that society had come to take for granted. Just as the Army's recruits were treated as halfwits in *Sergeant*, *Nurse* took a look at some of the authoritarian rules meted out by the NHS, then just over a decade old. Patients could feel terrified, hospital staff could be demeaning – 'this place is feudal,' says Kenneth Williams's character Oliver Reckitt.

Norman's script also pointed out the contradiction between the lifesaving jobs done by hospital staff and the way they were ordered about by their seniors – what the writer called 'archaic, hierarchic, meaningless restrictions'. He certainly had a point, when you stop to consider nurses literally held life and death in their hands all day, before being told what time they had to be in bed at night. In *Teacher*, he laughed at some of the pompous new guidelines being pedalled by visiting 'experts', while the school's teachers found nothing old-fashioned about merely wanting to teach. Norman didn't explicitly point any of this out, he relied on Carry On's audiences being able to recognise themselves and others in the stereotypical characters on screen, and raise a collective eyebrow to the comforts and blind spots of authority, the stifling officialdom, the patience of benevolent elders as well as the undervalued second-in-command who makes everything all right and ensures all finally comes good. Hierarchies may be disrupted but are ultimately preserved, individuals come a cropper alone but comradeship prevails.

> *'It's matron's round.'*
> *'Mine's a pint.'*

Even with all this material ripe for satire, Norman never forgot his initial instruction from Peter on *Sergeant* that he followed throughout his work on the series: 'turn it into a comedy'. Sure enough, for each title, the writer remembered, 'We set out to get as many laughs as we could in 83 minutes.'

Some Carry On purists insist on calling *Carry On Nurse* the first of the series, pointing out that *Sergeant* was initially intended as a stand-alone feature and only at this point did the franchise kick off. While respecting this viewpoint, I'm afraid this is not a hill I am prepared to die on. For the purposes of this book, *Sergeant* stays in!

Nurse was remarkable, however. Firstly, even by the speed for which the production of the series became known, Norman's efforts on this film were spectacular.

He was handed an idea based on the stage play set in a hospital, *Ring for Catty* co-written by Patrick Cargill and Jack Beale, with the words of Gerald Thomas ringing in his ears, that 'this film would be made along similar lines to the previous *Carry On Sergeant*'. Norman was initially stuck for a story and spent days staring at a blank page, often looking for inspiration to his wife Rita, a nurse with plenty of anecdotes from the wards.

But then he had a wonderful stroke of bad luck when he was taken urgently ill with an exploding appendix (writers are known to exaggerate, but we should probably take his word for it that he was in a great amount of pain!) and was admitted to Watford Hospital where, from his bed, he took in everything going on around him. Once safely back home, he set down his ideas for life in a men's surgical ward, a bunch of patients drawn from across the classes who wouldn't normally meet one another let alone conspire, but team up to defy the hospital rules. *Nurse* had less slapstick humour than *Sergeant*, although the hospital setting clearly made for more gentle innuendo, but Norman created a richer tapestry with more stories being told, including people of different classes, professions, and strong female characters.

There were some serious points being made. The film was released only a decade after the inception of the National Health Service, so such intimate portraits as this were still novel and interesting, and Norman didn't ignore patients' concerns about being treated (and behaving) like children, nor did he overlook the rigid, often arbitrary rules of hospital life, nor the harsh treatment of junior nurses by their seniors. However, as he pointed out, it is also a simple tale of 'horny men and lovely girls all in a room together, one helpless against the other'. He finished the entire script in ten days.

Once again, costs were kept low. Local hospitals provided medical and nursing equipment, while Heatherden Hall became Haven Hospital on screen. Peter Rogers confessed, 'I like to stay in my own back yard.'

For the first time in Carry On, established theatre and TV star Leslie Phillips joined in the fun. He had just returned from Hollywood when the script for *Nurse* was handed to him. He remembered, 'It was the funniest script I'd ever read. I told my agent I had to do it.'

Playing bunion-afflicted Jack Bell, he gave the world for the very first time his life-enhancing appreciation of a fine lady, 'I say. Ding Dong.' As far as I'm concerned, he could have retired at that point and still done more for British cinema and the nation's morale than many other actors of his or any generation. Instead, he stayed for three Carry On titles in total and remained one of Peter's favourite ever actors.

Several familiar faces were there with him, including Kenneth Williams, Kenneth Connor and Charles Hawtrey. With Dora Bryan unavailable, Peter Rogers recruited Joan Sims for her Carry On debut. Shirley Eaton returned, and recalled fondly, '*Carry On Nurse* was a little diamond, a lot more fun and comradeship than *Sergeant*.'

'Colonel, whatever's going on?'
'Come, come, Matron. Surely you've seen a temperature taken like this before.'
'Yes, Colonel, many times – but never with a daffodil!'

For the first time in the series, Hattie Jacques played Matron, which meant that, with immense difficulty, she had to give the film's memorable punchline, '… but never with a daffodil.' Was it really that funny? Audiences seemed to think so.

Peter decided to test the success of this bon mot plus all the other hospital gags by inviting to the first screening a group of real-life nurses. They happened to be very tired after night duty, but even so, the jokes based on their work caused them to laugh uproariously, and Peter could be confident he had another hit in the bag.

That was an understatement. *Nurse* became the country's most successful film of 1959 and was still playing to some cinemas three years after its release. The film found an equally receptive audience in America. At one cinema in Westwood, Los Angeles, it ran for a whole year. In a nod to the final punchline of the film, plastic daffodils were even handed out to cinema-goers after screenings. A true phenomenon had been created.

'What a fuss about such a little thing.'

Plus, it was the extraordinary success of *Nurse* that persuaded those big cheeses at Anglo-Amalgamated, Stuart Levy and Nat Cohen, that Peter had the right chops to make a success of a proper series. They gave him the go-ahead for three more films, even invited him to join their board. Just like that, Peter, Gerald and Norman had a franchise on their hands.

While taking his customary poke at a familiar institution, this time the education system, Norman wrote probably his most sentimental script of all with *Teacher*, his first entirely original script of the series. Set in a school, it has two love stories woven around the central peril of the headmaster of Maudlin Street Secondary Modern wanting to move to another job, while his childish staff and surprisingly mature pupils all want him to stay. The comedy comes from their mostly misfiring attempts to achieve this in the face of an official visit by a Ministry of Education Inspector (Rosalind Knight's Miss Wheeler) and a celebrated child psychiatrist Alistair Grigg (Leslie Phillips). As well as the troupe of now familiar faces, keen-eyed fans notice a young Richard O'Sullivan as senior pupil Stevens, along with a star turn from comedian and radio host Ted Ray as school principal William Wakefield. In recognition of his established success, Ted Ray was one of only a tiny number of actors Peter Rogers paid the compliment of bestowing a solitary credit in the opening titles. Bob Monkhouse also received this rare acknowledgement, as would Phil Silvers years later.

Teacher has the requisite romantic comedy of Kenneth Connor's reluctant seduction of Rosalind Knight, and Leslie Phillips' more open pursuit of 'Miss Allcock' Joan Sims, and it has the banana-skin antics of Miss Allcock's shorts-splitting PE scene and the staff all getting drunk after the pupils spike their staff-room kettle.

Because children help drive the narrative, much of the humour is deliberately juvenile, and it ends on a heartfelt, sentimental note, something Norman Hudis excelled at. The dynamic between Kenneth Williams and Charles Hawtrey hints for the first time at a competitiveness between the two, with Charles eager to please, and Kenneth subdued but snappy. Neatly slotted in are some more serious questions about education, such as the debate between traditional teaching and progressive methods, and the merits of the still-customary use of corporal punishment. Kenneth's Mr Milton makes this point acutely.

'Extraordinary theory – you bend a child double to give him an upright character.'

Ted Ray slotted in seamlessly with the rest of the cast and Peter admitted he would have loved him to continue with the series, but contractual obligations prevented it. Carry On needed a new leading male for the next title in the series, and Peter found just the person – Sid James.

Constable found Norman stuck once again for inspiration, until he sat down and watched *Dixon of Dock Green*. Straight away, he was able to come up with his usual winning recipe of a familiar institution, a bunch of incompetents, a little bit of romance and some personal and professional challenges that all came good in the end.

At the centre of the action, for the first time, is Sid James. As Sergeant Wilkins, he faces a similar challenge to that of William Hartnell's Sergeant Grimshawe, how to shepherd some disparate incompetents, in this case a bunch of reserve coppers called upon to fill in the ranks of the local constabulary depleted by flu. As with *Teacher*, there is also the promise of a better posting elsewhere until, predictably, Wilkins decides he's happier where he is. Sid James's casting, however, gives the formula a whole new vigour. He neither sets himself apart from his misfits nor falls for their nonsense, of which there is plenty. Leslie's PC Tom Potter asks a robber for directions to the police station. Kenneth Connor's Constable Charlie Constable believes he's overhearing a violent murder, which turns out to be a play on the radio.

Through Sid's everyman eyes, we see them for all that they are, both good and ridiculous, and from the first time we meet him on screen, we know we are in safe hands, even as his debut is anointed with a bucket of water in the face by PC Potter.

'Mars was in conjunction with Uranus at the time. How could we possibly do well?'

Making their Carry On debut alongside Sid were some bare bottoms – of the male variety, much to the distress of Charles Hawtrey, whose buttocks would be glimpsed on screen during a shower scene. Worried that he would look too pale in the finished version, Charles insisted on the application of a powder puff, and his cast mates joined him in becoming a little more rosy-cheeked.

A year after *Constable*, *Carry On Regardless* went off at a bit of a tangent from Norman's previous tight narratives. Set in Helping Hands, an employment agency with Sid's Bert Handy at the helm, the story follows the different jobs taken up by his staff – you guessed it, a bunch of disparate characters who would probably not have met each other otherwise – and the individual misunderstandings and mayhem that result.

As a result of this narrative framework, the film appears as a pot pourri of mostly unrelated funny sketches rather than a cohesive whole. There is no singular defining peril or challenge, and Norman himself considered it his least favourite of the series, although he conceded it had its share of priceless moments. In his memoir, he mistakenly credited a London taxi driver for a brilliant ad-lib when Kenneth Williams's character, Francis Courtenay, tasked with babysitting a chimpanzee, tries to hail a cab and is given short shrift by the cabby.

'I'll take you, but not your brother.'

This marvellous punchline wasn't in the script. However, Peter Rogers later revealed he'd been the one to come up with the bon mot on the day of shooting. Whoever first said it, it worked a treat and must have been a relief to Kenneth Williams just to wrap the scene, after his hairy co-star initially forgot his direction and started smashing up the house in which they were waiting for the cameras to roll.

The chimp wasn't the star of the show in *Regardless*, however, and nor were guest stars Fenella Fielding, Nicholas Parsons or new Carry On team arrival Liz Fraser. For me, that honour goes to Kenneth Connor who, as Sam Twist, embarks on the biggest job of them all. With inevitable misunderstanding, he believes he's been sent on a top secret spying mission involving a train, an encounter with an enigmatic femme fatale and finally his arrival at the Forth Bridge. With equally inevitable bathos, it emerges his only task is to make up a fourth at bridge – get it? – but not before Kenneth puts in a turn worthy of proper leading man status. Kenneth himself said *Sergeant* was his favourite of his Carry On turns – 'because of all the marching. All that square-bashing was a delight' – but I'm convinced *Regardless* was his finest hour. His whole wannabe secret agent set piece, as well as being a parody of *The Thirty Nine Steps*, *Strangers on a Train* and other crime noir offerings, was surprisingly ambitious compared with the other segments, and a teaser of all the spoof wonders of the series that were later to come.

If the team were becoming ever more polished, Kenneth Connor was the shiniest of them all during those first early titles. He doesn't get his own chapter in this book, but only due to lack of space and his relatively few roles. He dropped out of the series for much of the golden era before returning later for *Jungle* duties.

He definitely merits an 'Also Honoured' in despatches, for his versatility, his wealth of voices, his elastic expressiveness and self-deprecation. Norman Hudis was particularly fond of him and described him as 'a giant comedy talent, with glimpses of pathos and tenderness, rendered all the more wrenching for their understatement'. In the next film in the series he was on fine form as usual, as Dr Binn, the ship's quaking doctor.

'Binn?'
'No, that's the trouble.'

Cruising was the first Carry On film to be made in colour. Although this attracted a much bigger budget than previous titles, stretched to £140,000, sadly none of that went on exotic locations for the cast. The furthest anybody got was Southampton, and that was only director and producer to get some exterior shots. The cast remained in their usual spot at Pinewood.

One person noticeable by his absence on deck was Charles. Originally pegged to play the chef, Charles had developed ideas above his station after reading a critic's gushing compliment that no Carry On film would be any good without him. Basking in this praise, the actor decided such acclaim warranted a pay rise, and a star on his dressing room door to boot. Peter was having none of it. Not only was Charles not given a star or a raise, his role of Ship's Cook was replaced in the film by Lance Percival.

For everyone else, it was business very much as usual. In a set up very familiar to those of both *Teacher* and *Constable*, Sid as Captain Crowther wants to impress his guests, secure a new Transatlantic posting and leave his current brood behind, in this case, a brand new crew of seemingly inept misfits. Somehow, this unprepossessing lot overcome their limitations, help him earn his dream posting, only for him to decide he wouldn't be happier anywhere else after all. In the meantime, a couple of blossoming romances and misunderstandings prove Peter Rogers wasn't wrong – he really was making the same film over and over again.

After making twelve films for Peter in six years, including six hugely successful Carry On titles, even Norman Hudis began to flag. By his own admission, he tried and failed to deliver a script for *Carry On Spying* that was a worthy successor to all that had gone before. Looking back, it wasn't so much a failure as a different direction from the one expected of him. 'Creative differences' is usually the go-to euphemism for a pop group's less than edifying reasons for splitting, but it really does seem to describe what came to pass between Norman and the rest of the Carry On production team. Given the seed of an idea for *Spying*, he turned his customary gaze on the state of England and took the plot down a path leading to a CND demonstration, threw in some activist undertones for good measure, and came up with a script that was miles away from the chunky, chuckly spy drama spoof that Peter was envisaging. Who's to say he was wrong? *Spying* in its final form would become one of the great triumphs of the series, but Norman's more political version remains unmade and beyond criticism.

Norman reflected in his memoir years later that perhaps the time had simply come for a change. Of Peter's rejection of his script, he wondered, 'Did he realise that if the series was to take a slightly more fantasy-based comedy, then it was time for me to leave? It was a creative decision I cannot argue with.'

At the same time, his own amazing success with *Nurse* had drawn all sorts of requests from American studios, with Hollywood agent Lee Rosenberg even phoning him and offering to represent him. Fearing he'd run out of track at Pinewood, Norman decided to up sticks and take his chances. He took with him the support of Peter Rogers, whose only stipulation was that Norman refrain from using the phrase Carry On in the title of anything he wrote.

Instead, in the years that followed, Norman went down a mostly television path. His American writing credits included *The Man From U.N.C.L.E. CHiPs* and *Hawaii 5-0*.

Years after his auspicious debut work for the stage, *Here Is The News*, he also returned to theatre with the play *Dinner With Ribbentrop*, inspired by his own much earlier experiences of working in theatre with anti-Semitic actor Eric Portman, which found an unlikely but impressed audience in Santa Ana, California. Later, his play *Seven Deadly Sins Four Deadly Sinners* went round the world.

His producer on both these projects was Marc Sinden, son of Donald Sinden, godson of Peter Rogers and Betty Box. He tells me what an impressive figure he believed Norman to be, particularly in keeping his cool when faced with the likes of Portman's bigotry. 'I asked him why he stayed,' recalls Sinden. 'He told me, "It was money. I had a family to support." That takes a very strong man.'

I wonder if Norman was as funny away from work as we saw in all those early Carry On films? 'He was very dry,' remembers Sinden. 'Quite unfunny in his own way – until he came up with the perfect line, and then we'd fall about laughing.'

For the rest of his working life, Norman found audiences in film, TV and theatre. He died aged 93 in February 2016. For his own part, he reflected, 'I'd love to be remembered as somebody who had something of a hand in making millions of people laugh.'

In his formative contribution to the Carry On series, he did that and much more besides. He cast a generous but all-seeing eye on British society as it was moulding itself post-war, pre-sexual revolution. There was a modesty to his protagonists, Sergeants Grimshawe and Wilkins, Bert Handy and Peter Golightly, all men challenged by events and their own limitations, but ultimately coming through before … carrying on. Most of all, from *Sergeant* right through to *Cruising*, Norman Hudis celebrated a sense of comradeship and of being in it together, a recognition of the strength of cohesion and community I sometimes worry is long gone in our daily lives, even if fortunately we have films like these to remind us.

Of his particular gift of gently poking fun at national institutions and alerting his audiences to their inconsistencies and foibles, Norman remained humble, writing, 'We didn't know we were being significant or reflecting social or political mores of any kind. We just followed our noses and it led to fame and fortune, which was nice.'

Peter Rogers was more effusive. He described Norman as being the only writer he employed who could provide the 'tear-jerk' element that was so crucial in the early Carry On titles. He wrote in the foreword to Norman's own memoir, 'I told Norman that I wanted a laugh and tear-jerk script and that is what I got – one after another. Bless him.'

In 1998, at a reunion for Carry On cast and crew, celebrating the 40th anniversary, Peter took a moment to recognise publicly Norman's extraordinary contribution to the series. He introduced him as 'the man who pioneered the Carry Ons. He's here today and I want him to stand up for people to see what a genius looks like'.

At another event a few years later, Peter repeated his affection for Norman and wondered aloud why he had disappeared off to work in America.

'They asked me and paid me,' Norman answered. With perfect timing and also some delightful ambiguity as to quite whom he was chastising, himself or Norman, Peter replied, 'We all make mistakes.'

Norman's first six Carry On titles are full of community, togetherness, pluck and comradeship. They are warm-hearted, simple and old-fashioned, not perhaps what people think of anymore when they're asked about the Carry On films and often overshadowed by the bawdiness that came later, nevertheless they have a charm and lasting appeal all of their own.

And, despite the huge success that followed, it is one of these original six films that can still lay claim, after all these years, to being the most popular Carry On film ever. Of the profound and long-lasting success of *Nurse*, even the ever-humble Norman Hudis was moved to express his profound satisfaction.

He remembered, 'Acclaim like that happens once in a lifetime. It is at such rare moments that the most battered movie writer knows that there is a God and that he has a sense of humour.'

Chapter 5

Star Spotlight – Kenneth Williams

'Stop messing about!'

Charles Hawtrey's behaviour was as spontaneous as his screen rival Kenneth Williams's was furiously in check. Off screen, Kenneth was both contemptuous but envious of his colleague's acceptance of his sexuality, writing, 'He can sit in a bar and pick up sailors and have a wonderful time. I couldn't do it.'

If Charles led a life that tottered constantly into chaos, his more intellectual co-star led one of often miserable, tight-lipped control, at odds with his extraordinary on-screen contribution.

'I think we're here to entertain, to get laughs,' was how Kenneth once explained the Carry On team's mission in an aside to a reporter on a film premiere red carpet. He could equally have been describing his own professional raison d'etre – something he proved definitively by sacrificing quite early in his career the opportunity to realise his far loftier, more serious aspirations.

When Kenneth's diaries, covering forty years of his life, were published after his death, they revealed something we all instinctively already believed to exist – the deep chasm between the extrovert, often outrageous, public performer we watched steal the limelight whenever he appeared as a guest on any TV chat show or radio panel game, and the private, complicated, often deeply troubled man away from the spotlight. If there is any solace to be had from reading of his own battles with a multitude of demons, it is in the knowledge that, at least, his comic persona brought him all the success he so clearly deserved – with his elastic facial expressions, his mastery of timing and his unique enunciation.

The voice we hear in our ears whenever we think of Kenneth Williams is probably the one he selected most often from his armoury, in the way the rest of us might reach for a favourite coat or hat. These crisp, rich tones, bordering on aristocratic, were just one layer of his carefully created entity, but significantly the ones most at odds with his working-class London background. His father, a hairdresser called Charlie, definitely didn't sound like that as he ruled the roost in the family's one-room, no-bath flat just north of King's Cross Railway Station, nor did he have any truck with young Kenneth's gentle ways. Hearing Kenneth relate later how his father wanted to toughen him up and even once presented him with a pair of boxing gloves, well, it's hard to work out who to have more sympathy for.

Instead, like Charles Hawtrey, Kenneth forged an intense, lifelong bond with his mother Louie. Years later, he confirmed in his diary, 'There will never be anyone I love as much as her.' If the star's directness could be traced to his father's style, his mother's bawdy humour had an equal influence. The actor's old friend Peter Nichols often recounted an incident when he arrived to see Kenneth at his father's salon, and Louie asked if he had a television. 'Yes,' he told her, 'a 19-inch console.' '19 inches,' she replied, quick as a whip, 'that'd console anyone, that would.' A line surely to match anything Talbot Rothwell would ever come up with.

'Friends, Romans...'
'Countrymen.'
'I know!'

Kenneth got his very first taste for the boards at school where his Princess Angelica in *The Rose and the Ring* earned a cracking review in a local paper. 'Kenneth Williams, with his mincing step and comical demeanour was a firm favourite with the audience, to whom his snobbishness and pert vivacity made great appeal.' Pert vivacity! No later notice better summed up his entire career.

Although Kenneth initially adhered to father's insistence on entering a trade and became an apprentice draughtsman with a map-maker, this career path was interrupted by the war, when he was evacuated to a house in Bicester. He returned to London with a love of learning, books and a newly posh voice. By 1945, he'd signed up with the Army and been sent to the Far East to combat Japanese forces. While not a natural soldier, he found his metier entertaining fellow troops with his recitals, stories and, above all, impersonations.

'He became an absolute compendium of British types,' remembers Russell Davies, who later edited Williams's diaries. He tells me, 'There was his extremely posh voice, which he later used to represent himself on chat shows, and also the raucous cockney voice, which he inherited from his father. That might have been nearest his natural persona, buried deep underneath, although there was scarcely anything natural about him at all.'

Pretty soon, Kenneth was off to join the Combined Services Entertainment, where colleagues included Stanley Baxter and John Schlesinger. Even in this freshly liberal environment, Kenneth kept his own sexuality private, although he joined the others in realising the potential for entertainment in the high art of camp.

Back in London, he trained to be an actor in repertory theatre and was briefly set on running his own company. When that failed, he was forced to move back home where he continued to educate himself, much to Charlie's disdain.

Initially set on becoming a serious, classical actor, his big break came in 1954 when he was cast as the Dauphin in *Saint Joan*, a highly-lauded performance that drew attention from high, but very different, places. Radio producer Dennis Main Wilson spotted him and thought he'd be perfect for a brand new comedy show, *Hancock's Half Hour* and not long after, he was invited to appear in the 1955 West End production of *Moby Dick*, directed by no less a figure than Orson Welles. The Williams Diaries report that Kenneth so impressed the legendary director, he received an invitation to join his Company in America. When the actor turned this down in favour of staying in Britain and sticking to comedy, Welles' reply has gone down in history as indignant – 'You will tread the path to oblivion.'

However, playwright Terry Johnson believes any laments by Welles and others to Kenneth's lost classical career are not to be over-cooked. 'I don't think he could be bothered to take himself seriously. Once he realised he could make people laugh, he dedicated himself to being a comedian.'

Russell Davies agrees. 'As soon as he got his hands on what he came to call burlesque, he fitted into that perfectly.'

Sure enough, *Hancock* writer Alan Simpson remembered that the original plan for the radio show had been to play the lines straight until Williams walked in for the first reading and said, in his distinctively nasal way, 'Good evening.' Simpson added, 'Then of course, on the show it got an enormous laugh. Instead of having the courage to say we were trying to do away with funny voices, we said we'll use it.' Simpson reflected on Kenneth's skills in an interview for *The South Bank Show*, 'Carry On films were perfect for him. He wasn't the subtlest of actors, and he could overplay and be outrageous, and be really funny.'

Simpson once described Kenneth as having four basic voices – snide, rich and plum, the befuddled nonsense of an upper class twit and, finally, the broad Cockney he borrowed from his father – and this proved plenty for the millions tuning in. Kenneth's star was in the ascendant.

When Tony Hancock's show was moved to TV, however, the plan was to make it less farcical, which meant Kenneth's role was diminished, ironically to make room for one Sid James. Instead, he stayed in radio to join what would become *Round The Horne* – creating with Hugh Paddick a pair of outrageously camp characters Julian and Sandy. Bear in mind this was 1958, almost a decade before homosexuality was legalised in Britain, let alone widely socially accepted, and you realise just how radical they were. Kenneth's castmate Betty Marsden remembered, 'It was the first time that a couple of camp gentlemen had ever been heard on radio, and we were astounded that it got past the censor.' One of the show's writers, Barry Took, later called it a conspiracy of silent understanding between the players and their 8 million listeners.

Radio and revue work kept Kenneth in demand, and his success and clear talents appealed to writers as discriminating as John Mortimer and Peter Cook. However, by the early 1960s, Cook's own show *Beyond the Fringe* heralded a radical new era for comedy, one in which Kenneth might have found it harder to fit, had something else even more distinctive not come calling.

In 1958, he was spotted in revue by the producer Peter Rogers and offered a role in a brand new comedy film to be called *Carry on Sergeant*. He went on to appear in twenty-six in total, and became one of the series' most defining players.

Where to begin with Kenneth Williams's place in the Carry On firmament? Well, first, there is his unique look and sound. His voice is as large as his body is small. His eyes are invariably wide and round in optimism until his authority is usurped, when they become narrow in suspicion. Finally, they bulge in outrage, just as his nostrils flare and you can see the flames if you look carefully.

In body, like Charles Hawtrey, Kenneth appears super-slim, but less knock-kneed. Instead, he seems to slither and writhe around, whether in smooth superiority or agony. His voice, with its superb range and his mastery of control, remains silky and smooth until all semblance of control is lost, and the shrieks begin.

In style, he is constantly over-deliberate, self-important, suspicious until circumstances conspire against him and his barely-restrained apoplexy inevitably escapes. Is he really ever acting, or just extending his already developed public persona, relying on his comic timing and sense of the absurd? Alan Simpson described him once as 'a grotesque', while actress Sheila Hancock said he called to mind 'a malevolent elf'.

Whatever the most accurate description, his limitations as a straight actor served him excellently in Carry On. Noel Coward once told him, 'You are one of the few actors I know who can be outrageous and get away with it.'

Russell Davies reflects now on 'the outrageousness that he both chastised himself for in his diaries but he was also secretly proud of. He couldn't impose himself on the world in a physical and executive way, but being outrageous was a way of doing it by parody'.

His early Carry On co-star Leslie Phillips explained, 'They didn't want characters, they wanted the essence of what you had, so Kenny was like himself. He was very snooty, very grand, very erudite – he used to mug around, joke around, and he'd just do that on film.'

I believe that the tension between Kenneth's lifelong impulse for self-control and superiority and the manic cartoon that Carry On demanded of him is where the magic lies. We see it time and again in the films where his character begins as an outsider, a superior, an antagonist, who is ultimately brought down and inside, by events. His mania always explodes from a locked-in grenade that is bound to go off and, always, he takes it seriously, which means we as viewers don't have to. Actor David Benson who has brought Kenneth to life on stage in the play *Think No Evil of Us* and brought his perfect impersonation of him to many other TV and radio performances, pins it down beautifully with the phrase 'punctured pomposity'.

Along with Charles, Kenneth relied heavily on camp, but it was only one trick in his armoury. Benson explains, 'Kenneth had a much broader palette, probably because of all his reading. He had a broader imagination on which to build a character.'

Reviewing the series reveals this to be true. The early titles from *Sergeant* and *Nurse* through to *Regardless* channel Kenneth into a roll call of uppity, intellectual outsiders, sneering at others despite his own low station, telling William Hartnell in *Sergeant*, 'Sociologically, it's important for me to find out just how far one can retain one's individuality in the army.'

Cruising gives him more of a centre stage position as First Officer Marjoribanks, and the first colour film of the series brings the actor fully to life, with his voice, his mannerisms, that unique and instantly familiar voice, plus a hyena cackle to match Sid James's conspiratorial chuckle. Status-wise, he's central too, a mid-ranking officer seen helping equally the ship's captain, the surgeon and the chef. From here on in, though, he's promoted to roles of authority, from *Jack* through to *Dick*. Add to this list his various doctors in the medical titles, plus his frazzled school outing leader in *Camping*, and a pattern emerges – of authority undone, pomposity inevitably pricked.

'What's all this jigging in the rigging?'

Throughout many of the films, but particularly noticeable in the hospital titles, chaos comes to Kenneth in the form of female attention. He is constantly fending off the overtures of (matron) Hattie Jacques and (assistant) Patsy Rowlands, but the satire is clear. It is his status they covet, not his personality, which appears throughout as carefully asexual, if not alien, in comparison with any traditionally attractive male prospect. Much of the comedy he gives us relies on our sense of his palpable prurience faced with all this totty. 'No, no, Barbara,' he instructs his charge in *Camping*. 'Tent up first, bunk up later.' This is only funny because the thought of Kenneth bunking up is, well, unthinkable. The same goes for his follow up. 'It's fairly easy to get it up, it's getting it to stay up, that's what counts.'

Later on in *Dick*, as Captain Desmond Fancey, in the course of catching the famous looter Dick Turpin, he threatens to have his way with marauder Harriet. When she consents, he flees, an episode that cuts to the heart of the battle of the sexes in all the films.

'I'm Camembert, the big cheese'

The golden age of Carry On reveals Kenneth in all his revue splendour – from a wilting sea captain in *Jack*, a limp Caesar in *Cleo* to Police Chief Camembert in *Don't Lose Your Head*, or a bejewelled Rajah Khasi in *Khyber*. My favourite Kenneth Williams character is the teetotal town mayor Judge Burke in the colourful *Cowboy*, fully formed and memorable. 'That's another pot I've won,' he announces after a game in the saloon, before carefully picking up an actual pot. 'Mighty pretty it is too.'

Russell Davies points out, 'He had to work harder for that one. The voice wasn't in his repertoire, so he went and found it in old Hal Roach Western movies and worked it up from scratch, an unusual process for him, but enjoyable. He was rarely pleased by anything, but that one he did like.'

'Infamy, infamy, they've all got it in for me.'

Of course, even if you've never seen a Carry On film, you've probably absorbed two of their most definitive moments, both of which Kenneth formed a crucial element. *Cleo* finds him despairing as Caesar – 'I do feel queer' – before realising he has lost the confidence of his people.

Five years later, Williams is on duty again, leading his girls in a PE routine for *Camping*. It is his Dr Soaper who is on the receiving end of Barbara's bra when it pings across the field, and the joke would be nothing without his stricken face. He recovers his composure, at least enough to carry on the class.

'Stop laughing, now that Barbara's fallen out, we will continue.'

He seldom switched off, even when the cameras stopped rolling. Away from set, he'd pull up a chair and tell stories to all those around him and enjoy the strong reactions, whether they be approval or shock. He became notorious at Pinewood for his self-described 'vag trick' – pulling up his skirts and pretending to be a girl. He met his match in Edna, the tea lady, known for pushing her trolley around between takes. When he flashed her during *Carry on Henry*, she looked him up and down, eyed his crotch and said, 'One lump or two? Or in your case none at all, I should think.'

He wrote himself of his complex character, delighting in his public lewd talk, contrasting with his quiet self, a prisoner of the public persona that won him so much affection:

When I think of the shameless way I behave, anything for a cheap laugh … and the person that I really am at home with myself, it is almost a Jekyll and Hyde existence, and the first half gives me guilt and remorse. I am loathe to relinquish the laughs and crowd … I need them like a healthy person needs a partner.

Russell Davies adds now:

He had licence to behave outrageously in a way that many adults are prevented. He was allowed to get away with it because he was the bad boy, although the film-makers got their revenge, playing on his obvious primness, and fear of physicality. He was often dunked in gunge, and that was them putting physical discomfort in his way for the pleasure of his reaction.

His attitude to the films themselves had always been ambivalent. In January 1961, he wrote, 'What a fantastic paradise to imagine working in nothing but Carry Ons,' but the honeymoon didn't appear to last long. By the following month, he'd added, 'I'm not going to do another Carry On.'

'What a day, pelted by the populace, sat on by the senate, spat at by my wife, I don't know why I bother being emperor.'
'Why do you?'
'What else can I do? At school, I didn't even get my X.I. plus.'

His diaries record his increasing woe at how he felt they chipped away at his diminishing talent. He wrote, 'The scripts are schoolboy scatology … the most depressing sort of would-be funny rubbish.' He constantly pledged to depart the series, then signed up for the next film, finally appearing in no less than twenty-six, taking some sort of dysfunctional pleasure in continuing to take part, rather than walking away. Go figure.

If he was honest, though, he needed them as much as the reverse. As well as the regular, if small, pay cheques, they ensured his profile remained high. More significantly, working with the same team through the years brought him the closest thing to a sense of family he'd ever had.

While he respected the skills of Sid James, his personal favourites included Hattie Jacques, Peter Butterworth and Bernard Bresslaw. He even ended up going on honeymoon with Barbara Windsor – hers, not his. Russell Davies comments, 'He liked to drop in on domesticity that was functioning because he'd never had that. Kenneth Connor he liked as well.'

Increasingly, though, his venomous pen flowed. He wrote of his contempt for the productions, his co-stars, scripts and viewers alike, sparing no one. As Peter Rogers remarked later, 'Sometimes he wrote in a very loud voice.'

His frustrations grew with his feeling he was repeating himself, particularly as the films became broader over the course of the 1960s, and Kenneth's characterisations both more extreme but also more marginalised. He could sense he was becoming a parody of what had gone before, and each time he was offered a role, he vowed it would be his last. Finally, with *Emmannuelle*, it was.

Kenneth once explained to Joan Rivers on her chat show, 'I should have been a monk. Privacy is the most important thing in my life, and anything which invaded that would be a threat, so consequently I live a life of celibacy.' She probably thought he was exaggerating.

If his associates weren't convinced that was 100 per cent accurate, nobody doubted Kenneth's need for solitude, attested by the few visitors he allowed to his London flat, where they described his complete lack of furnishings, and even a kitchen hob covered in polythene. His friend Peter Nichols described his flat as resembling 'a beached liner', where even friends were made to feel unwelcome. It was Spartan and drab, in comparison with the colour of his public persona and vivacity of his language.

Probably the best outlet for both once he departed the Carry Ons was radio's *Just a Minute*, where his erudition and capacity for learning served him in wonderful capacity, endlessly amusing as well as occasionally letting rip. On TV, he found brief success as the compere of *International Cabaret*, but was disparaging about the acts sharing his stage. At one point, he wrote to the BBC, asking for his fee to be lowered.

With radio and TV work drying up, his platform was reduced even further. Michael Parkinson described him by now as 'that most forlorn of creatures, the person who existed because of gameshows and talkshows', although in the same breath, he credited him as 'God's gift to a chat show host', no doubt because of his ability to alchemise his own distress and strangeness into wonderful material. Kenneth once explained, 'If something is misery making, talk about it, make it funny, explain why the malaise occurs, and you can do that with comedy.'

That lasted for a while, but here the walls began to close too as new faces appeared, and he realised he had little else of himself to feed on, writing in his diary, 'The fact is on these chat shows, I've been eating at myself for years, just living off body fat, and people say, all he does is now is go on and tell stories we've all heard before... pathetic.' His friend Gyles Brandreth referred to Kenneth's evolution into 'a coarsened caricature of himself', and described it very sadly, 'From an enormous potential, he had boxed himself into a corner.'

Comedian and writer Robin Ince poses it to me as the eternal entertainer's dilemma. If you were Kenneth Williams, he asks, would you reveal more personal, deeper parts of yourself or would you put on the show you know everyone wants?

Ince adds:

And then of course be nauseated by the fact everyone is looking, and that he'd let himself down. Here was a reader of philosophy, he'd worked with Orson Welles, and none of that was accessible to him now, in no small part due to all those appearances in Carry Ons. Every now and then you'd see him when an interviewer gave him fresh respect, and he would rise to that.

With a career ever more restricted by typecasting, a despair at lack of creative fulfilment, plus a sense of his own increasing ailments added to his mother's failing health and dependency on him, the future must have looked properly bleak for Kenneth. He had mentioned suicide throughout his adult life, and by the late 1980s, his talk, both with friends and in his diary, became increasingly ominous. When he fatally succumbed to an overdose of barbiturates on 15 April 1988, the coroner recorded an open verdict, but few of his friends felt much doubt. His final diary entry, written the evening before his death, asked, 'Oh – what's the bloody point?' He was 62.

If he struggled to express his sexuality personally, Kenneth exploited it to extraordinary success professionally, thrilling fans on radio and then delighting millions more with his portrayals in Carry On. Sheridan

Morley explained, 'He was so suppressed that it came out in comedy.' More poignantly, his friend Miriam Margolyes reflected, 'I feel sad that his life wasn't as happy for him as he made it for all of us. He had the gift of creating laughter, but he didn't have the gift of creating it for himself.'

We must be grateful, though, for the former. When I ask playwright Terry Johnson to sum up Williams's enduring quality, he captures it in a word, 'Mischief.'

In this era of wafer-thin celebrity, it is hard to think of a contemporary equivalent to this extraordinary performer, with his unique combination of reading, learning – what people used to call unashamed erudition – that he brought with him and gave weight to even the most bawdy of material, bridging two very different worlds. Kenneth said himself, 'There's room for all sorts of entertainment, as long as it works on its own level. The only charge to be taken seriously is if the comedy [isn't] funny.'

David Benson wracks his brain before conceding, 'I can't think of anyone who comes close to that brilliance as a speaker, a performer, a raconteur. People don't seem interested in it, which is a shame.'

Despite the 700 pages of intimate diary he left behind, will we ever be able to say we really know Kenneth Williams? Was he the snooty vaudevillian he perfected, or the man seemingly most comfortable filmed joining in a knees-up in an East End pub? As Russell Davies asks, was he a guttersnipe or toff, or in some strange way, both?

The only thing we know for sure is that he was a performer with funny bones, with a mission he explained possibly better than anyone else could, when he said:

Acting is all about faith. Performing is an act of faith, believing that you can create reciprocity between the auditorium and the stage. That's why when the atheist says, what if life's pointless, what if it's all a joke, has to be answered by the comedian … if it is a joke, let's make it a good one.

It is such a shame for both Charles Hawtrey and Kenneth Williams, both so talented and able to transform the material they were given, that their biggest and enduring success with the Carry On films left such a bitter taste in each of their mouths, that becoming so unhappy themselves, they weren't able to share the joy they brought to millions, and continue to decades later.

They weren't the first men to turn up on stage or screen in a dress, and the debate rolls on as to what contribution they made to gay culture. As one half of Julian and Sandy on the radio, then in the Carry Ons and finally as himself, Kenneth was never anything but out and therefore possibly deemed a breakthrough artist, but we must qualify this.

Firstly, he was so unique in his personal qualities that he didn't really open up territory for others to follow. He was too complicated to be a prototype.

Secondly, on screen neither Kenneth nor Charles were ever fully formed gay characters with which the masses had to come to grips. As every girl knows, camp men are great fun to have around, being both funny and gentle, and none of this pair's Carry On characters were ever sexually assertive or even active. While they were shuffling across the mud of the campsite or struggling into high heels, they were hardly disrupting the establishment or ruffling audience feathers. That conspiracy of silence between performers and audience spotted by Barry Took could remain in place for a few more years at least.

However, for a young gay actor in a village in West Wales, both of them made all the difference. Jamie Rees remembers:

> For me, as a gay man growing up in the 1980s and 1990s, I did everything I could to hide my campness. I watched them in awe, thinking, how could they be so open, so revealing of themselves? It used to blow my mind. I think they did us all a great favour. They were seen, they didn't hide, they revealed who they were in all their glory, and by doing that they set the path for gay actors and performers to come after them.

Many have indeed followed. Names like John Inman, Larry Grayson, Dick Emery, Melvyn Hayes, Christopher Biggins and Russell Grant were topping the bill from the 1980s onwards, and the success of today's stars such as Julian Clary, Alan Carr and Graham Norton can make it difficult to imagine a time when it was more complicated to be down and out and very funny.

But over half a century ago, when it still wasn't legal to be gay, they brought with them a burst of outrageous camp energy into the mainstream for millions as they chased women, were chased themselves, oohed and aahed and constantly poked fun at traditional masculine stereotypes in a manner that was itself pioneering and, yes, brave. Plus they created big screen stardom for themselves out of two very unlikely, physically unpromising characters, in a way that pays testament to their skills as entertainers as well as to their personal appeal.

Let us console ourselves with that thought, and finish with David Benson's moving account of something that happened every night when he told Kenneth Williams's story on stage. Benson used to finish the night, exhausted, with the line, 'I didn't realise how much I missed him until he was gone.' He tells me, 'I used to turn to the audience and ask them, "Don't you?" and they'd all whisper, "Yes."'

Chapter 6

A Change of Tone

*'Put me and an engine side by side, and I'll give
you one guess which one he starts to strip down first'*

Liz Frazer in *Carry On Cabby*

*Lawrence of Arabia, The Manchurian Candidate, The Man Who Shot Liberty
Valance, To Kill a Mockingbird* and *The Loneliness of the Long Distance
Runner* – these titles and more are enough to convince veteran film critic
Stephen Farber of the thesis spelt out in the title of his book *Cinema '62:
The Greatest Year at the Movies*. For him, 1962 is a 'pivotal' moment in film
history – as he explained in an interview with *The Times*, he considered
it 'a rare confluence of art, studio craftsmanship and commerce that has
never been surpassed'.

Never mind all those Hollywood goings-on, 1962 was certainly a
pivotal moment in the history of British screen comedy, as it was when
Norman Hudis passed the Carry On scriptwriting baton to the writer
who would ultimately become responsible for the series the way most of
us remember it – Talbot Rothwell.

While each writer enjoyed an equally expressive funny bone, they
looked to very different traditions for inspiration. Whereas Norman had
kept one foot firmly in the real world, using his scripts to raise an eyebrow
to lampoon, always affectionately, the national institutions he saw
around him, Talbot Rothwell reached for something more fantastical,
increasingly colourful, increasingly veering into cinematic parody, spoof
and kaleidoscopic camp. I guess each of them were products of their own
era. While Norman's scripts belonged in the lighter, whimsical 1950s and
early 1960s, Talbot's could only be understood in the nothing-off-limits
decade that followed.

Many fans of the series, including its stars, describe the films in which
Talbot had a part as the postcards of Donald McGill brought to life.
These were vignettes of saucy British goings-on, depicting attractive

young women lusted after by middle-aged men. Frequently alongside them were plump old ladies, blushing honeymoon couples and, bizarrely specifically, vicars.

Long before the Carry Ons offered similar fare on the big screen, lifelong Londoner Donald McGill had created thousands of distinctively colour-washed, often seaside images which were then mass reproduced as postcards. He was praised for his acute observation of society and his knack for wringing the comedy out of everyday life.

Interestingly, the artist – who began his career as a naval draughtsman before dedicating himself to his saucy designs – ranked his own output according to their vulgarity, as either mild, medium or strong. And, similarly to the earlier Carry On titles, Donald McGill's work was initially influenced by the realities of life around him, in his case supporting the efforts of men serving in the First World War, and recreating the world from both their point of view and their loved ones back home.

Just as Peter Rogers battled often with the British Censor, so Donald McGill had his own trials with censorship committees, and was even convicted in in 1954 of breaking the Obscene Publications Act, before censorship eased in the late 1950s.

During his life, McGill was estimated to have created 12,000 designs, many of which visitors can still enjoy in a Postcard Museum dedicated to him on the Isle of Wight. His most popular postcard ever, estimated to have sold more than 6 million copies, shows a young couple, the man bookish, the lady pretty, sitting under a tree. The man asks the lady, 'Do you like Kipling?' She replies, 'I don't know, you naughty boy, I've never kippled!' It's a line that could have come straight from any of the Carry On films, especially those penned by Talbot Rothwell.

His arrival in the Carry On firmament signalled a fresh era, moving away from the gentle slapstick of Norman Hudis's scripts and towards increasingly bawdy innuendo and double entendre. He was richly inspired by the music hall traditions he had absorbed in his youth – including those of his own personal favourite, Max Miller. While Norman had invariably steered his narrative towards a drop-in-the-eye sentimental ending, Talbot preferred to go out on an upbeat gag following a series of bon mots and punch-lines you could set your watch to.

If there was someone who proved it was possible to find laughter in anything, even the most testing of times, it was Talbot Rothwell. A man with a lifelong love for the corniest of jokes, he grew up in Bromley, Kent where Peter Rogers's biographers recount one of Talbot's earliest memories of arriving home from an unsuccessful fishing expedition to tell his mother, 'No newts is good newts!'

Talbot's first job was as a town hall clerk in Brighton, before wartime service beckoned and he joined the Palestine Police, then the RAF. He was shot down over German-occupied Norway and captured, becoming a prisoner of war in the infamous Stalag Luft III camp in Sagan, Poland, 100 miles south-east of Berlin. It is best known now for two ambitious escape plots, both hatched by Allied prisoners and both of which had their stories told in films *The Wooden Horse* and *The Great Escape*.

While he was imprisoned in the camp, Talbot passed the time writing plays, concerts and comedy material for his fellow prisoners to perform. In one of life's great coincidences, one of his fellow POWs was future Carry On regular actor Peter Butterworth, who frequently performed in Talbot's concerts, and can lay unique claim to being the first of Peter Rogers' team to speak from a Rothwell script, and in remarkable circumstances.

In fact, three decades later, when Peter Butterworth was the subject of *This is Your Life*, host Eamonn Andrews introduced several of his Stalag campmates. Each of them, perhaps deliberately, made light of their experience in the camp, joking about how they'd passed the hours by putting on entertainment shows during their time as POWs. Talbot described their efforts, remembering, 'I think we had one production about once every seven to ten days, which ran for about four days.' Then, with perfect timing, he added, 'Let's face it, we had a captive audience.'

When he addressed himself to Peter, Talbot remained jocular, telling him, 'You could say we've been carrying on ever since.' He recounted fondly, 'Even if Pete wasn't in it … if he wasn't taking part, he was designing sets, mending the theatre or repairing the seating, even if the people were still in them.'

Two decades later on the set of the Carry Ons, even with the much-noted camaraderie of the entire cast and crew, one can only guess at the special bond between these two men with such a shared history.

Back in England after the war, Talbot found his footing as a comedy writer, both for the stage antics of the Crazy Gang, and also for radio stars including Arthur Askey, Ted Ray and Terry Thomas. By the beginning of 1963, everyone in the industry knew of the vacancy going at Pinewood, and Talbot's agent wouldn't have been doing his job if he hadn't sent one of his client's scripts about a nautical epic voyage in the direction of Peter Rogers.

When Talbot's script *Steady Boys Steady* arrived through the post, the producer realised immediately the potential of both the story and its writer. Although Talbot's initial script wasn't pitched as a Carry On film, Peter saw in it all the aspects of where he wanted his series to go next, and that Talbot was just the talent he needed. Over a jolly shared tea at the Dorchester, both men became happily engaged in opening a new chapter on the series.

With guidance from the veteran producer, Talbot set to work on the screenplay for what soon became titled *Carry On Jack*. Inspired by the visions of Errol Flynn and other stars going into battle on the high seas, plus the heroics of the popular Captain Hornblower novels, Talbot completed his first Carry On script in just three months.

With its exchange of Norman Hudis's contemporary British tableaux for a historical costume and setting, its tongue-in-cheek sending-up of big screen nautical epics, *Jack* served as a significantly transitional film in the series. Far away from the everyday settings of the previous six films, *Cruising* excepted, *Jack* took the stars and audiences on a journey all the way to … Frensham Ponds in Surrey, where the film was shot over a period of eight weeks in September and October 1963. For the 'battle' scene that came later in the story, the producers pushed the boat out and went all the way to Kimmeridge Bay in Dorset.

> *'I'm a midshipman.'*
> *'You're certainly amid something.'*

As well as a shift in setting and style, *Jack* stood out for some notable changes in casting. With no roles for Sid James, Joan Sims or Hattie Jacques and Kenneth Connor departed to join Frankie Howerd on the London stage, it was left to Kenneth Williams and Charles Hawtrey to bridge the gap between Carry On old and new.

Peter Rogers was particularly keen to cast Kenneth in the lead role of HMS Venus's Captain Fearless, what he called 'a part that would fully reflect Kenneth's great talent as a character actor'. Sure enough, Kenneth let loose in a performance where the humour lay in the chasm between his apparent authority and personal limitations including, most unfortunately for a ship's captain, seasickness whenever actually in motion, but also fainting and frequently reaching for the comfort of his seafarer's manual. While this wouldn't have been believable in someone as robust as Sid, Kenneth easily stole the film with his flashing eyes, his stick insect frame, his crisp voice and gradual delirium, leading to his distinctly out-of-place child's plea, 'Daddy, what were you doing with Nanny in the summerhouse?' It was quite the tour de force in a surprising setting.

There were other new Carry On faces. Jim Dale continued to climb steadily up the rankings with a small but significant role, while Juliet Mills took the central female role of Sally, following Liz Fraser's departure from the team. Fans to this day delight in spotting Donald Huston, Patrick Cargill and Anton Rodgers, but the real star of this one was the already tireless Bernard Cribbins.

'If you've got a heart of oak, it's got a worm in it.'

The hard-to-impress Kenneth Williams called Bernard 'the best droll I've seen in years', and he certainly brought a lot to his role of Albert Poop-Decker, still unqualified as a midshipman after eight-and-a-half years' training. Physically strong, versatile of voice, believable as the romantic lead, he fitted in perfectly, even though he remained matter-of-fact about his arrival in the team in his memoir, calling it 'just another job'. When I have the good fortune to speak to Bernard about his roles in the Carry On series, he continues in the same vein. 'I was a jobbing actor. I wasn't doing anything else at the time, so I said, "Yes, I'll do it."'

Unsentimental he may have been about the contract, but even Bernard couldn't resist what he called 'a very happy few weeks' jumping around on the boat, swinging between ropes and performing his own stunts.

Perhaps Talbot Rothwell was still warming up, but *Jack* is certainly less bawdy than many of the later films and plays more like a historical comedy than a classic Carry On romp, gags notwithstanding.

'Wouldn't you like to go to sea, friend?'
'See what?'

Despite this, Peter Rogers was intent on calling the film 'Carry On Up the Armada', but the sensitive censors of 1963 weren't having it, so *Carry On Jack* it became. This battle, plus the longer shoot and other production challenges meant that the film didn't make it to screen until February 1964, and it would be a very different film destined to become Talbot Rothwell's first Carry On release.

Considering how celebrated he became for his colourful, high-energy spoof epics of Carry On's golden age, it is remarkable that his first actual release would be a naturalistic comedy filmed from a script that he penned in the sum total of two weeks – *Carry On Cabby*.

> *'What you're going to do is wrong Charlie!'*
> *'Alright, so it's wrong, Charlie. And I'm a right Charlie!'*

After the move to colour film for *Cruising*, it was back to black and white for the deceptively simple but memorable tale of two rival cab firms – one run by Charlie Hawkins, and the other, secretly, by his wife Peggy. Originally planned as a non-Carry On film and inspired by the stage play *Call Me a Cab*, it became part of the series midway through development and is remarkable on several fronts.

It marks Jim Dale's Carry On debut, as well as that of regular composer Eric Rogers. *Cabby* has a jaunty theme tune, and a confident vibe all of its own, from the first opening scenes of Sid James as Charlie driving his cab, a scene familiar to fans of the TV comedy series *Taxi!*, which saw Sid in a very similar role. Veteran cabbies worked as extras and advisors on the set, although Charles Hawtrey, safely returned to Peter Rogers's bosom with the *Cruising* sulks now forgotten, would never be mistaken for one of these. In an unlikely biker's jacket, he even had to learn to drive, three hours of lessons every day for three weeks, for his role of Terry 'Pintpot' Tankard, and only passed his test on the Friday before filming began.

> *'What the matter with you? Can't you give a hand signal? Turns out he can.'*

There is plenty of room for innuendo, and *Cabby* has some familiar tropes to previous Carry Ons, with Sid doing his best to train an unruly mob of would-be drivers in his cab firm, but the film is deceptively progressive and, in its own way, as transitional as any Carry On title. Its line-up of strong female characters whose importance we shall discuss fully later on, includes that of new Carry On face Amanda Barrie, and most importantly Hattie Jacques as abandoned wife turned businesswoman Peggy. In contrast to her Matronly presence in previous titles, here she is equally indomitable, but also softer and more vulnerable. It is a good role, and a great performance.

While *Cabby* was closest in style of Talbot's scripts to Norman Hudis's previous titles, the giveaway is in the final scene. As Peter Rogers intimated, Norman would have always opted for the sentimental ending. Instead, here Talbot opted for the upbeat pay-off, 'Call me a cab.' His seal was stamped.

Although *Carry On Spying* contains several of Carry On's familiar elements – an inept band of trainees, some moustache-twirling figures of establishment, an alien threat that, despite themselves, our tireless heroes eventually overcome, plus the requisite amount of dragged-up debacles – there are also signs of a grander narrative landscape than seen in previous films of the series. When the British government receives word that a top-secret chemical formula has been stolen by the Society for Total Extinction of Non-Conforming Humans (STENCH), they must send their brightest and best to go fetch. Cue Agents Desmond Simpkins (Kenneth Williams), Harold Crump (Bernard Cribbins), Charlie Bind (Charles Hawtrey, in the first example of a character being given the same first name as the actor) and Daphne Honeybutt, the dazzling debut of peroxided, pint-sized Barbara Windsor.

> 'See, all ready to get off a slick draw, see.'
> 'Oh Mr Simkins, that was wonderful. I'm sure I'll never get my draws off as slickly as that.'

The story sees the agents travelling from Whitehall to Vienna, then onto Algiers and, despite Peter Rogers keeping his customary grip on his cast and crew remaining at Pinewood, in total fifty-four sets were used. Even his writer Talbot had someone to help him this time around – his friend Sid Colin, who'd worked with him before on radio scripts, and would later pen the film of *Up Pompeii*.

Spying is often referred to as a parody of the James Bond films, and Peter Rogers registered the title as early as October 1962, following the success of 007's first outing in *Dr No*. Peter had already sparred with Bond producers Cubby Broccoli and Harry Saltzman at Pinewood with the latter hinting he was inclined to make a comedy version himself, but when Cubby threatened to sue over Charles Hawtrey's character's name, 'Charlie Bond, Agent 001(half)', Peter willingly changed it to 'Charlie Bind, 000 (Oh! Oh! Oohhh!)' – thus creating one of the film's early big laughs. *Spying*'s poster also had to be changed, following complaints that it too closely resembled that of *From Russia With Love*.

'Don't be silly. How can they be on to us? We don't even look British!'

In fact, *Spying*'s noirish sequences, stealthy encounters and especially its undercover expedition from Whitehall to Vienna then Algiers, all make it more redolent of Carol Reed's *The Third Man* and also *Casablanca*, with the filming (the last Carry On to be made in black and white) only adding to the ambience. Instead of parodying just James Bond in particular, *Spying* took aim at countless espionage film conventions audiences had come to accept and expect. Talbot's script was an early example of his mastery of spoof, that of lampooning an entire genre (instead of parody, which is mocking one specific film or work of art in particular), something the writer and his Carry On team would continue.

As well as throwing in countless familiar tropes from those and other espionage thrillers, it also gave us a stonking good film in itself, although not remembered quite as fondly by returning leading man Bernard Cribbins, who suffered the excruciating pain of being hit at close range by the blank from an extra's gun.

'The extra was given the revolver with the blanks, and was firing it straight at Barbara Windsor and myself,' he tells me. 'A blank is not a safe gun at close range, because it shoots out burning particles. One hit me in the lip. Agony!'

Bernard remembers the crew were less than impressed with how angry he was at being hurt like that, and Peter Rogers himself described the actor's ranting as 'bad behaviour' which he couldn't tolerate as it undermined the director's authority. When I speak to him, though, the actor squarely defends his strong reaction that day.

'As soon as I started shouting, it was, "What's the matter with you? Come on!"' Bernard recalls the crew's lack of sympathy. 'The man who was shooting it hadn't been instructed to get above our heads or below, not to shoot directly at faces.'

Bernard also found the speed at which *Spying* was filmed – fifteen pages of script a day   quick and uncomfortable after the relative luxury of *Jack*'s eight weeks' production, a hectic pace he likened to 'standing up on an Inter-City train'. His great solace was working alongside his friend Barbara Windsor, whom he remembers today as 'a breath of fresh air'.

Apart from these un-fond memories, *Spying* was a remarkably successful step up for Carry On. Following the grittiness of *Cabby* and the historical epic of *Jack*, *Spying* offered a completely different experience for cinema audiences – the effective creation of a fully realised world, particularly when our protagonists reached STENCH's underground HQ. The plot even took a novel, surreal turn when we finally met super-villain Doctor Crow, played physically by Judith Furse but voiced by John Bluthal. Watched again in 2020, Doctor Crow's scenes remain striking, I think ahead of their time, and a revealing giveaway of the filmmakers' ambition.

Along with all its customary double-entendres and misunderstandings, *Spying* gives us some outstanding visual gags, such as when STENCH's HQ turns out to be directly underneath the offices of the British Secret Service, and when the gang tries to escape its imprisonment by STENCH through a hole in the ground that tunnels through – all the way to a hole in the same room!

Of course, the whole perilous story of international counter-espionage is ridiculous and unlikely, but no more so than many big screen counterparts who take themselves far more seriously. On its release, *Spying* enjoyed both big audiences and critical acclaim, fans responding to the zip-fast pace, the tongue-in-cheek references to other popular films and a palpable shift in ambition on the part of the cast and crew. For the first time, it seemed almost fashionable to admit to liking a Carry On film. As Kenneth noted drily in his memoir, 'Stick around long enough, and even the critics will come to accept you.'

To this day, *Spying* is still considered among the best of the entire series, while for many it signalled the beginning of Carry On's most celebrated era.

Talbot Rothwell went on to write an astonishing twenty of the Carry On films in total, before finally calling it a day in 1974. His bottomless well of jokes never appeared to run dry, with Gerald Thomas once remarking, 'I think he has a Victorian gag book at home.'

Unlike Norman Hudis, he didn't move on to another significant creative chapter. Already suffering from ill health when he left Peter Rogers's team, he confined himself to penning a few TV specials, and writing the first series of *Up Pompeii!* starring his old Carry On alumnus Frankie Howerd. Awarded an OBE for services to cinema in 1977, he retired around the same time and spent his final years in Worthing, where he died in 1981, aged 64.

His outstanding tenure at the creative helm of Carry On included many of the most defining and rightly beloved titles in the series. But right from the day he joined the team with his hastily submitted script for 'Up the Armada', it is clear he had a vision for how to put his stamp on the series, and he succeeded in taking it in a direction for which it will always be best remembered. With *Jack*, Carry On gave us its first belt-and-braces period drama, with *Cabby* the writer continued Norman Hudis's affectionate portrayals of everyday British life but painted with a much broader palette, particularly when it came to the role of women. Finally, with *Spying*, he gave Carry On audiences their very first taste of the genre for which the cast and crew would become most celebrated – the epic spoof. Talbot Rothwell may not have not known it at the time, but he and the rest of the Carry On team were about to embark on their golden age.

Chapter 7

Star Spotlight – Sid James

'Spoken like a true man!'

Forty-one minutes into *Carry On Constable* is when it happens. With so many officers off work due to illness, Sergeant Frank Wilkins is forced to join his inept underlings back on the beat. After one of his constables mistakenly thinks he overhears a murder being committed, the force breaks into a woman's apartment and chaos ensues. Wilkins arrives and clears up the misunderstanding, then goes to leave the apartment. Then, just as he is about to close the front door behind him, he opens it one more time and pops his head back round.

No more words are said, but there it all is in the double take, the glint in the eye and the naughty grin – Sid James sharing a silent joke with millions of fans, his character indulging his eye for the ladies, the actor giving us the benefit of a charm that appeared the gruff opposite of his co-star Leslie Phillips's smooth delivery, but would prove to be even more potent as Sid with his signature style became an anchor in the evolving legend of Carry On.

Sid James was always the first to play down his own looks. He once said, 'I've got a pug ugly face, so I get pug ugly parts. My face is my fortune. I knew it wouldn't win any beauty prizes, but it's never been out of work for long.' Sure enough, over the years his crinkled face and speckly features earned comparisons with 'an unmade bed' and 'a tangerine that's been left out in the sun'. Even on screen in *Carry On Regardless*, he was described as 'resembling a relief map of the Himalaya', while in *Loving*, his character was likened to 'an ancient and dissipated walnut' – and that was by the woman who went on to marry him! But none of these fond insults do justice to Sid's enduring appeal.

Physically, that came from the mischievous twinkle in his eyes, the gravel of his tones, the readiness of his smile. Along with those came the laugh, his delightfully amused, conspiratorial cackle that has come to define him, and in fact the Carry On films as a whole. These were all expressions of a personality that appeared to have been chipped and glued together somewhere in London's East End, but could fit in anywhere, hence his career as one of Britain's most prolific actors. Sid said himself, 'I've played a hell of a lot of roles, but they're all me, just with different hats on.' Sure enough, as he became one of our most familiar faces and voices, it seemed that his characters on screen were simply exaggerated versions of his real self – a lovable rogue, a bookie's best friend, an unassuming actor who eschewed the trappings of stardom and, despite years of success, always remained 'one of us'.

Perhaps, then, the biggest surprise of Sid James's life was that, in fact, he wasn't 'one of us' at all, at least not for his first three decades. This most beloved British Cockney-sounding Everyman started life as Solomon Joel Cohen nowhere near Bow Bells, but thousands of miles away in South Africa in May 1913 – born into his Jewish family living in a house in Hillbrow, Johannesburg to be exact, and in Hancock Street, to sound prophetic. Sid's parents Lou and Reine had emigrated from the East End of London three years before, and soon plied their trade as music hall performers.

Infant Sidney would accompany them on tour, sitting in a basket in the wings, from where before long he began to join in their act. In an interview many decades later at Pinewood, Sid remembered fondly his earliest days performing with his parents and a lesson he learned at their knee, revealing, 'My father taught me a lot when I was very young. He told me to smile when we were taking our bow. He told me, "You're not smiling until you feel it. Feel the smile."'

Growing up, Sid pursued a theatrical career while making money in a series of jobs – teaching dance, heaving coal, polishing diamonds and running his own hair salon. The performing bug got hold of him at a young age, taking him into repertory theatre in Johannesburg and carrying him through wartime service, which he spent entertaining the troops as a lieutenant in the South African Army. Following the end of the war, Sid decided it was time to take his chances in London, and he used his de-mob money to pay for one-way tickets for himself, his second wife Meg and their young daughter Reina. One close friend from his days in South Africa was Harry Rabinowitz, a musician who would go on to great success in London too, and he reflected later, 'I think Sid was coming home more than anything else. He was immensely English.'

Sid and his family arrived on Christmas Day 1946. He was 33 and was rewarded almost straight away with an extraordinary stroke of luck. A chance meeting on Shaftesbury Avenue with some old South African friends, Olga Lowe and her actor husband John Tore, led to them suggesting Sid meet with talent agent Phyllis Parnell, which in turn led to his very first screen role in the 1947 film thriller *Black Memory*, a part he landed just nine days after his arrival in this country. From there, Sid never looked back, soon becoming one of Britain's most prolific post-war actors.

Never unaware of his good luck, he was equally happy to give his old friends from South Africa a helping hand. Harry Rabinowitz arrived in England soon after him, but despite all his musical experience, struggled to find work until Sid stepped in, introducing Harry to West End impresario Jack Hylton, who gave Harry his first London job. Three months later, Harry was conducting a BBC orchestra and went on to an extraordinary career as a conductor, composer, arranger and pianist.

His daughter Karen tells me that Harry remained grateful to Sid for the rest of his long life. As the subject of *Desert Island Discs* in 2015, Harry himself reflected on his friend's support, 'He gave me a leg up.'

Meanwhile, Sid had two significant things going for him. The first was the post-war blossoming of London's theatre and cinema scene, where lots of films were being produced, swiftly made productions perfect for an actor as light on his feet as Sid. The other was his own attitude to his profession – that of an actor happy to work for the money, to move quickly between projects and be credited well beneath the title, what he called 'a safe place in the middle of the bill'.

Despite his relaxed approach to his craft, Sid clearly had great talent as a character actor, which meant he was always in huge demand. By the end of the 1950s, he had made what is conservatively estimated at around eighty films. He had shared the screen with Gene Kelly in *Crest of a Wave* and Charlie Chaplin in *A King in New York*, he'd turned up in *The Belles of St Trinians* and appeared in several Ealing comedies. He'd also made his name on radio and TV and appeared in a string of plays in the West End. The last brought him the role he said himself he felt closest resembled his own life – that of card-dealing Broadway hustler Nathan Detroit in *Guys and Dolls*.

By the mid-1950s, he also had a young family to support following his third marriage, to actress Valerie Ashton in 1952. The couple had met when they'd co-starred in the play *Touch and Go* and Sid had asked Valerie out to dinner. Despite her initial lack of interest in him – Sid was fifteen years older than her – Valerie finally agreed to a date and promptly, in her own words, fell madly in love with him. She said, 'He just had something about him that just won you over instantly' – more proof of Sid's unique charm. The couple had two children, Stephen and Susan, and were married for the rest of Sid's life.

At one point, he had a hefty tax bill to pay and so reluctantly accepted a role in the 1956 film *Trapeze*. Although his co-stars were big names Burt Lancaster, Tony Curtis and Gina Lollobrigida, Sid was reluctant to take the part he was offered as Harry the snake charmer. If there was one thing Sid feared it was snakes, but he gritted his teeth and spent six weeks with a snake around his neck, before happily paying off his debts. Sid was a grafter.

In many of his films, he played shady but distinctive characters who quite possibly ran a side-business or two. A classic of this type was his role in 1951's *The Lavender Hill Mob* starring Alec Guinness. Sid's character, the dodgy but cheeky Lackery, was perfect for him, and it was in this that he first caught the eye of writers Ray Galton and Alan Simpson. They thought he'd be perfect for their brand new radio series with rising star Tony Hancock.

Sid wasn't keen on the idea of radio work, saying 'I like to work with my hands and face,' and had to be persuaded to join the team, initially for just one episode then two. By all accounts, he was literally shaking to his bones with nerves at the prospect of performing before a live radio audience, but of course soon found his way. It was Sid's role in the weekly *Hancock's Half Hour* that made him a household name in Britain, along with future Carry On comrades Hattie Jacques and Kenneth Williams. The show's theme tune was conducted by his old pal Harry Rabinowitz – it's a small world.

As Tony Hancock's fictional sidekick and lodger, Sid's optimistic attitude, his character once again juggling side-lines of varying legality, perfectly complemented the title star's angst-ridden foibles, and the pair became a formidable duo, first on radio then on TV from 1954.

Alan Simpson said of their chemistry, 'It gelled perfectly.' In contrast with Hancock's lofty pretentions, Ray Galton praised what he called Sid's earthy realism. He remembered fondly of Sid's lack of curiosity, 'If it's not horse racing, it's of no interest.'

Messrs James and Hancock also became firm friends and Sid once gave an interview to the BBC, revealing how their characters' different aspirations were mirrored in real life. 'He was trying to improve my mind. He'd say, "For god's sake, learn a little." I'd say, "I know enough for what I need."'

During my research for this book, playwright Terry Johnson suggested I listen to the two men's similar cadences and speech patterns and notice how similar they became the longer they worked together. Terry tells me, 'Sid James is Tony Hancock sped up. Sid was a really good actor, and both he and Hancock grew out of each other. Actors often drive each other crazy, but they also improve each other.'

Alan Simpson remembered Sid telling him, 'I want to be a second banana. I don't want to be the star of the show.' Despite this, Hancock became increasingly distracted by his fear of becoming one half of a double act and by 1960, after six TV series plus radio, 160 half-hours in total, Sid was out. Galton and Simpson created for him his own TV show, *Citizen James*, by way of compensation, which was remarkably similar to *Hancock*, just without Hancock. It was a huge success and ran for three series, cementing Sid in fans' hearts as a jovial, gravelly Everyman character. His love for the horses, the dogs, everyone having a good time, were all incorporated.

At the time, the show's huge success offered small comfort to its star. His wife Valerie remembered Sid's abrupt departure from Hancock's team, 'He was very upset. He always hoped to get back with him but it never happened. That was his favourite television show.' Despite his great hurt, Sid reflected years later, 'Tony was the best I've ever worked with.'

If Sid taught Tony Hancock the art of television, Hancock repaid this debt with arguably a greater gift, for it was at his side that Sid learned the art of comedy. Until 1954, he'd been far happier as the straight man, but his years with Hancock polished him into confident performer of funny material, a pro who could deliver a gag with the perfect timing for which he would become only more celebrated in the years to come.

'Sid James's laugh, you can't copy it. Good artist. Quite right for the part.'

With such admirable understatement did Peter Rogers describe, decades later, why he signed Sid to the Carry On series in 1960. Peter had reluctantly realised contractual obligations meant he wouldn't be able to use Ted Ray again following the success of *Carry On Teacher*, so he was on the look out for a new leading man. Of course, Sid arrived at Pinewood a known and admired quantity, with an astounding eighty films to his name. As well as all his previous film, TV, radio and stage work, he had appeared in Betty Box's remake of *The 39 Steps* as well as her comedy *Upstairs and Downstairs*, both films released in 1959. With his versatility and proven talent for effortless teamwork, he was a natural fit for Peter's blossoming series.

Sid joined Carry On for film number four, and ended up making nineteen titles in total. While he continued to do lots of other work, it was for Carry On that he became best known, as he naturally became one of the series' most central stars.

Sid's debut as Frank Watkins in *Constable* was marked in typical style. In his very first scene, he received a Carry On christening with a bucket of water in the face. Director Gerald Thomas was immediately appreciative, remembering, 'The reaction and the freeze that comes after it is something you'll only get from Sid James.'

If writer Norman Hudis was responsible for starting this mucky tradition, Talbot Rothwell was happy to continue it. Sid took it in his stride, later remarking, 'I think in every single Carry On I've done, I've been soaked to the skin. I think Tolly Rothwell now does it on purpose. The lot. Cement, water, mud, manure.'

In fact, such constant spraying later caused Sid problems. His son Stephen remembers his father getting water in his ears during a typically watery caper in *Regardless*. Stephen tells me, 'From then on, he always had to wear plugs in his ears whenever we went swimming.'

Constable and *Regardless*, the two Norman Hudis-penned Carry Ons that starred Sid, both gave him a central role of benevolent authority, bridging the gap between the snotty seniors and inept juniors that had sparred in the earlier films *Sergeant* and *Nurse*. Ted Ray's role in *Teacher* had provided a similar template, but Sid brought his own qualities to inhabit a middle ground that was perfect, professionally and socially, for his persona on-screen and off – in charge but not frightening, paternal not patronising, conveying a sense of comradeship summed up by his unique chuckle that we heard properly for the first time in *Regardless* – mischievous, wry, conspiratorial and deeply infectious.

Was that a persona created for the cameras? His son Stephen says not. 'I can't remember him being any different on screen to what he was at home.' Sid's daughter Sue mostly agrees. 'He would enhance it, as he knew what was expected. But he also had the twinkle at home.'

'Blimus!'

Although he made nineteen Carry On films in total, to my mind his finest films coincided with the golden age of the series running from *Cleo* (1964) to *Camping* (1969). After so many re-runs on TV, we almost take for granted now the farcical comedy of the Carry On period spoofs, but viewing them again makes me realise afresh just how carefully the comedy was constructed and how critical Sid's contribution. Whether he is striding the forum as Mark Antony in *Cleo*, twirling his pistols as the Rumpo Kid in *Cowboy*, or even resorting to drag disguise as Sir Rodney Ffing in *Don't Lose Your Head*, Sid's deliberate underplaying of his characters, his earthy realism as Ray Galton had put it, even in such exotic surroundings, beautifully serve both to highlight the farce of the tale and to give a safe sounding board for his co-stars as manic and kinetic as Kenneth Williams and Jim Dale respectively. For writer Talbot Rothwell, Sid was a robust linchpin of the cast, around whom he could build a canvas of surreal schemes, lecherous capers and bawdy intrigue.

Asked once to describe his own craft, Sid typically played down his talents, explaining, 'I just make a habit of playing against the others. I'm not a comic at all. These other lads are comedians. I'm more of a reactor. So I let them do it, and then I throw a couple of counter-punches. That's all I can do.'

That may have been the case but there was no doubt what value he brought to the series, both for fans of the films and for cast and crew, and his apparently straightforward delivery belied a profound work ethic that propelled him into action every single day.

'He was always an early riser,' recalls his son Stephen. 'The postman would arrive with the script, then he would sit with his glasses on his nose, going through everything with his pen, making tiny changes here and there to make it more natural. He knew all the tricks and he was a consummate professional. What looked effortless on screen was the result of hours of preparation and years spent in front of the camera.'

His daughter Sue remembers early mornings when she and her father were the only ones up in the family home:

Dad was shooting at Pinewood and I went to school in central London, so we'd both be in the kitchen at six in the morning, hardly saying anything to each other. We were both focused on our days ahead, very quiet, no fuss. That was when I learned from him: don't ever be late, always be prepared. He didn't show any anxiety that I saw, he was just calm and measured, so that's what I learned from him. Looking back, that was our special time together, all those early, quiet hours.

The charm of his screen characters was based on Sid's remarkable real-life popularity. Sue and Stephen both remember people everywhere constantly calling out to him on the street, and critics even now marvel at his unlikely appeal, his grizzled face and very ordinary physique belying extraordinary charisma.

'What they got you in here for then, something nasty?'
'No, not really, just a pain in the back.'
'Last bloke in that bed had the same thing.'
'Did he?'
'Right up to the end.'
'That's cheering. I'll say one thing for them, it's a nice warm bed.'
'Should be, they only took him half an hour ago.'

Stephen remembers one occasion when Sid fancied going out incognito. 'He put on a disguise, a hat and a moustache, and off we went for a walk. About two minutes after we got out of the front door, someone shouted, "Hi Sid, how are you?" He looked at me and just said, "Well, that worked."'

Throughout his career, men felt happy to share a pint with him, while women of all ages threw themselves at him, and he quite naturally became the narrative cornerstone on which all sorts of unlikely Carry On stories could be built.

Gerald Thomas called him 'a remarkable actor', explaining, 'We never wrote funny lines for Sid. Sid's comedy came out of situation and his reaction to other people's funny lines. Sid was a great reactor, his timing was superb.'

Peter Rogers was equally admiring, describing Sid in his memoir as a unique actor and fine artiste, someone who could play any character they wrote for him, and always wonderful to have on set. He called Sid the series' 'anchor man', and credited him for a sense of safety that Peter felt whenever his beloved actor was around.

If Carry On was a repertory team, Sid was undoubtedly its leading light. In her memoir, Barbara Windsor described Sid as the series' number one man. She wrote that without being at all dominating, Sid naturally engendered his colleagues' respect, saying, 'He had made so many films, people would listen to him.'

Off screen, male and female co-stars alike to this day can't say enough nice things about Sid. His co-star in *Convenience* and *Matron*, Kenneth Cope, describes him to me as 'a very generous man, very funny and easy to work with', while Anita Harris described him as 'so gentle and so sweet'. She said, 'I was terribly young and he was a bit like a father figure.' Liz Fraser remembered him as extremely protective. Sally Geeson, who appeared with him first on TV before he recommended her for Carry On, recalls his gentle voice as he guided her in the art of timing. Hattie Jacques called him 'the most unselfish of actors' on screen and chivalrous off it. She said he was 'a gentle man in the truest sense'. To Joan Sims, he was simply 'a darling man'.

Sid James and Kenneth Williams were very different types of people, of course, both in their acting styles and in their off-screen interests, but if there were cliques at Pinewood, Sid didn't get involved. While Kenneth was off holding court, Sid was usually to be found somewhere else with his head buried in *The Sporting Life*. Apart from work and family, Sid's great love was putting a bet on the horses, a habit his wife Valerie calmly kept in check by managing her husband's accounts, even as she explained afterwards, 'It was something he loved and you can't take away from somebody something they love.' To help oil these wheels, Sid was famously open to offers such as the whisky company who furnished him with cases of his favourite tipple, on condition it appeared in every film he made. (Fans of *Carry On Again Doctor* will be especially familiar with the brand.)

'Whiskey – where did that come from?'
'That came from an old wreck.'
'What old wreck?'
'The last doctor we had here.'

The affection in which Sid was universally held was clear after he suffered a heart attack in 1967 and wasn't able to work for six months. In an interview afterwards, Sid explained how he'd been forced to slow down, taking just one job at a time, which previously he would have considered unthinkable. He joked, 'I keep myself fit, workouts every morning, but fairly gentle ones. You don't need muscles to pick a bottle up.'

Gerald Thomas and Peter Rogers were so desperate to have him back in their fold, they wrote a part around Sid's need to rest. Fortunately the setting for 1967's *Carry On Doctor* made it quite natural for Sid's character, Charlie Roper, to spend almost his whole time lying in bed. Of course, he still managed to make mischief, whether trying to get a cuddle out of Valerie Van Ost's Nurse Parkin, or warming his thermometer in his tea under the nose of Anita Harris's Nurse Clarke.

'Come on Nurse, just a quick one while Sister's out of the ward!'
'Mr Roper, Dr Tinkle says it's not good for you.'
'But I've been smoking for years.'

Peter Rogers was delighted to have Sid back on screen, crediting his unique ability as an actor for the fact that fans didn't realise how little time Charlie Roper was actually in the film, and how much of it was spent lying under a blanket.

Fortunately for Sid and the team, his health rallied sufficiently not only for him to continue with the series, but to go on to enjoy some of the films' finest moments. His comedic legacy would be secure if only for his contribution as *Khyber*'s Sir Sidney Ruff-Diamond, with his penchant for Tiffin-time, and his wonderful working-class guffaws undermining the self-aggrandisement of the British Empire as completely as any army regulation woollen underpants.

Sid enjoyed donning old costumes discarded by Richard Burton for *Carry On Henry*, just as he had previously for Marc Antony in *Cleo*, but his favourite role of all was Rumpo the Kid in *Cowboy*, which thrills me as it's also my dearest film of the whole series. With its Wild West setting (at Pinewood, naturally), horses, guns and his character's American accent, *Cowboy* stretched Sid's skills, which delighted him. 'Out of all the Carry On series so far, I think I liked this one most of all,' he said at the time. 'Rumpo was the sort of part I enjoy.'

His daughter Sue remembers her father's glee in this role. 'Dad would come home in costume, which he didn't do for any other film, but he knew I'd enjoy it. Then he'd rehearse his gun-slinging in the back garden, dressed up in all his gear. Being the perfectionist he was, he wanted to practise, practise, practise.'

She adds, '*Cowboy* was definitely one of his favourites, and he enjoyed playing the character, with its grit. It was like the films he'd been in originally, it was as straight and dramatic as the Carry Ons would permit, and he ran with it.'

In the more contemporary films of the series such as *Camping*, *Loving* and *Convenience*, Sid represented every man in real-life Britain being forced to come to terms with changes in society, gradually evolving from the lecherous cackler he had brought to the earlier films into somebody less brazen, more befuddled by the world and women around him. We can compare the sexually insatiable Gladstone Screwer of *Carry On Again Doctor* (1969) with the put-upon, cheeky but ultimately faithful husband Sid Plummer of *Convenience* (1971). By the following year's *Matron*, his small-time crook Sid Carter is preoccupied with bounty rather than booty. Turning up in a nurse's bathroom, he even apologises, 'It's very nice of you, but I don't have the time.'

This change in style matched Sid's increasing discomfort on screen where he was constantly being cast as an older lech gawping at younger women. Somehow, he'd got away with it in the super-successful *Camping*, despite the story being one of a man in his late fifties attempting to seduce a schoolgirl. It may have helped, of course, that Barbara Windsor wasn't exactly that young, either. However, Sid was always worldly wise and acutely aware that public tastes were changing and it was time for him to change track.

Eventually, and with other projects filling his diary, Sid realised it was time for him to bow out of the series altogether, but fortunately, not before he gave us one more tour de force in *Carry On Dick* in 1974. Back in period garb and central to Talbot Rothwell's final screenwriting turn,

Sid delighted in the double role of dastardly highwayman Richard Turpin and his alter ego, the more restrained clergyman Reverend Flasher, running rings around Kenneth Williams's Captain Fancey before finally outwitting his captors and making a dusty dash for the border.

This period in Sid's life was complicated by an affair with his co-star Barbara. Although this particular carry-on became the subject of gossip at the time, then later a play and even a film, Sid's wife Valerie always remained elegantly sanguine on the subject, saying only that, like so many other people in this world, the couple had experienced a hiccup in their marriage and, fortunately, got over it. As it was, Valerie stayed by Sid's side for what would prove a hectic postscript to his Carry On career.

Throughout his fourteen years of making the films, Sid had remained busy with other projects on both big and small screen. Following his departure from the Carry On franchise, he became nearly as well known for the role of Sid Abbott, the patriarch of ITV sitcom *Bless This House*. Playing the family man on screen for five years from 1971 as well as in a film version in 1982, Sid was no longer the lewd, bawdy character of the Carry Ons, but instead a bemused and often baffled spectator to the antics of his children, themselves the new front-runners of the permissive society. By contrast, he presented a figure of resignation as well as responsibility. He was still a charmer ready for a drink and a laugh, but it seemed his screen role had finally caught up with real life. Audiences responded in their millions, with Sid remaining one of the nation's most popular funnymen.

Despite his massive TV success in the later days of his career, his daughter Sue reveals that he never drew an absolute line under Carry On duties:

> It wasn't that cut and dried ... *Bless This House* was getting 25 million viewers, and I think he just recognised that path was working well for him. Whether he'd have chosen to do another Carry On if one had come along that was right for him, I'll never know. But he made dozens of episodes of *Bless This House*, plus the film of the show, plus theatre work. He was getting older, and the type of character he was becoming recognised for was a different person.

Sally Geeson played his daughter Sally in the TV show and her admiration is enduring of both Sid and his ability to reach fans like no one else.

'Other actors have tried to manufacture it but he was unique,' she tells me. 'He had this marvellous face and lovely way about him. He was a very sophisticated man, dressed beautifully, but also very easy-going and relaxed.'

To anyone who asked, Sid said he still worked because it was easy, but that his favourite pastimes were actually sunbathing, fishing and being with his family, that his dream was to retire at 65 and put his feet up.

Sadly, he never got there, instead continuing to push himself through a gruelling work schedule even as his health began to fail and his full-to-the-brim life caught up with him. Finally, in April 1976, he took on one project too many with the British tour of *The Mating Season*, a comedy he had already performed in South Africa, Australia and New Zealand.

It was the play's first night at the Sunderland Empire when he collapsed on stage and passed away a little later, aged 62. Poignantly, his co-star beside him left waiting for her cue was Olga Lowe, one of his oldest friends and fellow thespians from those days when he was just starting out, in long-ago and long-forgotten Johannesburg. In interviews afterwards, Olga described how the audience in the theatre that night were slow to realise the truth of the situation. Because it was Sid they had come to see, they were instead happy, relaxed and waiting for him to make them laugh, just as he had done for so many years. But it was horribly real, a terrible shock for fans, and even more devastating for those who loved him.

If Carry On was a repertory company, Sid James will always be remembered as its leading man while his charm, modesty and warmth remain his personal legacy.

Many people have tried to sum up the unique appeal of such an unlikely screen legend as Sid James – made even more difficult by Sid's own refusal to describe his level of success as 'stardom' – a word, he said, that was often misused. In 1972, during the making of the film of *Bless This House* back at Pinewood, he told his interviewer Keith Howes that he 'just got lucky', adding, 'I didn't think I'd ever be responsible for a show... All I ever wanted was first feature or first supporting player.' Sid reasoned, 'You got a long life in the game if you do it that way.'

He added, 'You've got to be very lucky, but when you get lucky, you've got to use it. You can't keep going if you're a lousy performer. You don't find bad performers lasting very long.'

Bless This House producer, the late William G. Stewart, later famous for hosting quiz show *Fifteen to One*, once speculated that Sid could have been a great straight actor, had comedy not got hold of him and, as he put it, 'taken him over'. Terry Johnson agrees, reminding me that 'Sid was a really good actor. Watch his work with Hancock. It's superb'.

Stewart's view was, though, that Sid's familiarity would have worked against him. 'If you'd cast him as a doctor in a murder drama, nobody would have believed it. He didn't have a chance.'

Sue James reflects on how times have changed for actors, given more choices these days. 'Dad definitely loved his straight parts, but the comedy just worked for him. His warmth always came across and that was an enormous part of his appeal. I think people just expected him to make them laugh, he knew that and he delivered.'

And Sid's daughter Reina once shared a conversation she'd had with her father when she'd asked him if he ever wanted to act in serious things. 'He said, "There's no point. They'd laugh the minute I came on."'

Instead, for thirty years, he epitomised a very familiar type of English bloke, one we've all met down the pub, in a shop, walking along the street, checking the racing results in the paper, one who had emerged from the chaos of wartime into a society of traditional values and stereotypes and then stood scratching his head as things speedily changed around him, yet always saw the funny side.

Terry Johnson explains it to me like this:

There's barely a run of footage anywhere of Sid James being unhappy. He could be combative and disgruntled, but he was never unhappy. His disgruntledness was as attached to his love of life as everything else he had. He was such a positive character, and a funny man.

He was very much like a family member, when they were having a good time. We all have relatives like him. You'd quite like to go on holiday with him. He always seemed to be having a good time in life, and I hope he did. His appeal was in the familiar and the fun-loving.

It's no coincidence that, more often than not, Sid's characters were also called Sid, what the actor termed 'an insurance policy', meaning the audience could always identify with both the character and the man. Sid once reflected:

> If the customers like you, it makes a big difference and you're part of the family. Nobody ever calls me Mr James. One fellow did the other day, I felt like I'd been promoted. Perfect strangers in the street I meet yell out, 'Wotcha Sid. How's it going?' I like that. I think that's real nice.

Cultural historian Matthew Sweet comments, 'There is something of his own nature in all the characters he played. He more or less plays himself every time he appears.'

If Sid made it look effortless however, you only have to look at the yawning gap he left in the later films of the series to realise the depth of his contribution, the delicate tightrope he walked to bring cheekiness without leeriness to the bawdiest of tales, to be in charge without ever being a bully, to be mocked and thrown in muck without ever being properly humiliated. It was the mark of an intelligent actor with the lightest of touches, and of course the chuckle helped, that distinctive calling card Sweet delightfully tags 'the dirtiest laugh in cinematic history'.

Terry Johnson also points to Sid's great sense of decorum and humility. 'He was unassuming. The world of acting is divided between those who know their luck and those who don't. Sid knew his luck. There wasn't a trace of pomposity about what he did. He was modest, and he was true.'

If there was a secret formula behind all the apparent ease, Sid wasn't giving anything away. To anyone who asked, he kept it simple. 'If the lines aren't funny enough, you've to do something funny. Wear a funny hat.'

For Carry On's leading man, that seemed to be enough. That, plus the tip he'd learned from his father all those years before, the lesson he took into every one of his hundreds of roles, but was equally apparent in his life off-screen. 'You're not smiling until you feel it. Feel the smile.'

Chapter 8

The Golden Age

'Infamy! Infamy! They've all got it…'
Kenneth Williams in *Carry On Cleo*

Gerald Thomas once explained, 'Basically our pictures are of the same format, the same people, different locales and different incidents that happen, but basically it is a formula which the public expect.'

Peter Rogers put it more bluntly, 'We just made the same film over and over.'

This was their deceptively simple answer to the question of how the Carry On series travelled, seemingly effortlessly, from one box office triumph to another throughout the 1960s. With their saucy seaside humour, reliance on double entendre, references to female anatomy and bodily functions, the films could have retained the charm of the early titles but inevitably soon run out of ideas. Instead, by the middle of the decade, the films were bigger, their landscapes broader and more colourful, even while the familiar faces and genres kept them grounded well within audiences' reach.

For many fans, the golden age of Carry On began with their move away from the affectionate but cheeky portraits of contemporary institutions and customs such as those we saw in *Teacher* and *Constable* into a world of spoof and history, sending up the genre cinema of James Bond and Hammer Horror, but also the real bygone world of monarchy and empire.

Half a century later, the gift of hindsight makes it seem an obvious formula for success: assembling a reliable, consistent cast and crew, creating instantly familiar character stereotypes, leaning on film tropes equally recognisable to cinema-goers, borrowing plots from the original serious storylines but adding countless comedic twists along the way to make for nonsensical, hubristic capers guaranteed to bring the house down. Even as Gerald revealed the team's approach above, it appears abundantly straightforward. Yet every filmmaker in the world knows how difficult it is to strike gold once, let alone repeat the feat for a decade or more. It clearly took the bold eye of Peter, the unwavering direction of Gerald, the seemingly bottomless well of Talbot Rothwell's gags, plus some special alchemy between all three and their performers, to create these worlds and bring them to such vivid life on screen over and over again.

Now we're all clued up on the difference between a spoof and a parody, I think we can safely put *Carry On Cleo* in the latter camp, a mockery of one particular film, although, just to confuse us, Kenneth Williams actually referred to it in his autobiography as 'a burlesque', i.e. an absurd or comically exaggerated imitation of something, which would also appear to fit perfectly.

Rich in colour, characterisation and story, *Cleo* is for many the definitive Carry On film, and it is clear that when they made it in 1964, the team was firing on all cylinders. A mountain of luck came their way, with the disastrous British filming of the Elizabeth Taylor-Richard Burton epic *Cleopatra*. When 20th Century Fox gave up trying to shoot this big screen behemoth at Pinewood, packed up and moved their production to Rome, they left behind their sets and costumes, all used to glorious effect by Peter and his crew for their own telling of the story of the Nile's great Empress. With exteriors from *Cleopatra*, and interiors from a stage production of *Caligula*, it all made for a swanky and impressive setting and not just by Carry On standards.

'I cannot tell you any more about this woman. She is absolute perfection. They call her the Siren of the Nile.'
'Ooh, I hope she don't go off!'

Amanda Barrie, in her second Carry On outing after *Cabby*, dazzled as a beguiling Cleopatra, while Sid, Kenneth and Joan all outdid themselves as a sanguine Mark Antony, wilting Julius Caesar and complaining Calpurnia respectively. Charles was cast against type as a lecherous Seneca, variously inviting women into his bath and disguising himself as an urn for a bit of peeping-tomfoolery. If the actor was somewhat under-used in comparison with Sid and Kenneth, nevertheless it was in the service of a great film. Jim Dale burst into glorious Carry On technicolour for the first time as captured caveman turned hero Horsa, and he was aided and abetted by the whimpering Kenneth Connor as Hengist Pod. While this proved to be Kenneth's last Carry On outing for a few years, Jim's star was clearly on the rise.

'There must be some way we can get rid of him.'
'I have a poisonous ass.'
'I wouldn't say that.'

The stellar performances were matched by arguably Carry On's finest ever script, influenced not just by *Cleopatra* and Shakespeare's *Antony and Cleopatra*, but also Stephen Sondheim's *A Funny Thing Happened on the Way to the Forum*. Talbot Rothwell outdid himself with ancient allusions, characterisation and poking fun at iconic figures. The writer was operating at the height of his powers, reaching high for the classic material and then bringing it down to earth with a perfectly timed bump and be-dum. *Cleo* was also where he gave us, probably, the greatest ever Carry On line of all.

'Infamy, infamy! They've all got it in for me!'

Although Talbot rightly got the credit for giving this line to Kenneth Williams's Julius Caesar, it originally came from the pens of Frank Muir and Denis Norden. The pair worked in the same building only a few creative desks away from the Carry On writer and, one day, pushed for a line, he asked them if they could help him out. Frank and Denis were each of the opinion that a joke no longer belonged to anyone once it was out there, and happily dug out one of their original gags for radio show *Take It From Here*. Both of them spoke always of their gratification of later seeing it voted the best, most archetypal Carry On line of all – 'rewarding' was how Frank Muir put it, in his inimitable fashion.

Two little bits of controversy did nothing to harm *Cleo*'s publicity campaign. First, 20th Century Fox, clearly sensitive to anything *Cleopatra*-related by now after the booming budget overspend on their epic, plus censure both from critics and the Vatican on the extra-marital goings-on between their two enraptured co-stars, attempted to sue for copyright over the poster for *Cleo*, which clearly aped their own, except with Sid James and Amanda Barrie replacing Burton and Taylor. However, Fox's own poster turned out to be based on an ancient painting, which meant nobody could sue anybody – but not before many column inches had been devoted to the imminent release of *Cleo*. Similarly, when a journalist pointed out that the film's market traders Marcus et Spencius were using the same colour green on their banner as a certain high street department store, Peter had to fend off an inquiry by the latter. This too came to nothing, but with more column inches secured, thanks to what Peter described as 'some kind critic who thought he'd make a fuss'.

'Potolome'
'I am telling you!'

The film premiered in London on 10 December 1964 and went on to be one of the country's most popular films of the following year – not bad for a production budget of £165k, and pretty impressive when you compare it with the costs of, say, *Cleopatra*, on which 20th Century Fox ended up spending more than $44million in total. Bigger isn't always better.

If Peter and Gerald were never going to write cheques on quite that scale, nevertheless, even they weren't completely infallible and on their next film, for the only time in Carry On history, they too went over budget. I have to say, though, I believe it was worth it. *Carry On Cowboy* is the undervalued gem of the entire series, I believe, and it turns out I'm not alone in my thinking.

For the eleventh film in the series, Peter, Gerald and the team embarked on a spoof Western, which required the construction of an entire dusty set on the back lot of Pinewood. Additionally, locations were found at Chobham Common in Surrey and Black Park, north of Pinewood in Buckinghamshire. The unique dip in the finances came about when shooting moved to the latter, where the rain came down on the American desert scenes. Even Gerald could not make his usual sun-shining magic happen, and shooting went over-time and hence over-budget. Despite this, the director's daughter, Deborah, tells me of her father's great satisfaction with this particular film. 'He loved the boys' adventure of it, plus the fact that Sid loved his role,' she remembers. 'It was a good script and they had a lot of fun making it. Everything just worked.'

Sure enough, the storyline was very strong, offering the team the chance to showcase all the Western film genre's most clichéd tropes – the glamorous moll who could hold her own but remained somehow in thrall to the resident bad boy, the corruption rife in such a tiny town, the unreconstructed relationship with surrounding Native Indians, plus the arbitrary rivalries that always cropped up in those films. It's interesting to note that while *Blazing Saddles* is always pegged as the ultimate spoof Western, Mel Brooks' masterpiece actually arrived in cinemas a good nine years later, and trod much of the same territory explored by *Carry on Cowboy*.

Most notable of all, though, were several of the series' finest performances by regular cast members. Joan revelled in her role of former saloon owner Belle Armitage, not least for her beautiful sequinned dress, particularly in the scene requiring her to flirt with the town's new arrival Johnny Finger, aka The Rumpo Kid, played by Sid. She admitted later, 'I was working out a lot of fantasies.'

Meanwhile, Sid was perfectly cast as the lonesome cowboy, bringing an authentic Steve McQueen or Gary Cooper vibe to the part, speaking in a laconic drawl which included the familiar cackle which kept his comedy fans happy.

For Kenneth, the role of Judge Burke, the beleaguered Mayor of Stodge City and yet another figure of undermined authority, required a whole new look and sound. He used greying sidepieces and a moustache to look older, and adopted the gravelly drawl of Hollywood veteran Hal Roach. Unfortunately, adopting this voice throughout filming, speaking out through one side of his mouth, took its toll, causing Kenneth's jaw to go out of alignment. In his memoir, he described receiving help from an unlikely source, when he shared his predicament with a Baker Street newspaper seller. That wise man recommended he to go to bed with his face tied up with a scarf. Despite the random source of such medical advice, Kenneth reported that it did the trick.

'My, but you've got a big one.'
'I'm from Texas, ma'am. We've all got big ones down there.'

Cowboy was the most physical of all the Carry On titles to date, with Sid, Kenneth and Jim all appearing on horseback. The filmmakers even brought in special trainers to show the actors how to ride their horses, American-style.

Jim, in the role of Marshal P. Knutt, a sanitation engineer mistaken for a peace martial (even after his plunger oh-so-inevitably got stuck to the inquiries desk!) and so unwittingly sent to save the town, brought it all – physical energy, perfect comedic timing plus the good looks of a classic leading man, and this was a clear promotion to Carry On's centre stage. Following the press screening of the shoot, Sid James's agent was moved to tell Peter Rogers, 'I think you have done miracles for Jim Dale.' His star was rising ever higher.

Alongside him as Annie Oakley was Angela Douglas, making her Carry On debut after a rushed invitation from Peter and Gerald to join the team. Angela recalls this moment for me, 'I was in bed, early in the morning, and I had a call from Peter Rogers asking me to meet him and Gerry at the Dorchester Hotel, to discuss a role. I did my hair, put on some mascara and off I went.'

Angela remembers not being remotely overwhelmed by the prospect of joining the celebrated team – 'Because of the arrogance of youth, and I'd been working since I was 13 or 14, so nothing fazed me' – and that she was actually more inspired by the role they were discussing. 'To be offered the role of Annie Oakley was a great part. I didn't care who was making it.' One nice lunch at the Dorchester later, and she was in.

This was the first Carry On film to have a sung main titles theme, as well as a number in the bar where Annie Oakley sang 'This is the Night for Love'. Cowboy also welcomed Bernard Bresslaw to the team, making his debut as Little Heap, son to Charles's Big Heap. The physical disparity between the pair meant the joke wrote itself, just like some others.

'This is my new squaw, Kitikata. I bought her for two buffalos in...'
'How...'
'Never mind how, where?'

Cowboy may have enjoyed richer portraiture and scenery than anything previously in Carry On, but when it came to the serious side of delivering the gags, it was clearly business as usual.

For many fans of the series, Carry On Screaming! is right up there with the best of them. While I'm not in this camp, I do appreciate the production values on show, although I believe loving this film probably depends on being a fan of the Hammer horrors it was sending up, with its tale of young people going missing in the wood, abducted by the mysterious Oddbod, a sort of Frankenstein's monster created by electrically-charged scientist Dr Orlando Watt (Kenneth Williams) with the help of his enigmatic sister Valeria, played by Fenella Fielding in her second Carry On outing after *Regardless*. This kind of narrative would have been familiar as well to fans of American sit-coms like *The Munsters* and *The Addams Family*, shows popular on both sides of the Atlantic. In fact, Bernard Bresslaw's character of Sockett the butler in the spooky mansion was so similar to Lurch in the latter show, the crew took to calling him by the same name.

Carry On's director of photography Alan Hume had previously worked on Hammer's *Kiss of the Vampire*, so he brought a palpable sensibility that meant, while *Screaming* is a perfectly pitched send up of the Hammer horror films, it manages to be just a little bit frightening in some places, such as Doris's spooky appearance as a mannequin, as well as funny.

'Fangs ain't what they used to be!'

The film's Edwardian setting didn't prevent Peter Rogers making his usual search for bargain-bucket props. This time, he was able to arrange to borrow vintage cars from the automobile enthusiast Lord Montagu of Beaulieu, including a grand 1910 Into Taximeter Cabriolette, which was one of the stars of the show. Where he *was* forced to splash out, though, was on his leading man.

The central role of DS Sidney Bung, a henpecked husband of a detective charged with investigating the mysterious disappearances, was written with Sid James in mind, naturally, but the actor was busy working with Tony Hancock, so Peter Rogers approached Harry H. Corbett – star of *Steptoe and Son* and another favourite of Hancock's writers Ray Galton and Alan Simpson. To fill the gap at short notice, Peter offered Harry H. a record sum at the time for a Carry On film – a reported £12,000 for six weeks work.

One of my reservations about this film is the reduced space given to Kenneth Williams as the quivering ashen-faced scientist, and to Joan Sims as Bung's complaining wife Emily. Coming straight after their great performances in *Cowboy*, *Screaming!* doesn't give Kenneth enough screen time for my liking, and undermines Joan's great comedy with her character's one-trick tyranny. The running joke is her lack of lovability with no real let-up even by the end.

An actor not expected to appear in the film at all was Charles Hawtrey. However, a critic discovered this and wrote a piece saying he hoped it wouldn't affect box office returns. When Peter got wind of this, he took note and was quick to reassure his distributors at Anglo-Amalgamated that Charles would, in fact, appear – as Dan Dann, gardener turned attendant in some underground lavatories. Later, Peter conceded that Charles had brought something special to the role. He also had one of the film's best lines, remarking as unsuspecting pedestrians walked on the glass ceiling above him, 'Business here is looking up.'

If Charles had the best line, Fenella Fielding was convinced she had the corniest, when her character Valeria, the spooky mansion's mysterious mistress, seduced DS Bung, asking him if he minded if she smoked – just as puffs of smoke came up around her. She remembered asking Gerald Thomas, 'Do I really have to say this corny gag?' to which he replied, 'Don't worry about it, darling – children will love it.' And of course they did. So delighted was the actress by that great cinematic moment, 'Do You Mind If I Smoke?' became the title of her own autobiography.

'Oddbod, what happened to your ear?'
'Oh never mind. Ear today, gone tomorrow.'

From the very start of the series, Peter Rogers always said he relied on his own gut instinct for what was funny and what wasn't. He didn't need to go to film screenings or premieres to check on the audience reaction, preferring to rely instead on his own funny bone to tell him. He hadn't even broken his own rule back when *Carry On Nurse* was filling cinemas all over the US, and he could have been excused the ego trip of travelling to America to receive the overseas acclaim that was his due. Instead, he enjoyed the fact that he was a film producer who never once went to Hollywood. His choice to remain behind the scenes meant that his face remained almost unknown beyond industry circles, despite everything he achieved.

History clearly records Peter's role as the backbone on which the entire series was built, never more so than in 1966, following the successful release of *Screaming!* when change was in the air for the films' long-time distributors. Over at Amalgamated Partners, the death of Stuart Levy prompted the company's decision to cease carrying on with the Carry On series, and Peter's biography records his shock on learning this over a lunch meeting. However, he picked himself straight up and went instead to the Rank Organisation, which proved unsurprisingly enthusiastic to take up the baton of distributing these guaranteed cinema-fillers. There was just one fly in the ointment at this stage – they were wary of continuing their rival's brand and didn't want the films to be called Carry On! This was later ironed out, but explains why the next two titles in the series were originally Carry On in everything but actual name.

It is a shame *Don't Lose Your Head* didn't initially have the series epithet because it is everything a Carry On film should be: a strong story in its parody clearly leaning on the legend of The Scarlet Pimpernel (even though Peter once again dodged the lawyers by claiming it wasn't), a colourful period setting of eighteenth-century France and England, cracking performances from all the regular cast, and beautiful National Trust manor houses for locations.

'Camembert has her emprisoned, The Bastille.'
'I know that – where's the girl?'

Apart from its title, this film broke other Carry On conventions too. An unseen narrator introduced the plot giving it more faux-gravitas, and Sid James as Sir Rodney Ffing (pronounced Effing, naturally) even broke the fourth wall and addressed the audience at one unexpected point. Story-wise, though, it was business as usual, with the plot giving the cast plenty of opportunity for flamboyant costumes, nonsensical disguises and energetic displays of physical comedy, including a final sword fight remarkable for both its length and the amount of beautiful pottery, tapestry and finally even a harp that had to be sacrificed.

This is one of my favourite films of the series, an often overlooked gem, with its strong single narrative, bottomless bucket of good lines and visual vibrancy. The heavy lifting was shared between Sid's double role as Sir Rodney and his fugitive alter ego the Black Fingernail, Jim Dale's action heroics as his sidekick Lord Darcy Pue and Kenneth Williams as the secret police chief Citizen Camembert, who he reminded us was 'the big cheese'. However, I would argue that, in her role as Desiree Dubarry and later the Comtesse de la Plume de ma t'Ante, Joan Sims enjoyed her very finest Carry On hour. She certainly had the film's best line.

'My brother, the comte...' (It was all in the enunciation)

Honours must go, too, to Charles Hawtrey, yet again stealing the show as the Duke de Pommefrite, haughty and ridiculous in a periwig, chuckling and waving all the way to the guillotine, demanding 'short back and sides, not too much off the top'.

The next film in the series similarly gave a literary hero the special Carry On treatment, and also excluded Carry On from its title. *Follow That Camel* was a parody of the adventures of Beau Geste as told in P.C. Wren's 1924 novel. Jim Dale played central protagonist Bo West whose reputation and lady-love were both lost to him in England, hence his decision to join the French Foreign Legion with his faithful manservant Simpson, played by the ever-reliable Peter Butterworth. Their enlisting took them to a fort in the Sahara Desert, which meant cast and crew making a rare excursion from Pinewood all the way to Camber Sands near Rye in East Sussex.

Sid James was not among them. When Peter Rogers was sorting out the casting, he learned that Sid was tied up with TV work, committed to his sit-com *George and the Dragon* with Peggy Mount, which left a gap centre stage. This gave the bosses at Rank the chance to flirt with the idea of introducing an American celebrity into the series, no doubt believing some international stardom would help them secure an American distribution deal.

Peter was against the idea, certain his very British films didn't need this kind of element, but they got the support of writer Talbot Rothwell who was convinced the part of pleasure-loving Sergeant Nocker was meant for Phil Silvers, saying he couldn't stop seeing the *Bilko* star in his mind's eye the whole time he was creating the script.

Sure enough, Phil Silvers came on board, for an astronomical fee by Carry On standards, and from the moment everyone arrived in Rye, Peter was proved right by the lack of ease on display between Silvers and his fellow performers. In his memoir, Kenneth noted how the American veteran's long jokes failed to find an appreciative audience when they all dined together. Their co-star Angela Douglas remains more compassionate about the difficulties Silvers faced. She tells me, 'We were a tightknit group. It must have been difficult for him.'

'I haven't had this much fun since, what was his name? Bow Legs or something.'

If Silvers proved a challenge on set, there was one star who turned out to be even more of a diva, and that was the camel. For a start, it turned out he'd led a peaceful zoo life, and couldn't actually walk on sand, so special tracks had to be laid down for him, and then he spat at everybody on set, with the understandable exception of Charles Hawtrey.

The location shoot was not without its complications. As well as the camel's antics, this being the British seaside, a Sahara-like sunshine wasn't guaranteed, in fact filming had to be halted more than once because there was snow on the sands.

Silvers did bring something different to this Carry On title, and it was more than his familiar *Bilko* bluster and the fact he even kept his American accent intact. In his hands, Sergeant Nocker was more confident, less self-deprecating than previous protagonists in the series. The way he treated his lady, café owner Zig-Zig played by Joan Sims, was less than chivalrous, or maybe Silvers just had to perform without the magic weapon of the Sid James chuckle, which somehow always made the British star's equally outrageous lines acceptable.

With Silvers at centre stage, everyone else took their usual positions. Kenneth was once again a figure of foiled authority, this time the Legion fort's Commander Burger. When he wasn't trying and failing to keep order, he appeared more physically active than in previous films, participating in the fort's defence and even falling from the battlements. If Sid's most surreal Carry On moment so far had been when he addressed the audience in *Don't Lose Your Head*, Kenneth's turn came in *Camel*, when he turned up in the final scene as a baby in a pram.

Jim Dale customarily split his duties between physical comedy and romantic interludes, and his affections between Angela Douglas's surprisingly worldly Lady Jane Ponsonby, and Anita Harris's belly-dancing temptress Corkpit.

Follow That Camel did well at the box office, but also served to show just how essential Sid James was to the atmosphere, both on screen and off. Although TV duties had prevented him appearing in the film, he'd gone on to suffer a serious heart attack in May 1967 which meant when he did return to work, he was under strict doctors' instructions to remain a lot less active as he slowly recovered. So keen were Peter Rogers and Gerald Thomas to have him back, though, they quickly came up with a plan for his next Carry On role, one that meant he could bring all his charm and star power to screen without even getting out of bed.

The golden age of the series wouldn't be complete without a medical title, and *Carry On Doctor* was special in several ways. With Rank still seemingly reluctant to continue with the films, Peter thought this might just be the last one, and the poker-faced boss for once allowed a thread of sentiment to be woven into the production. Kenneth Williams noted in his diary at the time that Peter had intimated that, after fifteen films and a decade of box office triumph, he'd like to make *Doctor* and then sign off from the Carry Ons. The usually critical Kenneth admitted, 'Rather sad really.'

Peter's wife Betty Box had enjoyed dazzling success of her own, particularly with her *Doctor in the House* franchise, starring first Dirk Bogarde, then Leslie Phillips. In a nod to this achievement, Peter arranged for a portrait of that series regular James Robertson Justice to hang in the foyer of the hospital setting for his own *Carry On Doctor*. I'm sure Betty was just as moved by this acknowledgement as by Peter's present to her of a percentage of his film's profits.

If the *Doctor in the House* series had helped acquaint audiences with all the tropes of hospital comedy fare, cinema goers would have found the new face on the Carry On team just as familiar. When Kenneth rejected the central role of 'faith healer' Francis Bigger, Peter gave it to Frankie Howerd, although he expressed concern that with Kenneth also in the cast albeit in a smaller role, that might be too much camp even for Carry On.

'Mr Bigger, whatever are you doing down there?'
'Waiting for a Number 13 bus.'

As it turned out, Frankie proved a natural addition to the usual crew in the role of Bigger, a faith healer forced to surrender himself to the medical experts after taking a tumble. Frankie's talent for wide-eyed ooh-ing and aah-ing meant he could easily hold his own without crowding out the regulars, who all did their usual thing around him: Sid may have been bed-bound as Charlie Roper, shamelessly faking illness to stay in hospital, but the strength of his personality meant he made as much impact as ever. Charles was as believable as usual as Mr Barron, a patient apparently suffering from sympathetic labour pains while his wife waited to give birth, and Bernard Bresslaw as Ken Biddle seemed more desperate to get to the ladies' ward than to recover from whatever ailed him.

> 'I dreamt about you last night, nurse.'
> 'Did you?'
> 'No, you wouldn't let me.'

Tending to these unlikely patients, Jim Dale put his talent for physical comedy to work as the clumsy but charming Dr Kilmore, secretly adored by Anita Harris's Nurse Clark. And Barbara Windsor returned after a three-year absence to play junior nurse Sandra May, who of course innocently decided to go sunbathing on the hospital roof and cause chaos for everyone, particularly the well-meaning Dr Kilmore who inevitably ended up falling through the ceiling and into the bubble bath of another surprised nurse.

Peter's concerns about having Frankie and Kenneth both in the cast were alleviated by the pair sharing little screen time, and in fact they balanced each other very well. While Kenneth's documented obsession with his real life ailments might have lent him naturally to play hypochondriac Bigger, instead he revelled in playing Doctor Tinkle, the hospital registrar quick to brush off his anxious patients' fears. His best scenes were with his great real-life friend Hattie Jacques, returning to the team for the first time since *Cabby* and once again in situ as lovelorn Matron, deaf to Tinkle's pleas that he was 'once a weak man'. You know the rest.

This jolly caper was essentially a more colourful, speedier and energetic version of the enormously successful *Carry On Nurse* a decade before, just with more focus on the medical staff and a lot saucier as befit the newer age. The earlier film received two allusions in *Doctor*, firstly with the subtitles, which read 'Nurse Carries On Again' and 'Death of a Daffodil'. Then, in an even cheekier nod to the previous hit, Francis Bigger reserved his biggest ooh and aah for when he was offered a daffodil by a nurse.

'Oh no, you don't, I saw that film!'

Making this blatant reference to their most popular ever title, the Carry On crew were treading unchartered territory here, but clearly knew they were playing to an appreciative home crowd. Sure enough, *Doctor* was Britain's third biggest film of 1968, behind *The Jungle Book* and *Barbarella*.

Finally, six months later in November 1968, crowning this dizzying era of Carry On, came what many consider to be the very best of the entire series, one that probably deserves to be tagged the team's towering creative achievement. Even Peter Rogers ultimately judged it his favourite, for what he called 'the colour and anachronism'. The cast all looked magnificent in their richly layered period costumes. There was also the script and unusually acute satire on display, lamenting the hubris and complacence that accompanied the sun setting on the British Empire. I refer, of course, to *Carry On Up the Khyber.*

The storyline of the casual rule of the jewel in the crown of the British Empire, specifically by one of Queen Victoria's governors over the Indian province of Kalabar, might seem an unlikely patch in which to dig for a Carry On comedy, yet it proved to be richly fertile soil, particularly in the direction Talbot Rothwell's script took it. The men of the Third Foot and Mouth Regiment, charged with guarding the Khyber Pass, suffer a collapse of their reputation as 'Devils in Skirts' after the advancing Burpa tribe, led by Bernard Bresslaw's warlord Bungdit Din, has an altercation with one less than intrepid soldier, Charles Hawtrey's Private Widdle. When they come across him on duty, guarding what is basically a wooden gate representing the whole of the British Empire, they discover that, contrary to myth, the British soldiers have been keeping themselves warm under their kilts with woollen underpants. The problem, as Widdle tries to explain to his superiors, is the way the wind whistles up the Pass. Thus is the surreal narrative for this madcap look at Britain's empirical past set in motion.

'Who's the turban job on the throne?'
'You mean the Khazi.'

Meanwhile, back at the Governor's mansion (in real life Pinewood's always stately Heatherden Hall so familiar to Carry On fans) Sid James and Joan Sims are in residence as Sir Sidney Ruff-Diamond and his wife Lady Joan. While Joan is in posh if frustrated mode, Sid remains very much Sid despite his luxurious trappings, doing very little and counting the hours until 'Tiffin time', referring of course to the local tea.

Already snapping at their heels by the beginning of the tale is Kenneth Williams's glittering Khasi of Kalabar, a native ruler intent on defying his British overseers. Even as he gives Sir Sidney the benefit of his crocodile smile at the polo, he is describing him to his daughter Princess Jelhi (Angela Douglas) as a governor 'whose benevolent rule and wise guidance we could well do without'. There is a lot going on in this deceptively light-touch film.

In Jim Dale's absence, the role of wide-eyed young lead went to the equally versatile Roy Castle. While Roy was just as handsome and talented as the Carry On regular, to my mind he lacked the physical comedy, the sense of elastic confusion, that Jim brought to his parts. Or perhaps the role in *Khyber* was a stiffer one. What's for certain is that Roy was just as charming, and delighted in entertaining the locals when the cast went filming on location. Yes, once again, they managed to get past the gates of Pinewood for a rare production excursion.

Both cast and crew were no doubt cheered by the fact that they got to shoot away from home. To create the Karakoram Ranges of British Imperial India, everyone hotfooted it all the way to Snowdonia in Wales, for a whole ten days – which was really pushing the boat out by Carry On standards – as the Watkin Path was deemed to look sufficiently similar to the Khyber Pass in Afghanistan. Fortunately, Peter Rogers was still able to save money in other ways, for example hiring soldiers' costumes already used in the 1964 war classic *Zulu*.

The team's trip to Snowdonia in the spring of 1968 has become the stuff of local legend, following their filming beneath the summit of Mount Snowdon and their stay in hotels in nearby villages Beddgelert and Llanberis. Since 2005, there is even a plaque in the latter spot, marking the time Carry On came to town.

With all the external shots safely in the can, it was back to Pinewood for the definitive *Khyber* scene, the dinner party at the Ruff-Diamonds' residence while, outside, the Khasi leads the charge of rebellion – at least, until they are held off by the men of Sir Sidney's Regiment lifting their kilts. There, the Khasi's men stand horrified before beating a hasty retreat. We will never know what they see that day, but the Khasi's horrified face says it all.

The extraordinary final exterior scene is matched by the ribaldry inside the mansion, as the governing class continues to dine despite the din of the guns going off outside, despite the Fakir's head (still talking) being served on a platter and even the walls and ceilings falling in on them. Sid and Joan seem to be having a whale of a time, barely staying in character as they grin at their guests, sip at their soup and drink their wine. Joan finally crowns this unforgettable display of misplaced British bravado with her glorious cheerful ad-lib in the face of falling masonry, 'Oh dear, I seem to have got a little plastered.'

Khyber became the UK's second most popular film at the box office in 1969, after Peter Rogers withstood pressure from Rank to change the title to 'Carry On The Regiment'. Angela Douglas, who did the honours of unveiling the Welsh plaque in September 2005, remembers fondly, 'The film just hit the nation's funny bone,' but her role found fans further afield too. She reported once receiving a fan letter which somehow found its way to her, despite being addressed only 'Princess Jelhi, England'.

Bernard Bresslaw, who played Burpa tribal leader Bungdit Din and got to deliver the timeless line 'Fakir, off' – careful to stress enough of a pause where the comma was to get past the Censor's eagle eye – once visited an Indian restaurant. The owner ran up to him in delight, and instantly pressed a free meal on his honoured guest, telling him what a delight it had been to see his home country on the screen. Bernard recalled, 'I didn't have the heart to tell him it was filmed in Wales.'

'My father, who are those people?'
'That, light of my darkness, is Sir Sidney Ruff-Diamond, the British governor whose benevolent rule and wise guidance we could well do without.'

Uniquely, this title has stood the test of time and found a sweet spot with even contemporary critics nearly half a century later. They point to the element of satire that had been present in some of the previous titles, but never so artfully aimed.

The film's sub-title 'Or the British position in India' gives us our first hint of this, pointing both to Carry On's smutty roots, but also to something far more cheekily satirical. And the same is true of the final scene, which for many Carry On fans and cultural commentators alike, sees the team operating at the height of their skills.

Of course, the team doesn't neglect to do what they do best, offering us the outrageous physical comedy of the Fakir's detached talking head, the lifted kilts, the falling plaster. But underneath bubbles something quite different. With the blatant patriotism of the still-standing Union flag and its motto 'I'm backing Britain', plus the victory of the Regiment over the Afghan rebellion, there seems to be an upstanding patriotism familiar to all cinema audiences of the time. And yet, made twenty-one years after India itself had started the de-colonisation process, *Khyber* still invites us to wonder at the misplaced pride of the Brits, the randomness of their hierarchy, the nonsense of a be-skirted and under-panted Regiment far away from home keeping guard over a wooden gate, the blatant absurdity of the whole self-important thing.

For culture critic Toby Young, *Khyber* is far less susceptible to the charge of promoting racism and bigotry than other films of the period. He tells me, 'On the contrary, it takes the mickey out of the British Empire and the idea of the White Man's Burden. It could have been called Carry On Kipling.'

Khyber is frequently tagged the best of the Carry Ons (along with *Cleo* and *Screaming!*), and in 1999 it even sneaked onto the British Film Institute's list of the top 100 British films ever made. Matthew Sweet describes it today as 'one of the most interesting films about de-colonisation ever made'. He explains, 'There is so much going on in that film, a particularly fantastical space where decolonisation can be momentarily denied but not in any serious way. It both softens the blow and allows it to be managed. It shows its absurdity on both sides, but at the same time it's slightly consoling.'

All in all not bad for the sixteenth in a series of films, which the producers always maintained were simple in concept, efficient in execution and relied on audiences knowing what to expect when they came to fruition. *Carry On Up the Khyber* proved that while all that was true, the team could nevertheless also create something complicated in idea, rich in production, challenging to experience. To put it simply, without even seeming to try that hard, this team of vaudeville throwbacks could still pull off something very special.

Chapter 9

Star Spotlight – Joan Sims

'My intimate friends call me Ding Dong'

Joan Sims and Hattie Jacques were by no means the only female stars to shine in Carry On. The faces of many beautiful women leapt out of the screen over the two decades of the series – Shirley Eaton, Dilys Laye, Angela Douglas, Amanda Barrie all come to mind, plus of course Barbara Windsor (don't worry, we'll get to Babs). But I think Joan and Hattie did something unique in the films – they brought a sense of real-life beauty to the screen. They weren't there as totty. They provided something far more substantial, both physically and emotionally.

As well as being great friends, they shared a background in London's theatre and a work ethic that saw them flourish on stage, screen and radio before they brought their very distinctive talents to Pinewood and became indispensable additions to the Carry On cast.

'She was a stationmaster's daughter so never went off the tracks and always knew her lines.' With the pithiness of a Carry On punchline did Joan used to like to explain how her upbringing made her just right for a life in showbusiness. Even so, it was an unlikely background for someone whose career would go on to encompass stage, TV, radio and dozens of film roles including, most importantly for us, twenty-four Carry On titles.

An Essex girl long before that epithet brought with it any cultural connotations, Irene Joan Marion Sims was indeed the daughter of a stationmaster. The only child of John and Gladys Sims, she was brought up in the station house at Laindon Railway Station, twenty-two miles down the line from Fenchurch Street Station in London.

Much beloved by her doting parents but often lonely as a youngster, Joan kept herself and others entertained by dressing up and putting on a show for the waiting passengers at Laindon Railway Station. There were no theatrical connections in the family, but Joan's mother Gladys was a fine singer and pianist, while her friends later believed she inherited her comedic talents from her father John. She said herself of those formative years, 'I had a built in audience, because I always had all the passengers.'

After taking part in local amateur productions, she persuaded her parents she was only cut out for the stage, and they supported her efforts. Sweetly, her friends remember the scrapbooks they kept from the beginning of their daughter's career, every cutting a souvenir of her growing success.

Joan herself was nothing if not determined, getting into RADA at her fourth attempt and emerging with both her certificate and an agent almost straight away. Peter Eade would continue to guide her career for the rest of his life, and became one of Sims' most trusted friends and mentors.

A star had been born. Instantly signed up as an understudy for one production, Joan proceeded to step in and steal the show, according to her friend, composer Ronnie Cass. From then on, she became a leading lady, with one stage hit following another, bringing Sims both critical praise and a growing fanbase.

She joined in several of Brian Rix's farces at the Aldwych Theatre but, like Charles Hawtrey and Kenneth Williams before her, Joan flourished in revue where the combination of humour, sketches, songs and frequent ad-libbing brought out the best in her. Appearing as a scantily clad young thing one minute, dressing up as a toothless old granny the next, it was clear she had many skills to her name, a versatility that would stand her in great stead in the Carry On years to come.

Joan made her West End debut in 1953 with *High Spirits* – much later the title she gave her own memoir – and followed this with the massively successful Intimacy at 8.30 revue, where her audience included big names like Noel Coward and Gene Kelly. By now, she was an established star, stunningly pretty, broadly talented, flawless with her comedic timing and versatile. She had it all, with two small caveats.

One was Joan's own boredom threshold. Although she enjoyed huge success on stage, she revealed she didn't have the stamina for extended runs. By the end of her career, she admitted, 'No actor should really say this, but I don't like the long stage runs. I find it very difficult to keep each performance fresh and besides, I like getting up early in the morning.'

This meant that, despite getting theatrical offers, she frequently sought other outlets. Her returns to the stage became increasingly rare as TV and film work kept her constantly employed throughout the next two decades.

The second was her physicality, specifically her round, cute-as-a-button face. The film director Anthony Asquith probably thought he was being nice when he reportedly told Joan, 'You can't play a dramatic part, it's such a happy face.'

The actress said herself, 'I've been told my bun face fits the comedy parts better than anything else.'

This, and her penchant for film and TV over stage, meant that despite her enormous talent, her career seemed destined to follow a comedic path.

Joan's handful of early film roles included two titles, *Will Any Gentleman?* and *Dry Rot*, whose cast included Sid James. Other co-stars around this time included Norman Wisdom, Leslie Phillips, Terry Thomas and Peter Sellers. By the end of the 1950s, Sims was well established as a star on Rank's books and specialised in characterful cameo roles, something that continued even after she began making her regular trips to Pinewood.

In 1954 she was cast as the singularly uptight Nurse Rigor Mortis in *Doctor in the House*, where she struggled with the attentions of a suave Dirk Bogarde. Making quite an impression in the small role, Joan went on to appear in three more films in the series, including *Doctor at Sea*, which saw her cast as a love rival to Brigitte Bardot. In her autobiography she wrote, 'I was cast again as the Plain Jane character. Joan Sims versus Brigitte Bardot. I'll leave you to guess which of us got her man.'

More happily, the films were produced by Betty Box, which meant Joan soon came to the attention of Mr Box, the tireless Peter Rogers.

In 1958, with his *Sergeant* star Dora Bryan unavailable, he sent Joan a script for *Carry On Nurse*, the second in the series. The actress would go on to become one of the franchise's leading lights, appearing in twenty-four films over the next two decades.

Fellow Carry On actress Dilys Laye said of Joan Sims, 'The mark of a true comedienne is one who does it real, and everything Joan did was real. She followed it through. I don't think I ever saw her caricature anything.'

Joan's long tenure with Carry On saw her move from playing flirtatious bombshells to nagging wives, and she may have lacked the defining singularity of some of her male co-stars, whether it was Sid James's lecherous chuckle, or Kenneth Williams's waspishness. As a result, she became more of a liquid presence in the series than them, but she never fell into being typecast, and this was down to what Dilys Laye had noted, Joan's ability to bring a full-bodied characterisation to each part, whether she was playing a mid-West saloon-owning femme fatale in *Cowboy*, or a faux-aristocratic memsahib in *Khyber*.

What was consistent was her hint of bawdy naughtiness beneath a veneer of high-pitched hoity-toity. She also brought huge physical energy, which enhanced every scene she played.

From her first Carry On appearance in *Nurse*, as Trainee Nurse Stella Dawson, Sims played a series of cheerful, seemingly innocent characters, her sweet cherubic face meaning she could easily play younger than her real years.

'Are you satisfied with your equipment, Miss Allcock?'
'Well, I've had no complaints so far.'

In *Teacher*, she was effectively the female lead as the shapely gym mistress Miss Allcock, sent to distract Leslie Phillips's visiting child psychologist, particularly after she took a gym lesson and her shorts inevitably split, a full decade before Barbara Windsor suffered a similar PE-invoked wardrobe malfunction in *Camping*.

Regardless saw her character Lily Duveen attending a wine-tasting session, where she of course ended up taking part. Unbeknownst to the actress, Gerald Thomas had replaced one of her many samples with neat gin, and Joan had to 'take it easy' most of the rest of the day. Despite this, she gave gusto to one of the most sneakily progressive lines in the film with Lily's indignant remark, 'There aren't any interesting jobs for women. It's about time someone did something about it.'

Joan's other work kept her away from the series until 1964, when she returned for *Cleo* and was thrown into Carry On's golden age of cinematic spoofs and period romps. Throughout the series, she never really had a contemporary glamour, more a sense of beauty from a bygone age, and Joan looked her finest in period splendour. In his biography of the actress, Andrew Ross cites her friend Nicholas Ferguson who describes it well, 'Style more like an eighteenth century – sort of a cuddly lady in frills.' This promise of frilly cuddles made Sims a perfect fit for many of Carry On's very best titles.

'You've always had magnificent balls and I wouldn't miss one of those.'
'Thankyou, Lady Binder.'

Where writer Norman Hudis had played to Joan's youthful playfulness, Talbot Rothwell brought out a domineering but authoritative side in her characters. Fortunately, although she often played the demanding, cuckolded wife, her sense of fun was palpable. In *Cleo*, she was Calpurnia, married to Kenneth's Julius Caesar, who was intent on seducing Cleopatra. Similarly, in *Cowboy*, she played Belle (one of Joan's favourite roles in the series), a saloon owner who could shoot straight and would have easily held her liquor had the townsfolk been allowed any. She looked absolutely stunning in her sequinned dress and enjoyed a wonderfully dramatic entrance.

'So you're Belle.'
'My intimate friends call me Ding Dong.'

In *Don't Lose Your Head*, she looked equally fine in a film replete with cracking one-liners, none better than her character Madame Desiree Dubarry's retort to a suitor, 'I'm all for Equality and Fraternity, but I'm not having you take any Liberties.'

Joan later revealed her own favourite Carry On film was *Khyber*, and it's easy to see why. As well as a good plot and the chance to shoot on location (okay, Wales), her role of Lady Ruff-Diamond brought her passion, betrayal, fury with her cuckolding husband, and finally, the gift of one of the film's greatest lines as the roof of the Empire appears to be caving in above their dining heads.

'Oh dear, I seem to have got a little plastered.'

Carry On's hospital titles didn't demand as much of the actress as of her co-stars, although it meant she got to share screen time with two of her greatest cast chums, Frankie Howerd in *Doctor* and Kenneth Williams in *Again Doctor*. In the former, she played, almost unrecognisably, frumpy Chloe Gibson, the assistant to Howerd's charlatan faith healer Francis Bigger. The pair famously could barely shoot a scene together without corpsing, reducing each other to the same fits of giggles as they would later on in *Jungle*.

Of that quasi-tropical caper, Joan's great friend, choreographer Eleanor Fazan, remembered, 'Joan and Frankie Howerd couldn't look at each other, they'd end up looking at each other's foreheads or eyebrows, or they'd burst out laughing.'

In the later film, *Carry On Matron*, Joan spends her entire screen time in bed, as an overdue expectant mother Mrs Tidey who seems far more interested in eating than producing a baby. It would be cruel to believe the filmmakers were poking fun at Joan's appetite as they did at Charles Hawtrey's drinking in the following title *Abroad*, but there was no doubt the actress was self-conscious about her weight. The woman whose legs had dazzled West End audiences now burst into tears at the thought of being in a corset for *Carry On Again Doctor*, and refused point blank to wear a bikini for *Camping*.

Joan's place in the Carry On firmament had also evolved, as she shared the screen with younger, fresher faces, and increasingly was reduced to the role of nagging, dissatisfied wife (*Screaming, Abroad, Convenience*) or frumpy prefect-type girlfriend, sent to ruin everybody's good time (*Camping, Girls*). This naturally followed what had come before for Joan – a wronged woman in *Cowboy, Jungle* and *Khyber* – but now with less fun and fewer powers of revenge.

She was often cast as the romantic partner of Sid James, despite his being seventeen years older than her, and this may have strengthened the perception that Joan was no longer the series' spring chicken. By the time she filmed *Behind* in 1975, she was cast as Patsy Rowlands's interfering mother, even though Joan was only a few months older than her co-star. Somehow, she had become Carry On's resident battleaxe matriarch, in only a few real-life years.

Fortunately, towards the end of her Carry On tenure, Joan was able to return to the historical genre where she excelled, in *Henry* as the garlic-chewing French Queen Marie (where the crew swapped her peppermints for real garlic and gave both her and her passionate suitor Henry, played by Sid James, quite the shock) and in her last period romp for the series, *Dick*. This was the final Carry On outing for both Sid and Hattie and, for many purist fans, the beginning of the end.

Why did Joan Sims stay so long with the Carry On films, even after many of her friends had departed? Eleanor Fazan explained, 'She loved her working environment. She particularly enjoyed filming, the car coming to fetch her, the dressing room.'

Joan herself spoke fondly of the atmosphere at Pinewood in a 1987 interview, remembering, 'We were like kids at school, everybody got on with everybody else. There was nobody with a big head. We worked jolly hard. We used to have half an hour rushes a day.'

Of all her beloved co-stars, there was one whom Joan relied on the most, and that was Hattie, whom she described later as 'a wonderful person – I looked on her as a sister come mother'.

Decades later, she remembered:

When I'd get my script, I'd sometimes phone up Hattie, 'We're not going to do this load of rubbish. It's the same old gags, Hattie.' Hattie would say, 'What are you on about you silly thing? We'll have fun.' And of course we always did. We always loved it.

For Joan, unmarried and without her own family at home, it was the company at Pinewood as much as anything that kept her going back for more, even after the departures of Hattie and Sid, Charles and Barbara.

Unfortunately, this meant she stayed on the roll call for Carry On titles that were a poor shadow of previous triumphs.

If Joan's very last outing for Carry On in 1978's *Emmannuelle* was unworthy of her great contribution to the series, there is small consolation in the fact that her role of housekeeper Mrs Dangle was a tad stronger than the one which preceded it. In 1976's *England*, Joan played Private Jennifer Ffoukes-Sharpe, a supporting character that brought her little pleasure in a limp title that only brought home how far the series had departed from its initial chirpiness, let alone its golden age.

Emmannuelle was, at least, gloriously bad. As Mrs Dangle, Joan was reduced to living vicariously through the saucy antics of others, peeping through keyholes and landing a series of saucy one-liners. The best scene in the film was Sims's version of a launderette seduction, but even this was a parody of everything good that had come before. It was time for her, and everyone else, to go home.

Joan had no trouble finding work afterwards, a few forays to the theatre, but mostly in TV comedy. She had already made her mark in *Till Death Us Do Part* as Gran, Alf Garnett's mother-in-law. Considering she was actually four years younger than the show's star Warren Mitchell, this was fresh proof of Joan's willingness to surrender any vanity for a role. She was so distinctive that writer Johnny Speight had plans for a spin-off comedy, just for Gran, but Joan demurred. Her reluctance was, reportedly, down to her real-life fears. 'That character depresses me. One day I might be like that.'

Many comedic roles came her way, in shows including *On the Up* with Dennis Waterman, *Only Fools and Horses* plus a special of *One Foot in the Grave*. Later, she became known for her role in *As Time Goes By* after she joined Geoffrey Palmer and Judi Dench in the popular sit-com. Years before Patricia Routledge delighted millions as Hyacinth Bucket, Joan perfected outraged pomposity in children's shows *Worzel Gummidge* and *Simon and the Witch*, playing Mrs Bloomsbury-Barton and Lady Fox Custard respectively.

On only a couple of occasions did she reveal the darker potential of her talents, playing Amelia Elizabeth Dyler in an episode of *Lady Killers* in 1980, and later in the Agatha Christie tale, *A Murder is Announced*. I would have loved to see her play to these depths more often. Imagine Joan in Kathy Bates's role in *Misery*, or Judi Dench's in *Notes on a Scandal*. Priceless.

By now, though, Joan's health was sadly failing her. As well as physical ailments, she suffered from loneliness in her later years as she was confronted with less work and the loss of loved ones. Her friend, songwriter Myles Rudge, remembered, 'When she needed a friend, she turned to the bottle,' and in her memoir, Joan revealed the depths of her sorrow and agoraphobia.

Later, she said, 'When you have lived to work, and I have been a workaholic, I'm happiest when I'm working. The danger was when I didn't work. The depression starts.'

Mercifully she pulled through it and became more content in the last couple of years before she died. She said then, 'I'm a much happier person now.' She was back in demand, too, taking on voiceover work and securing one of her best ever parts, again with Judi Dench. In *Last of the Blonde Bombshells*, a nostalgic TV drama, she played bandleader Betty in what proved to be her final acting performance.

Sims went into hospital in November 2000 for a routine operation, but complications caused her to fall into a coma and she never properly recovered.

One of her long-time best friends was Norah Holland, an actress she had first met decades before when a stand-in was required for her on the Pinewood set. It was Norah who was sitting with Joan when she died in June 2001. She said later that just ten minutes before, 'I was talking to her all the time – you go and find Hattie and Kenny, all the gang, they're all up there.'

Joan's co-stars really were her family, her closest friends, and Kenneth had even once proposed marriage. She reflected later, 'If Kenneth had been livable with, I might have said yes, for companionship. But poor Kenny, he never stopped, he would sap your energy. No regrets. It would have been impossible.'

Her biographer Andrew Ross details Joan's shyness, the difficulty she had being recognised in the street, despite her popularity. She said herself, 'I've never been shy as an actress, but terribly nervous as a person. Being an actor, there is something unreal about it.'

The film set was, simply, her happy place, her escape from the personal challenges of real life where, despite a few relationships, she spent much time alone. Her friend Eleanor Fazan described it like this, 'She was lonely, but she wouldn't have wanted any relationship to stop her going out to work. She loved her work, loved her colleagues. I think they came first.'

It is telling that in her autobiography, Joan wrote, 'I was always useless at flirting and simply did not know what needed to be done in order to snare my target. I always ended up resorting to jokes, and most men don't like funny women.'

In the world of Carry On at least, she found a place where that wasn't the case. Let me give the final word to Joan, who wrote in that same memoir very movingly, 'The last couple of years have seen more lows than highs. My long-held view that whether you're up or you're down, there's only one way to react to whatever life throws at you. Carry on.'

Chapter 10

The Joy of Sets

'After all, we're all in the same boat, aren't we?'

Sid James in *Carry On Cruising*

'I'm big in Japan,' Charles Hawtrey once claimed, and it was true. He could have added Los Angeles, India and Australia. Kenneth Williams was presented with a souvenir film poster from Sarajevo, and received fan letters from Cuba. Kenneth wrote that the biggest puzzle for him was why the films proved so popular even in Communist countries. Somehow, by the end of the 1960s, this most British of film series had found audiences all over the world and made global stars of its regulars.

Back in Buckinghamshire and in the corridors of Pinewood, however, they remained a bunch of hardworking actors who rose at dawn, made their way to the studios where they prepared to hit their marks, deliver their lines and get the shots in the can, invariably in one take, for between six and eight weeks, twice a year.

Cast and crew alike were all familiar faces, greeting each other at the start of each film like children returning to school after the holidays, proof that Peter Rogers really had created a kind of repertory company for the cinema, which he put to work twice a year, productions timed for the actors' calendar gaps between Christmas pantomime and summer theatre season.

Despite Charles's occasional diva antics, Peter always made it clear that no one person was essential to Carry On. Instead, he had a roster of mostly regular faces, with new names being added as the series evolved – Jim Dale, Bernard Cribbins, Roy Castle, Patsy Rowlands, Esme Cannon, Harry H. Corbett, Amanda Barrie and so on – all actors with comedy chops rather than traditional comedians and, significantly, nobody very posh. Playwright Terry Johnson considers the class element key to the films' appeal. 'These people were non-aspirant working-class folk,' he says. 'They were grafters, and the working-class audiences particularly could relate to them, as they could sense the origins.'

The troupe's capacity for hard work is clear, with the enduring stories of how speedily, and also efficiently, the films were invariably completed. For the actors, as Kenneth explained in his memoir, this meant capturing the character, relationships, expressions and humour of a scene, regularly in the first take and often very early of a morning. In these circumstances, he reflected, there was no room for any ego, just hard, good-humoured work.

Not everyone enjoyed it, as Bernard Cribbins describes it for me:

> They were never easy to film. You were always being called to hurry up, hurry up, because they wanted to complete them in six weeks, a very short time for a feature film. I think *Jack* was a big one for them, nearly eight weeks. When we did *Spying*, even though it was a big production for them, it was still 'Take one, okay, one more before lunch, take two, done.' They were not luxurious. They simply got people they knew could do it and do it quickly. We had to be proper pros.

Others were in their element. Sid James, always aware of the precarious financial state of an actor's lot, saw it as an opportunity to wrap up the job quickly and move onto something else, while regular guest star Frankie Howerd actually relished the speediness:

> Filming sometimes months on these great epics, a lot of time is spent hanging around, whereas if you work quickly, and you do these scenes, you keep this air of spontaneity going and I think this is what comes over in the Carry On films, this kind of spontaneous air. ... They make it look easy and that's the clever thing. I admire them very much.

Even as the writers increasingly wrote around the actors they knew would be cast, regulars like Joan Sims loved the element of dress up, the chance to play all sorts of roles, in her case moving from Wild West saloon dame to French aristocratic duchess. As the cast kept returning and the writers got to know them, so the actors' timing and chemistry became even better. The whole production process was a well-oiled machine, everyone knowing exactly what was required of them and delivering it with a consistency that has gone unmatched in the British film industry. Kenneth Connor once likened it to 'a well-run ship ... so professionally done, everyone right through carpentry, props, they know where they are'.

If it was a well-run ship, the all-seeing eye of Peter Rogers made sure it was also a tightly-run one, when it came to both the shooting calendar and the locations. On one occasion during the filming of *Carry On Constable*, Sid James tripped and fell down the stairs. He prepared to go again, only to be told that there was no time for a second take, the shot would simply be cut from the finished whole. 'Going again' was the stuff of legend, it so seldom happened.

As for location, Peter and his director Gerald always found a way of staying as close to home as possible, whatever the story. Spain for *Abroad*? Pinewood Car Park. An African clearing for *Jungle*? Kew Gardens. Pre-Revolutionary France? Buckinghamshire. *Camping*? Back to the car park.

When Melvyn Bragg once asked Peter why he didn't splash out and take his cast any distance beyond the gates of Pinewood, he got the reply, 'Where would you have gone, the Sahara?'

There was no doubt that Peter broke the mould of the typical flamboyant film producer. Eschewing the swagger and cigar-chomping movie talk espoused by others in his position, he also avoided film premieres, even press screenings and other occasions where he could have been forgiven for glorying in his success. Similarly, he could be cynical about his competitors' methods of bumping up their budgets, opting for cheap, lowbrow productions even when it was unfashionable to say so. He told *The Times* newspaper as early as 1959, 'One hears people saying that you can't make a film which will show a profit for under £500,000. I did not believe this, and I think I have proved my point.'

The shadow that has hung for decades over the flawless production chain of Carry On is the money, or lack thereof, for the artists involved. Kenneth described it as having star status without star money, while Charles was even more succinct in an interview in 1984, summing it up, 'We worked for a bread ticket, and I don't eat much bread.'

He wasn't exaggerating. The figure of £5,000 paid to the leading men back in the 1950s didn't increase in over a decade. For the women, it was half that. The huge profits returned by the films became increasingly galling to the cast members as the titles were shown repeatedly all across the world without bringing them a bean in royalties. Worse, once the series began to be shown on television as well, the biggest stars found they had trouble securing other roles, victims of their own success. Barbara complained that, when she went for auditions, she was told, 'We can't use Barbara Windsor – she's never off the box!' Years later, Joan Sims complained, 'People think I'm rich and retired, but I'm still trying to scrape a living.'

Jack Douglas once recounted his agent asking him whether he wanted the good news or the bad news. The good news was he'd been cast in *Carry On Matron*. The bad news? 'You're not getting paid.' The myth went that Jack ended up being paid with a crate of champagne, although Peter Rogers later disputed this.

Angela Douglas remembers her first day on set, when Peter welcomed her, 'Anything you want, just ask.' She tells me:

Well as it happened, I had a little Mini, and it had broken down. So I asked him for a car to bring me to work. Everyone held their breath, and it seemed as though Peter had somehow vanished into the bushes. Sid James came up to me and said, 'You'll learn.'

Most strikingly, there endures the tale of Charles making his way on foot with his carrier bags from nearby Uxbridge train station and being scooped up for a lift by Laurence Olivier in his limousine. Once arrived at the studio, he reported that the great dramatic knight had been shocked to see such ordinary treatment being meted out to Pinewood's biggest stars, and that Olivier had said he wouldn't stand for it. 'That's why they don't cast him,' was the reply he received.

Peter was similarly brisk in his dealings with his writer Talbot Rothwell, when the latter's agent Kevin Kavanagh angled for his client to enjoy a cut of the profits for *Carry On Cowboy*. The warmth of the relationship between producer and writer is revealed in a series of letters between the two men, now housed at the British Film Institute, but this affection didn't impede Peter's businesslike approach. Fortunately for him, he was dealing with a man who clearly didn't feel happy having such discussions, as Talbot delightfully expressed it to him, 'As you well know, where money is concerned, I'm about as ambitious as a eunuch at an orgy.' Peter countered by pointing out a cut in profits would mean an initial lower fee for his writer's efforts. Any financial ambition Talbot might have had was thus nipped in the bud.

There remains some uncertainty around the finances. It was clearly a repertory system of casting, Peter's rationale being that, without a single star above the others, no individual could take either blame or credit for the films, instead they were all in it together. However, he also always maintained that he had, very early on in the series, offered his principal cast members a percentage of the profits in return for a cut in their fees, but that they'd all said no. Leslie Phillips, who walked away from the series due to the lack of funds coming his way, said he'd never heard of that. Peter retorted that perhaps his agent hadn't told him. Certainly no paperwork relating to this offer has ever been produced, and it would have been unusual in that era for actors to be offered such a deal. As recently as 2008, Peter told the *Daily Express*, 'I know I've got a reputation for meanness but it wasn't my fault.' The jury will have to remain out.

Some of the cast were philosophical. Sid James, on a buyout like everyone else, set about making up the shortfall in his pay packet with some blatant product placement – check out the amount of a certain whisky brand on display in *Carry On Up the Jungle!* – while Barbara was among those who soaked up the good with the bad. She remembered:

> Most of the time you arrived at the studio and you were happy because you were going to see everybody. There were other times, you'd think, we've got this terrible location, well it wasn't a location at all, it was a field at the back, and you knew it would be freezing cold, then suddenly Peter Rogers would swan by in his Rolls Royce and bib-bib you, 'Hello,' and you'd think, oh gawd, it's all right for some.

Kenneth Williams had his own moment of public indignation, with Jim Dale recounting him once screaming at Peter about the wages. Elsewhere, though, Kenneth rationalised that, as the producer who had put all the risk in the film to begin with, Peter deserved to reap the profits. In the same vein, avowedly anti-socialist, Kenneth once regaled a surprised Michael Parkinson and TV audience, no doubt expecting some camp Sandy jokes, with a rant against egalitarianism. So it's not really surprising that he had no argument with Peter's approach. Kenneth said, 'If a man sinks his savings into a well, he's got the right to charge a penny for the cup of water that comes out of it.' It's a view.

Sunny-tempered Anita Harris was able to put things into perspective too, pointing out, 'Georgie Best didn't get paid what David Beckham gets paid. It was part of that time. It would have been wonderful if we all got paid a bit more, but what came out was a lot more than payment in money. What came out of those movies were legends, longevity of work load, being part of something that is British heritage.' Oh, if we could all look at the world a bit more like Anita does, wouldn't we be happier!

Marc Sinden, actor turned filmmaker with much experience on both sides of the camera, defends his godfather's position when it comes to the monies and the swift, unemotional way in which he made his decisions. 'It goes with the territory,' Sinden tells me:

> Somebody has to be in charge, call the shots and say, 'No, we're not going over budget.'
>
> It comes as a terrible shock for an actor to discover their true worth, but I'm afraid that that is the reality. If you can get someone for £20,000 a movie, why would you pay them £50,000? It is a business.
>
> Many of the actors involved became household names because of it – isn't that what every actor wants? People unfairly hold him up as a bit of a miser, but the answer is simple: don't work for him, it's not compulsory.

Indeed, some didn't. Leslie Phillips was soon off, admitting later, 'I was very fond of Peter Rogers, but he was so bloody mean.' Jim Dale departed to take his chances with the National Theatre and then overseas. Bernard Cribbins remained relaxed about the whole exercise. 'I was very happy to do them, but if something else came along that I wanted to do, I went and did that instead.'

For many others, though, including the crew as well as cast, two guaranteed films a year amounted to a small but safe salary they were loath to part with. Playwright Terry Johnson explains now:

> For a lot of the team, living in either Denham or Iver, it was a kind of paradise. If you were one of the cast regulars or even a jobbing film

craftsman, why would you bother going elsewhere? It probably came down to how much you wanted to live in Iver.

Peter himself never attempted to justify or amend his attitude, reflecting years later, 'I've heard it said I made cheap pictures. I didn't. I made economical pictures.'

He considered it very straightforward – that his job as the producer was to make sure the films came in on budget and on time. Years later, at the 40th anniversary party of the films in 1998, Peter joked to a room packed with over thirty of his leading men and ladies, 'I loved them all dearly and would do anything for them except pay them more money!' Ouch!

There is seldom a creative duo throughout history who amount to anything without one person tending to the art, and one person backstage somewhere counting the beans. I don't think there's a person within a hundred miles of Pinewood who would argue that Peter Rogers served in the latter capacity, and showed nerves of steel when negotiating with both Anglo-Amalgamated and Rank to ensure the films kept being made. He was, by all accounts, a bit shy, but clearly ambitious from the start. He said himself, 'I never negotiated. That's the way to lose control.'

At the office, there was no doubt about it, he ruled with a poker-faced rod of iron, as Charles Hawtrey discovered when he requested his pay rise and a star for his dressing room door on *Cruising*, and was soon despatched for his troubles. On another occasion, one of his cast demanded, 'I should have more fun lines, I'm a comedian.' Peter told him, 'Your secret is safe with me.' And that was that. Kenneth's memoir also describes an incident when he was short with a costume man, and Peter upbraided him, insisting he apologise. When Charles once complained that Peter was 'drunk with power', Peter retorted that if anybody was drunk on those sets, it wasn't him.

Peter was unapologetic about the lack of awe in which he held his starry cast. He said performers were required to be experienced professionals to 'stand the heat of making the Carry Ons', particularly working on such a tight budget. 'Unprofessional behaviour couldn't be tolerated because it would put the entire film in jeopardy.'

Despite many accounts of this ruthless businessman persona, we shouldn't ignore the other facets of Peter's personality that no doubt contributed to the success of Carry On.

With wife Betty and their beloved dogs, Peter shared the beautiful home of Drummers Yard in Beaconsfield, an enormous listed building bought from their friend Dirk Bogarde. It was so big, the pantry was famously 35 yards away from the living room and their godson Marc still remembers the beautiful glass in the house, with its Russian Imperial coats of arms.

There, Peter devoted his spare time to his great passions of music, literature and animals. Gerald Thomas's wife Barbara remembers spending time socially with her husband's colleague:

> We talked about music a lot, and he was very knowledgeable. He had dogs whom he loved, possibly more than people. He also had highland cattle, which he liked because they were so picturesque in the paddock. He gave them names like Marks and Spencer, and Freeman, Hardy and Willis.

For Gerald's daughter Deborah, who often accompanied her parents to Drummers Yard, Peter and Betty seemed incredibly sophisticated. 'They had an enormous interest in everything – theatre, music, the arts, everything. Everyone dressed nicely, and went to lovely restaurants. They just seemed to be having a wonderful time.'

Away from production, Peter often met up with Gerald to plan their next shoot. Besides his constant collaborator, Peter's closest Carry On comrade was probably Kenneth Williams, with whom he would discuss literature at great length. Marc Sinden remembers how hurt Peter was when Kenneth's diaries were published after his death, and he read the terrible things his star had written about their working life together. He asked Marc, 'Why did the little bastard carry on making the movies if he hated them that much?' He told his godson, 'He really was duplicitous. He would fawn over me and have great fun, and then it came out in the diary that he was so bloody miserable.' Marc tells me of the effect this had on Peter. 'I know that hurt him a lot.'

However, the capricious Kenneth also credited Peter for seeing the potential for the long-lasting success of the series, 'undreamt of by the rest of us'. Marc believes it was the producer's ability to choose a team and then lead it so effectively that set him apart from every other film-maker who's ever dreamed of owning a franchise.

Marc tells me he once asked his godfather about the Carry On films, 'What's the secret, why do you keep doing them?' Peter replied, 'When you get to the point of owning a Rolls Royce, never bother looking under the hood.'

And he didn't. Instead, Peter just kept going, as he said himself, making the same film over and over again. Marc laughs, 'He used to walk around Pinewood as though he owned it, and in a funny sort of way, I suppose he did.'

Fortunately, at the producer's side throughout the series was a man with enough warmth, charm and humility for both of them. Director Gerald Thomas, while delivering every film of such quality and with such efficiency that he earned Peter's complete confidence and respect, was equally able to guide his flock of cast and crew with the authority and good humour required to earn their complete trust.

Even the often solitary Charles Hawtrey was effusive in his praise for his director, telling a BBC documentary crew, 'Gerald Thomas is as responsible as anybody for the success of the films. He keeps us in order, quite rightly we have to do what we're told and we discuss everything together as friends would and he's got a firm hand over the controls.'

If any actor was unsure whether Peter would be asking them back, Gerald was on hand to reassure them they'd be welcomed, and of course they mostly were, making for a regular and happy cast and crew. The shooting of *Carry On Jack* down at Frensham Ponds in Surrey, September 1963, was typical of a day's shooting. Under the blue sky, surrounded by smiling faces, Bernard Cribbins remembered the cameraman saying, 'The sun always shines for Gerald, doesn't it!' This was obviously before they made *Carry On Camping*.

Peter was a very creative man, for whom the most exciting parts of making the Carry Ons, or any other production, were the script and the music. For him, 'the film in the middle was just routine'. For Gerald, though, it was the opposite. Right from the first minute of shooting, the director had a plan and he never swerved from it, treating the script and schedule with great reverence, explaining, 'It's virtually a Bible, there's very little deviation, so we know when we start exactly how long it's going to take and where we're going to go from there.'

It helped, of course, that he'd started out in the cutting room. His wife Barbara tells me:

He was always an editor at heart, and that made it easier to be economical later on. He invariably knew exactly what shot he wanted from each scene, where he was going to cut, and his planning helped keep the budget down and brought the film in on time, which kept Peter happy.

The hard-to-please producer reserved his highest praise for Gerald, whom he nicknamed Speedy Gonzales for zipping through the shooting schedules at such a rate. Fenella Fielding once remembered asking the director to go again in a scene. 'You've had your retake,' she was told. 'That meant for the rest of my life.'

Possibly Gerald's most dizzying achievement was *Carry On Spying* which, spread over fifty-four sets in total, was in the can after six weeks one-and-a-half days. Even Peter called this 'a little extraordinary'.

Such a high production rate meant packing a huge amount into his working day, but Gerald never brought his job back from the studio with him. On the contrary, it seems he always made sure to break from filming in time to come home and see his young children, pour a drink for himself and Barbara and relax for the rest of the evening. Although Norman Hudis once wrote that Gerald had once revealed to him he'd never spent five minutes at ease during the whole time of the Carry Ons, it seems the director never outwardly showed any signs of stress about the huge projects he had to carry creatively. Barbara Thomas recalls:

Sometimes there was a bit of angst over the scripts, or a bit of a problem with the Censor, but I don't think he ever lost any sleep over it. He very rarely talked about work once he got home. As far as he was concerned, once he left the studio, which he always did in good time, that was all behind him.

At the start of each film, I bought him an appropriate present for good luck. There was a gun holster for *Cowboy*, an action man for *England*, complete with a tin hat, little things like that. And he had a beautiful script cover he'd use for each production. He always did his homework and was meticulously prepared, but it never took over his life.

The main reason for Gerald's confidence as a director was his trust in the team around him. Deborah remembers her father 'doing his budgets almost on the back of a brown envelope. He knew what he needed, and could rely on his technicians. He had the support in all areas of production'.

She describes it:

> When they turned up on the first day of shooting, it was like a family reunion. Everyone knew exactly what was required of them, so that took a lot of the stress out of the job. There were difficulties in the British film industry at the time, and they might have felt under pressure to deliver, but my father never let it show.

Her sister Sarah Hollywood remembers too their father's faith in his team, telling me, 'For him, it was a collaboration at all times. He adored and respected his crew who were, in exchange, loyal, talented and individually creative.'

If Gerald was Speedy Gonzales to his producer, he was 'The Headmaster' to the cast and crew he had to manage who, besides being a group of the most hardworking, talented professionals in the business, were also known to conduct themselves like a bunch of unruly school children.

'It's one hysterical laugh from start to finish,' remembered Sid. 'Not at the jokes, but at each other. I walk home every night, my eyes puffed up from laughing.'

Joan herself described returning to set once or twice a year as 'like coming back to school after the holidays. You know the people you're working with and there's a very happy atmosphere'.

This camaraderie was evident from the very first days of Carry On, when the practical jokes began on *Sergeant*. As new recruit Charlie Sage, Bob Monkhouse found he couldn't climb the rope on the assault course, most probably because Kenneth Williams had secretly smeared it with butter. On *Regardless*, Joan launched herself into the wine-tasting scene, not realising the team had swapped her totty for neat vodka. She ploughed on like a pro, and her shocked reaction made it into the finished version.

Angela Douglas's strongest memory of her time on Carry On is, she tells me, of the 'laughter off the set – non-stop, all day – sitting in our chairs or on the floor, chatting, laughing, listening to the jokes'.

Jacki Piper described the group as 'like a family, seeing each other twice a year', and as with every family reunion, members soon settled into their usual spots, Hattie sitting with her crossword and so on. Jon Pertwee, who appeared in three Carry On films (plus *Columbus*), recalled the atmosphere on set, 'Every single day, Charlie Hawtrey had his plastic bag with his crossword and his Tizer. Every single day, Kenneth Williams hid it. The first assistant would come on and say, "Right, chaps, be loyal."'

Barbara Windsor also likened it to being at school, but for her, the most wonderful aspect was the lack of jealousy between the actors. She explained, 'We weren't selfish. If a line suited someone else, we'd give it away. If … Kenny thought [a line] was better for Charlie, he'd give it to Charlie, like I would give it to Joan. It was a great feeling.'

This closeness extended beyond the studio. Gerald lived close to Pinewood in the picturesque village of Burnham Beeches, and his daughter Deborah recalls her parents' frequent gatherings, where they hosted the Breslaws, the Connors, the Butterworths and the Douglases. Often with the other adults downstairs, regular visitor Kenneth used to delight in sitting down to read bedtime stories to the Thomas girls. A thrilled Deborah remembers, 'One time he attempted to kidnap my doll Bluey and told me her ransom would be Daddy upping the size of his role in the next film!' Later on, Kenneth was happy to sponsor Deborah for her Equity card, although he insisted on her doing her hours.

While Gerald had every respect for Peter's business skills, his closest colleague throughout the Carry On years was Sid James. 'They were the best of friends, true kindred spirits,' is how Sid's daughter Sue describes it. 'Both utterly professional, and both completely unpretentious.' Their families used to gather at weekends, even holidaying together in the south of France, and Deborah and Sue have remained lifelong friends to this day. Gerald's wife Barbara describes Sid as a true gentleman. One day they were sharing a car along with Sid's wife Val, when a cab cut across them. She remembers the actor getting out and speaking to the cabbie, explaining very politely that he had ladies in his car, and asking him to please drive more carefully.

Barbara Thomas once received a beautiful fountain pen as a gift from Sid. Years later, she was sitting on the sofa, using it to write a letter when the television news came on, breaking the sad report of their friend's death on stage at the Sunderland Empire. Just at that moment, Barbara discovered that her pen had stopped writing, a strange moment that she has never forgotten.

Pinewood, a much smaller and more intimate operation in the 1960s and 1970s than the commercial juggernaut it is now, was a paradise for the children. Young Deborah relished meeting everyone from Cubby Broccoli to Sylvia Anderson and 'helping' the Carry On make-up artists by applying pancake to the stars between takes, while her sister Sarah remembers 'the sheer joy that permeated the set as I grew up'. But for Sue James it was all about the ponies. Her riding school was on the Pinewood lot, and her biggest treat of all came when Sid allowed her to ride her pony over to Black Park, where he was filming *Cowboy*. 'The combination of seeing Dad at work, and being allowed to take my pony out, was unbelievably exciting,' she recalls.

Sue's brother Steve, a couple of years older, was actually allowed to sit on his father's own horse during the same production. 'I used to love going to work with him,' he remembers. 'The first stop was the mobile café, where we had a bacon sandwich and a cup of tea. Never mind the filming, for me it was all about the sarnies.'

With even the reserved Peter Rogers years later describing the atmosphere as one of 'a family, always together', inevitably that could make things difficult for some late arrivals. As Sid once remarked, 'I always feel sorry for a newcomer, it really is like coming into someone's family.' He added with a grin, 'We've never had any trouble with newcomers, we just belt them.'

The thing about Carry On was that, as Peter made sure, there was never any one shining star. As Jacki Piper described it, the atmosphere was one of 'give and take, no one tries to stand out. They wouldn't be allowed to if they did. People who came in and did were cut down'.

One such person to discover this was Phil Silvers, drafted in at short notice for *Follow That Camel*, to replace Sid who had committed to filming a TV series. Kenneth's memoir painfully relates the American veteran star's failure to gel with the rest of the cast. It's hard to tell what infuriated Kenneth the most, Silvers's refusal to learn his lines in time for a take, or his indulgence in relating long, unfunny stories at dinner while the rest of the cast suppressed their giggles. Angela Douglas, also on duty for *Camel*, tells how 'the only bad apple was Phil Silvers, but that maybe wasn't his fault. It just didn't work at all, we weren't used to a new star coming in, we were a tight unit'. To make matters worse, Silvers kept losing his contact lenses in the sands of Camber. It seems the poor man couldn't get a break.

Even the far less starry British actor Hugh Futcher, who appeared in six Carry On films in total, found some of the regulars could be prickly with newbies. On location in Brighton for *Carry On At Your Convenience*, Hugh joined the rest of the cast in the hotel one evening, where everyone was taking turns to tell a funny story. When it was Hugh's turn, he was gratified to find his anecdote got lots of laughs, from all except one person, that is:

> Kenneth got up to leave and as he went past me, he got me by my cheeks and said, 'You will remember I'm the funny one, duckie?' Then he smacked me on the face, and it stung. Bernard Bresslaw noticed and said, 'Hey, what was that all about?' I suppose coming from Kenneth it was almost a compliment.

Back in the dining hall at Pinewood, the literary Hugh had a wonderful description for Kenneth and Joan Sims, perched in their usual seats near the door so they didn't miss a soul passing by. 'They were like a pair of Madame Defarges, Dickens's knitting woman at the guillotine in France, ready to tear someone off a strip. Everyone else would be wondering whose turn it was that day.'

Hugh enjoyed a far easier time with Sid, who frequently invited him to cast his eye over the racing columns in the paper. 'We'd go over the horses together, and I still believe that's why he asked the producers the next time around, "Is there anything for Hugh?" We had a great rapport. He had innate charisma, and he was always very nice to me.'

Sid, it seemed, was universally appreciated for his kindness to everyone new and old. In 1971, actor Kenneth Cope arrived on set for the first of his two appearances in the series. In *Carry On At Your Convenience*, Kenneth played bolshy union rep Vic Spanner, who had a relatively long piece of dialogue in a scene with Sid's character Sid Plummer (naturally). As is customary on shoots, Kenneth needed someone to stand by the camera for his reverse shot while he was making his big speech. By then, Sid was the established elder statesman of the set and could have easily asked for an extra to stand there while he went for a rest. Kenneth tells me the opposite happened:

> God bless him, he stood there the whole time with me, looking at me, giving me an eyeline, and it was a very generous, professional thing to do.

> Plus he was constantly nodding and encouraging me because it was my first day on the set. I've known a lot of people walk off because they're so-called stars, but Sid stayed put. I've never forgotten it.

For actress Sally Geeson, who'd appeared with Sid in the TV sitcom *Bless This House* before she appeared in two Carry Ons, *Abroad* and *Girls* (following a child walk-on role years before in *Regardless*), the atmosphere at Pinewood was equally welcoming:

> My first day, I walked along the corridor to makeup, and I could hear great howls of laughter coming from there. When I got there, it turned out to be Barbara Windsor and Charles Hawtrey just shrieking, and that was what it was like right through filming. I'd felt very lucky to be in a Carry On, because I'd been such a big fan as a little girl, and my parents loved them, but I'd had no idea it would be such fun as well. I used to come home each day, just exhausted from laughing.

Angela Douglas tells me exactly the same thing. 'We'd laugh until our mascara ran, then the makeup department would get cross because they'd have to put it all on again.'

It is a huge testament to Gerald Thomas's skills as both a director and a gentleman that, amid all this revelry, he nevertheless managed to get the films in the can as efficiently as he did. Sally recounted shooting one scene for *Abroad*, when a lot of the cast had to be squeezed into a prison cell, and they could barely get through a sentence without someone setting off everyone else's giggles:

> Eventually, Gerald had to clap his hands and say, 'Now, now, children!' We all shut up but we could still hear someone laughing. Gerald asked, 'Who is this who keeps laughing?' It turned out be

And they're off…
Carry On Sergeant unknowingly leads the way for the historic franchise (1958). (*Carry On Films Limited*)

Anglo-Amalgamated's Nat Cohen shares some laughs at Pinewood with Sid, Gerald, Hattie and Peter. (*Kindly supplied by the Gerald Thomas family*)

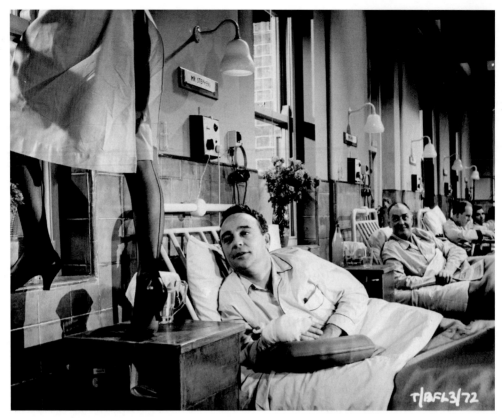

Carry On Nurse (1959) is the first of the team's medical titles, soon to become their stocking trade. (*Carry On Films Limited*)

Charles, Hattie and Kenneth have an itch to scratch after a powder plot by pupils in *Carry On Teacher* (1959). (*Carry On Films Limited*)

Sid keeps everything ship-shape in *Carry On Cruising* (1962). (*Carry On Films Limited*)

Sid has a bee in his bonnet about Hattie's secret business, but love wins out in *Carry On Cabby* (1963). (*Peter Rogers Archive, kindly supplied by Morris Bright MBE*)

The serious business of comedy – Peter confers with tireless screenwriter Talbot Rothwell. (*Peter Rogers Archive*)

They came, they saw, they conquered! *Carry On Cleo* enjoyed critical and commercial success following its debut in 1964. (*Peter Rogers Archive*)

Hands down, to this day *Carry On Cleo* remains one of the most celebrated titles of the franchise. (*Carry On Films Limited*)

Sid at his happiest playing Rumpo the Kid – 'Feel the smile'. (*Peter Rogers Archive*)

Bubbly Angela Douglas's debut in *Carry on Cowboy* (1965). (*Peter Rogers Archive*)

Two new stars join the legion of Carry On regulars for *Follow that Camel* (1967). (*Peter Rogers Archive*)

Valerie Van Der Ost's bedside manner is just the tonic for Sid in *Carry On Doctor* (1967). (*Carry On Films Limited*)

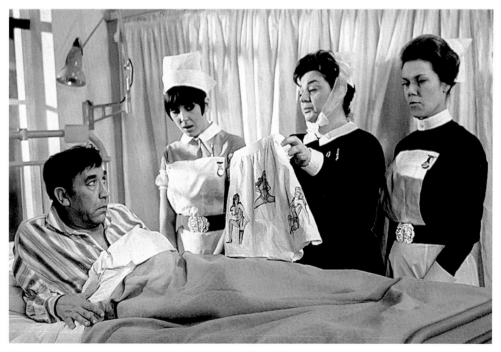

Matron tears a strip off reluctant patient Frankie Howerd in *Carry On Doctor* (1967). (*Carry On Films Limited*)

Gerald and Sid enjoy one of their many chats backstage. (*Gerald Thomas Family*)

Who's that on the throne? It's the Khasi! Kenneth on top form in *Carry On Up the Khyber* (1968). (*Peter Rogers Archive*)

Whatever the Devils in Skirts had under their kilts saw off any resistance in what many still consider the very best of Carry On. (*Peter Rogers Archive*)

The funny side of acting – Charles and Terry share a moment on the set of *Carry On Khyber*. (*Peter Rogers Archive*)

Paradise or bust? Barbara springs into action for *Carry On Camping* (1969). (*Carry On Films Limited*)

Hello Campers! Barbara, Kenneth and Hattie share a joke on set. (*Peter Rogers Archive*)

Kenneth has no time for Nookey in *Carry On Again Doctor* (1969). (*Carry On Films Limited*)

Charles suspends disbelief as Lady Puddleton in *Carry On Again Doctor*. (*Peter Rogers Archive*)

By the time of *Carry On Again Doctor*, the team has perfected the magic formula. (*Carry On Films Limited*)

Titter ye not! Joan and Frankie's giggles meant re-takes were in order whenever they filmed together. (*Peter Rogers Archive*)

Valerie Leon causes temperatures to rise in *Carry On Up the Jungle* (1970). (*Kindly supplied by Valerie Leon*)

Gerald joins the cast of *Carry On Henry* in an impromptu knees-up. (*Gerald Thomas Family*)

All in a day's work for director Gerald 'Speedy Gonzales' Thomas – the shooting schedule for *Carry On Henry* (1971). (*Peter Rogers Archive*)

PETER ROGERS PRODUCTIONS LTD

'CARRY ON HENRY'
7/APL/154

PROGRESSIVE SHOOTING SCHEDULE NO.1

From Monday 12th October to Friday 27th November 1970

25/9/70

DATE	STGE	SET NO.	SET	SCENE NOS.	CHARACTERS
OCTOBER Mon. 12th	D	322	INT. A CELLAR	21N, 68N	HAMPTON, FAWKES, PLOTTERS 1 & 2 CROMWELL
Tues. 13th	Loc.	315	EXT. COUNTRYSIDE	13	HENRY, SIR THOMAS, 3 COURTIERS, 2 Hounds LASS, Horses. 2 Dog Handlers.
Wed. 14th	Loc.	317	EXT. BARNYARD.	14,16,18.	HENRY, SIR THOMAS, 5 COURTIERS, LASS, FARMER, Horses
	Loc.	316	INT. BARN.	15,17.	2 Hounds + 2 Handlers
Thurs. 15th	Studio Gdns.	307	EXT. PALACE GARDENS.	51,53,55,60.	MARIE, BETTINA, HENRY, SIR THOMAS
Fri. 16th	"	311	EXT. CROQUET LAWN.	60A,61,62.	BETTINA, HENRY, MARIE, HAMPTON,
	PADDOCK TANK	303	EXT. SPEAKERS' CORNER	33	HECKLER, DANDY, YOUNG MAN, 20 Extras.
Sat. 17th. Sun. 18th.			NO SHOOTING		
Mon. 19th	D	310	INT. QUEEN'S BED-CHAMBER. (S/By W/C for 13th Oct.)	5	MARIE, SIR ROGER, HENRY
Tues. 20th	D	310	INT. QUEEN'S BED-CHAMBER. (W/C for 14th Oct.)	7,12,22N.	MARIE, WOLSEY, SIR ROGER, HENRY.
Wed. 21st	D	310	INT. QUEEN'S BED-CHAMBER. (W/C for 15th Oct.)	24N,26N, 28N,74N.	HENRY, MARIE, HAMPTON, SIR ROGER, BETTINA, PLUNKEY, FAWKES, 2 PLOTTERS.
Thurs. 22nd.	D	310	INT. QUEEN'S BED-CHAMBER. (W/C for 16th Oct.)	76N,84N, 90.	HENRY, BETTINA, FRANCIS, MARIE, HAMPTON. (WOLSEY'S Face as Baby)

Just your bog-standard behind the scenes shot from *Carry On At Your Convenience* (1971). (*Peter Rogers Archive*)

Smiles all round – the team on set for *Carry On Abroad* (1972). (*Gerald Thomas Family*)

Bernard, Gerald, Sid and Peter enjoy some down time on the set of *Abroad*. (*Peter Rogers Archive*)

The end of an era – after 20 years, the team prepares to bring down the curtain in *Carry On Emmannuelle* (1978).

Backroom boys Peter and Gerald presided over an astonishing 30 Carry On films and a unique chapter in British film history. (*Peter Rogers Archive*)

Alan Hume, our director of photography, at which point I think even Gerald gave up.

Of course, there's another way to look at it, as Bernard Cribbins pointed out about the way the Carry Ons got made, 'Because we were filming so quickly, there wasn't really any time for arguments. We had to get on with each other.'

Either way, the Carry On set at Pinewood was clearly a sweet spot where talent met teamwork. 'There's nothing better than a bunch of hardworking people in a room respecting each other. It's very hard to achieve,' is how Terry Johnson puts it, and he's an Olivier Award winner.

'We were a very innocent bunch of thesps,' remembered Joan. 'There was a great camaraderie, and they were just happy times.'

Like his great pal Sid James, Gerald Thomas also knew he'd struck gold, according to his daughter Deborah, who remembers her father as remaining very humble:

He was of that generation who are almost gone now. He'd landed on the D-Day beaches when he was young, he'd done his time, he adored his wife and he loved his family.

He knew Carry On was a great opportunity and he did his damnedest to make it work every single day. He was in awe of the talent around him and recognised the sheer good fortune of all those amazing people coming together like that. He used to say to me often, 'Darling, we are lucky people.'

Chapter 11

Star Spotlight – Hattie Jacques

'I want to be wooed!'

Joan Sims first met Hattie Jacques in repertory theatre, where they shared the stage often in their pre-Carry On years. It was to herald a working camaraderie and dearest of friendships flourishing through the decades ahead.

Hattie was eight years older than Joan and had made her own stage debut at London's Players' Theatre in 1944. By the time the pair became friends in the early 1950s, Hattie was already an established leading lady of the boards, as well as making her presence felt on radio and film.

Josephine Edwina Jaques was born in February 1922 in Sandgate, Kent. Her mother Mary was an amateur actress and singer, her father Robin was a flight lieutenant in the RAF until he was killed in a flying accident when Hattie was only 18 months old, her brother, also Robin, just a little older.

The bereaved family moved to London, where Hattie went to school and soon caught the performing bug, taking parts in amateur theatricals until war broke out. Hattie proved versatile and tireless, training as a nurse in the Voluntary Aid Detachment, attending to casualties of the Blitz, and even reportedly helping deliver a baby in a telephone box. She later found work as a welder in an arms factory.

Following a failed wartime romance with an American soldier, she joined the revue troupe at the Players' Theatre, underneath the arches at Villiers Street in London, where she soon became one of the company's stars, dubbed 'Queen of the Players' – appearing in sketches, singing and performing many of the old music hall tunes for which the theatre was celebrated. Later in life, Hattie became publicly defined by her comedic battle-axe persona, but at this point in her career, she bubbled with sex appeal and vitality. Some compared her allure with that of Marilyn Monroe, while others likened her look to Ava Gardner's.

Hattie's future long-time performing partner Eric Sykes first saw her in action at the Players' and he remembered, 'It was magic. I was intoxicated.'

There are a few different suggestions of how Josephine became 'Hattie', but the version the actress shared herself was that it came about after a Players production in 1946. She appeared in a minstrel show, *Coal Black Mammies for Dixie*, where she was blacked up in a way unthinkable today. Her buxom appearance led one of the backstage staff to remark on her similarity to Oscar winner Hattie McDaniel in *Gone with the Wind*, and she became Hattie to everyone from then on. Her surname had enjoyed a makeover too by then – both she and her brother Robin had added an extra 'c' for a bit of French exoticism.

In 1946, she toured with the Young Vic company, made her film debut in *Green for Danger* in 1950 and four years later made her mark on screen in *Chance of a Lifetime*. But it was radio where she really made her name in a trio of hits – firstly *It's That Man Again* starring Tommy Handley, then *Educating Archie* where she first worked with Eric Sykes, finally *Hancock's Half Hour*, where she was cast alongside Sid James and Kenneth Williams. It's fair to say young Hattie was much in demand. Bob Monkhouse remarked of her appeal at that time, 'It was difficult to find women at that time in radio who could do what Hattie could do. It was a limited pool.'

Certainly, her obvious skill in communicating with an audience was rare. Eric Sykes later described it like this, 'Hat to me had so much talent it was oozing out.'

Such appeal made her an obvious choice when Peter Rogers was casting his very first Carry On film in 1958. *Sergeant* has very few female roles, mainly romantically pursued or pursuing, in an otherwise dominantly male setting (save for the all-female brass band at the end) and Hattie's role of medical officer Captain Clark is pretty fleeting. Her hair up in an intimidating beehive, she has to deal with the invented ailments of hypochondriacal officer Horace Strong, played by Kenneth Connor. Only the twinkle in her eye hints at all she has to offer over the course of the series.

Hattie brought to her character what she did to all her Carry On roles – a sense of taking no nonsense, often as sole grown-up in a room of overgrown children, but always with warmth bubbling closely underneath.

Writer and broadcaster Tony Bilbow noticed this same disarming contrast between her screen persona and her real-life charisma when he sat down with Hattie for an in-depth interview. What does he remember most? 'Her sense of fun and bubbling naughtiness,' he tells me. 'She fizzed like champagne.'

Leslie Phillips called her 'a splendid comic actress, perhaps because she always played it straight'. While she fulfilled the cartoonish needs of her Carry On characters with a mixture mostly of authority and bluster, the depth of her humanity also came shining through. This meant that, whatever the role, she made sure to share the joke with the audience with a tip of her chin, a barely perceptible side-eye and a smile permanently hovering somewhere around her lips. Plus, with her maturity and intelligence, she helped ground the films where she appeared into some sort of reality.

> *'Younger birds may be soft and tender, but the older birds have more to them.'*

Over the next decade-and-a-half, Hattie became a mainstay of the series, while continuing her work in theatre, radio and TV. She appeared in fourteen Carry On films in total in a variety of roles, although there's no doubt how most of us see her in our minds' eye and that's as bristling Matron, a role she perfected in the five medical titles.

Her first matronly outing was in the second in the series, *Carry On Nurse* where, as Peter Rogers described her innate screen authority, 'She didn't have to open her mouth as Matron, she just had to appear. And she did appear.'

Hers was actually a relatively small role, but she presided over one of Carry On's most memorable ever scenes – the finale, when the fed up nurses take their revenge on their demanding patient, the irascible Colonel. Hattie gets the punchline, 'Yes, Colonel, many times, but never with a daffodil,' and serves up an iconic scene that became the stuff of legend even on the Pinewood set, where the usually professional Hattie couldn't get through the scene for laughing.

Rogers recalled, 'Poor Hattie got a fit of the giggles, and when one wag on the set made a noise like a champagne cork popping out of a bottle, as she lifted up the daffodil, she was a complete goner.' Almost uniquely for the tightly scheduled Carry On crew, everyone had to come back the following day to complete the scene.

Hattie was again formidable as maths mistress Grace Short in *Teacher*, a role marked only by her deceptively progressive plan of 'beating the men at their own game'. *Constable* finally gave her a softer moment, her Sergeant Laura Moon warmed by a gently blossoming romance with Sergeant Frank Wilkins, played by a personable Sid James in his Carry On debut.

Illness prevented Hattie from fulfilling her cast role in *Regardless*, with her spot given instead to Liz Fraser. Hattie later returned for a smaller cameo role as a hospital sister.

Her next Carry On title gave her a real chance to shine. 1963's *Cabby* was the first script by new writer Talbot Rothwell, who adopted a more risqué tone, but also brought a more focused narrative structure. In it, Hattie takes centre stage as Peggy Hawkins, the emotionally neglected wife of taxi firm boss Charlie who decides to set up her own rival firm, GlamCabs, especially after he tells her, 'Get a job? I've never heard anything so ridiculous in my life.' Peggy duly tells her girls, 'Get out there and grab all the business out from under their smug noses.'

Hattie shines in the role, trading in the traditionally formidable stereotypes of her previous Carry On roles for something more full-blooded – twinkly, nuanced, sad to be foiling her husband but determined to find her own way. It is a progressive role in a treat of a film, and Hattie herself later named it as her favourite of the series.

Throughout her time working on the Carry On films, Hattie was one of the most popular figures on the Pinewood set, becoming a close friend to many of her co-stars, and an earthy, welcoming mother-hen figure to everyone who crossed her path.

Barbara Windsor remembered, 'All of us knew Hattie as warm, kind-hearted, endearing lady ... with her posh paper, doing her crossword and smoking her cigarette…. We all loved her. A most glorious lady, sexy, full of fun.'

Co-star Patsy Rowlands once described Hattie's infectious giggle, 'If she started to laugh, it was terrible, it was painful, because you couldn't stop, and she couldn't stop.'

Even producer Peter Rogers appreciated the strength of Hattie's capacity for friendship. He said, 'In our family, she was what you might call the mother confessor. You wanted to be in her company, and didn't want to leave.'

This warmth she revealed on set extended to her home life with her husband John Le Mesurier and their two sons Robin and Kim. The couple had been married since 1949, and formed one of the entertainment industry's most popular partnerships. Their home in Earl's Court had long been a welcoming sanctuary for many of their friends to congregate.

Her friend, later John's wife, Joan Le Mesurier, remembered the embrace of the place. 'Hattie's house was the sort of place you wanted to move in. You felt you could be so comfortable there. It was cosy, tasteful. There was an abundance.'

Their son Robin recalled years later:

All the time I lived at home it always seemed like an ongoing party. You never knew who might drop in. It became normal for me to see famous people. I was in awe because I had seen them on film and TV. Peter Sellers was always joking around. Then there was Tony Hancock and the charming Sid James.

Joan Sims's memoir makes clear just how much she depended on her friend's support, and she wasn't alone. Kenneth Williams and Charles Hawtrey were also regular guests at her dinner table, and frequent visitors for parties and Christmas feasts, which were often three-day events and planned by Hattie well in advance. Robin called it 'a magical time of year. She'd have two kitchens going for all the guests. She'd start thinking about it months ahead'.

He also reflected on their Bohemian lifestyle, 'My family was wonderful and loving but dysfunctional. Although mum and dad both had affairs they loved one another. My character was shaped by their kindness, generosity and tolerant natures.'

Joan Le Mesurier agreed, explaining, 'Hattie was splendidly emblematic of the fact that her love does not have to be rationed, that giving to one does not necessarily mean depriving another. She always had enough for everyone.'

Hattie's zest for life plus the challenges it brought her were captured in the 2011 BBC drama *Hattie*, with the leading lady played by Ruth Jones, whom Robin said 'captured my mother perfectly'.

The drama followed the complications that unfolded when Hattie began an affair with John Schofield, whom she met when he was booked to drive her to a charity event. Still extremely fond of her husband but deeply in love with Schofield, she tried to keep two very different men happy. For a while, all three even lived in the family home, with Le Mesurier consigned to the spare room before moving out and soon marrying Joan. Stephen Russell, who wrote the award-winning drama, tells me what drew him to it. 'It was a good and unusual story. Most divorce stories are vicious, and it was actually about two pretty nice people, trying to work out how to break up in the nicest way possible.'

In researching Hattie's life, he noted the contrast between her on-screen persona – prim and standoffish – with her real-life warmth. 'Plus she was obviously sexually driven and passionate. It led to her breaking up with her husband, which at the time was quite a big thing to do.'

'I'm a simple woman with simple tastes and I want to be wooed.'
'Pooh, you can be as wude as you like with me.'

Following their divorce in 1965, Hattie remained close friends with her ex-husband, but the relationship with Schofield only lasted another year, before he left her for another woman. Hattie was reportedly devastated by the split and, never slim, became heavily overweight as she sought comfort in her food. As well as making her unhappy, her shape went dramatically against the look of the time, when models Jean Shrimpton and Twiggy were all the rage, and no doubt contributed to her being increasingly typecast as 'the funny fat girl'.

Bob Monkhouse, her co-star in *Sergeant*, lamented that this was the case:

Her career was restricted by that male dominance, by the way she was cast, the way she was written for.

I never much liked jokes about Hattie Jacques being overweight because that wasn't the point with Hattie. She was much more than that…. She became later a target for those jokes in the Carry Ons because the writer Talbot Rothwell was a joke writer.

As early as *Cabby*, Hattie had played along with such focused gags. One scene in that film saw her, dressed only in a towel, weighing herself on bathroom scales and sighing. 'Who would have thought a towel would have made that difference?'

Later on, if Hattie felt increasingly vulnerable about her size, as her friends and son later revealed, she was game and professional enough to play to the gallery as her Carry On bosses required, particularly in the hospital titles that peppered the late 1960s. For some reason, Joan Sims had originally been cast as Matron in *Doctor* but she had declined, saying Hattie's interpretation as seen in *Nurse* couldn't be bettered. In the bawdier second half of the decade, Matron's authority was given an extra dimension, that of the sexually frustrated big girl, frightening smaller men with her passions. She chases Kenneth's Dr Tinkle around the room in *Doctor*, trying and failing to seduce.

'No, no, Matron. I was once a weak man.'
'Once a week's enough for any man.'

Camping reprises the dynamic between the pair, this time with the name of the finishing school Chayste Place written across her ample bosom, and again in *Carry On Again Doctor*. 'Young chickens may be soft and tender, but the older birds have more on them,' she tells Kenneth's Doctor Carver seductively. 'True, and take a lot more stuffing,' is his curt response.

From then on, Hattie invariably played a series of tyrannical, dissatisfied battle-axes, either telling people off or chasing unwilling men in films such as *Loving* and *At Your Convenience*. These narratives were mainly male-led, but Dan Zeff, who directed the drama *Hattie*, points out the scale of her contribution to every scene. 'The dynamic between her and Sid James was particularly effective,' he notes. 'She was letting him be funny, and that's a wonderful actor's gift. Her intelligence shines through.'

If the work failed to delight her, her friendships at Pinewood always drew her back. Tony Bilbow believes she found it reassuring to be part of that unique repertory company. He believes she stayed longer than she wanted to 'out of passionate loyalty to her friends'.

He once asked Hattie the same question. 'For fun, not the money,' was how she explained it to him. 'Lovely, like a shot on the arm, all those chums. We've all grown up together in the business. There's no rivalry, it's like belonging to a club. You're all together and you have loads of laughs.'

Off screen, however, her health problems began to concern producers, particularly after Peter Rogers could no longer get her insured. For a while, he cast her anyway – 'It was a risk of course, from the distributors' point of view, but I never told them,' he revealed – but her days on set were clearly numbered. Her screen time as Floella the fiery Spanish cook in *Abroad* was minimal, and her final Carry On appearance came in 1974's *Dick*, a film that also proved to be the swansong of Sid James and Barbara Windsor. It was the end of an era.

Fortunately, Hattie remained a respected figure with her creative peers, beloved by British audiences. Throughout her time with Carry On, she'd remained a TV sitcom star, in *Our House* and even her own show, ITV's *Miss Adventure*.

Now an old sparring partner was on hand to give her a role that sealed her popularity throughout the 1970s. From 1972, she teamed up again with Eric for the return on TV, this time in colour, of *Sykes*. For the millions of viewers that tuned in for their antics, they may as well have been real life brother and sister. Perhaps just as importantly for Hattie, she said that Sykes 'hardly ever made any joke about my size which was a refreshing change'.

Although her success was beyond doubt, Hattie's daily life was becoming more and more difficult. By the late 1970s, her weight-related issues were leading to other physical problems, which also meant no insurance for films. As her health deteriorated, personal happiness eluded her and her career faded, she found satisfaction instead in huge amounts of charity work.

Additionally, surprisingly strained relations with Eric Sykes, particularly on tour, hurt her feelings during the second half of the decade, although the pair continued to work together until 1980. That April, she took a small part in Sykes's comedy short *Rhubarb Rhubarb*. It would turn out to be her final screen performance.

The following month, a planned holiday to Greece had to be called off after the actress's doctors advised she was too ill for such extended travel. Instead she went with her friends to Ireland and on the way home on the ferry, confided in her great friend, Bruce Copp, 'You know I'm not going to live long.'

Sure enough, she died of a heart attack on 6 October, aged only 58 and leaving an enormous gap in the lives of so many who knew and loved her, including her devoted Carry On coterie. John Le Mesurier's wife Joan said afterwards, 'Joanie [Sims] was heartbroken. When I think of all the people that knew Hattie, apart from very close family, I think Joan suffered the most from losing her.' Sims was too upset even to attend her friend's funeral. A month later, Hattie was remembered at a memorial service at St Pauls Church in Covent Garden, described by John Le Mesurier as a 'joyous occasion'.

Years later, Bob Monkhouse summed up the secret of Hattie's professional success, 'She was a lovely, lovely person and I think the public can tell when someone's decent, kindly and has some gold within them.'

He added that, while her weight had greatly helped her career – 'she was a great roly-poly, and roly-polies are funny' – he lamented that it had limited her scope to stretch her talents. 'She was an actress of far greater range than she was ever allowed to employ.'

Her biographer Andy Merriman agrees, telling me, 'Hancock's writers, the great Ray Galton and Alan Simpson, told me that, looking back, they felt guilty about mentioning her weight. They didn't milk it a lot, but there were a few lines, and they felt very bad.'

He mentions the role Hattie always wanted was that of Nurse in *Romeo and Juliet*, but he adds, 'Of course she never got the chance. Her weight ballooning up and down meant she missed out on things and ended up typecast, sadly.'

Dan Zeff is of the same opinion. 'There was certainly a frustrated performer in her. She could have easily been the lead in a musical, but she wasn't asked. So she threw herself into other things, like charity work.'

Hattie herself reflected, 'It would have been nice to have done something a little bit straighter, but if you're fat you're funny, it's as simple as that. You just have to be a funny fat lady.'

She added, 'I'm not complaining, because I love comedy and I really enjoy it, but I haven't had an opportunity of finding out if I can do anything else, if I can extend myself, if you'll pardon the expression.'

Both she and Joan Sims found their careers were limited by their weight – Hattie consigned to play the 'funny fat lady', Joan losing out on a lead role in *Nurse on Wheels* because of a few extra pounds – in a way that might or might not happen these days.

Could they have become dramatic stars, fully developed talents of stage and screen? Joan showed us her potential for straight, dark drama in *Lady Killers* and Hattie had easily the right charisma, the wherewithal, the knack of finding the truth in the script. These days, their fulsome bodies would have proved less of a challenge to overcome. There are more stories to tell, more roles to fill, audiences more open to possibilities and a far greater admiration for beauty in all its shapes and sizes. The sad thing is, we'll never know. They may have had the potential to transcend their funny bones, but tragically, Hattie died too soon to fulfil it and Joan wasn't confident enough to try.

Both women, like several of their male co-stars, also had their share of personal demons behind their laughs, and it was this vulnerability as well as their sense of fun that shone through on screen to powerful effect. It is gratifying that, whatever was going on away from the set, they both found somewhere to channel their great charms and talents.

Chapter 12

All 'Asses Must Be Shown

'It's not getting it up. It's getting it to stay up, that's what counts'

Kenneth Williams in *Carry On Camping*

For many, *Carry On Camping* is the definitive Carry On film, and includes the definitive scene. There is many a hardened cultural critic and social commentator of a certain age, mostly male, who, when asked to remember their first experience of watching Barbara Windsor doing her exercises, blushes becomingly and remembers the excitement of a more innocent, long bygone age.

Some people argue that, never mind a bra pinging off, something slightly more important happened elsewhere in 1969. Apparently, we went to the moon, or at least, Neil Armstrong and Buzz Aldrin did. The world was united in awe, even as down on Planet Earth, we remained horribly divided in places like Vietnam and Northern Ireland.

Politically, all over the globe we saw a changing of the guard – out with Charles de Gaulle and Lyndon B. Johnson, in with Yasser Arafat, Muammar Gaddafi and Richard Nixon.

At home in Britain, there seemed to be a sense of an era drawing to a close. Sir Matt Busby departed his managerial duties at Manchester United after twenty-four years, while Harold Wilson was on his last year at Number 10 after a tenure that had lasted most of the 1960s. Brazilian superstar Pelé scored his 1000th goal while English fans clung on to the Jules Rimet trophy won three years before. The Beatles gave their final public performance on the roof of Apple HQ. Meanwhile we had the purchase of the *News of the World* by an Australian newspaperman called Rupert Murdoch, the maiden flight of Concorde and, everywhere, mini skirts giving way to maxi skirts.

Musically, it was a mixed bag of old and new sounds. Britain's bestselling song of the year was the Archies' 'Sugar Sugar' while Frank Sinatra's 'My

Way' made it into the top 10, along with the mournful laments of Peter Sarstedt's 'Where Do You Go To (My Lovely)' and Bobbie Gentry's 'I'll Never Fall In Love Again'. Other massive sellers were 'Get Back' by the Beatles, and the Rolling Stones' 'Honky Tonk Women', although neither band made it to the line-up for the year's biggest get-together at Woodstock. Perhaps the most defining soundtrack of the era was provided by the oohs and aahs of Jane Birkin and Serge Gainsbourg on their room-stopping 'Je T'aime... Moi Non Plus'.

On TV, the Looney Tunes brigade told us 'That's all folks!' and for once it really was, as the animated series signed off for good. Instead we got *Scooby Doo* and the inexplicably enduring *Monty Python*.

The biggest box office hits showed an appreciation for rebellion, with the top slots filled by *Butch Cassidy and the Sundance Kid*, *Midnight Cowboy* and *Easy Rider*, but also... *The Love Bug*, where somehow an American comedy about a pearl-white Volkswagen Beetle with a mind of its own and matchmaking proclivities held its own against the horses of Paul Newman and Robert Redford as well as the Harleys of Peter Fonda and Dennis Hopper.

Socially, the Brits were still for the most part pretty happy before the 1970s' winds of discontent blew in and producer Peter Rogers, as ever, had his finger firmly in the breeze when he realised the nation's appetite for holidays on damp rural campsites would make the perfect context for a Carry On caper. In fact, he had registered the title as far back as 1962, and the film was originally planned to follow *Don't Lose Your Head*, which was completed in October 1966. Instead, after Peter had finished wrangling with the Rank Organisation over whether or not to continue with the Carry On name, Talbot Rothwell set to work on *Carry On Camping* or, to give it its alternative title, 'Let Sleeping Bags Lie'. For once, Kenneth Williams and Sid James had the same reaction to the script, Kenneth expressing his delight by letter to Peter and Gerald Thomas, and Sid also writing to say he'd driven his wife potty by laughing out loud as he read the lines for the first time.

After the historical complexities and nuances of *Khyber*, with its period setting costumes, props and location shoot (even if it was only Wales), *Carry On Camping* is disarmingly simple, with a stripped down (cough) narrative, smaller budget and tiny number of homegrown locations.

The story is as straightforward as any of the titles in the series: Sid Boggle (guess who) and his friend Bernie Lugg (Bernard Bresslaw, naturally) take their girlfriends Joan Fussey (Joan Sims) and Anthea Meeks (Dilys Laye) to the cinema where they are moved by the charms of a nudist camp caught on film. They scheme to visit the camp with their less relaxed partners, whom they hope will be influenced by the liberal mores of the Paradise Holiday Camp. However, much to their chagrin, they've made a booking error and they end up at a normal, fully-clothed site instead, and a pretty unglamorous one at that. Even more disappointingly, the girls have got wise and the 'boys' (Sid was 58, Bernard 34) end up with a tent to themselves.

'Joan may think you're a gentleman, but personally I've got sore misgivings. 'You ought to put some talcum powder on them.'

Meanwhile, other campers include a group of girls from Chayste Place Finishing School with its blonde and bouncy ringleader Babs, supervised by the easily flustered principal Dr Soaper (Kenneth Williams) and his lovesick matron Miss Haggard (Hattie Jacques). And there are middle-class miseries Peter and Harriet Potter (Terry Scott and Betty Marsden), somehow joined by rogue first-time tent-erector Charlie Muggins (Charles Hawtrey). The customary antics of these happy, and some unhappy, campers are disrupted further by the arrival in the next field of a group of hippies, who embark on an all-night jamboree led by a band called The Flowerbuds. The squarer holidaymakers must put aside their personal grievances to club together and drive the ravers away, before settling back into their respective rejuvenated romances. And that's it.

Production took place between 7 October and 22 November 1968 – calendar dates the meteorologists among you may have noticed are not those of the reliably glorious British summer. Of course, the ever-canny Peter Rogers had planned it exactly so, to make the film in winter in readiness for the following summer's huge cinema audiences, however even he would admit this made for conditions less ideal for actors forced to prance around, do exercises and kneel down on the ground to erect tents dressed just in flimsy cottons, sometimes less.

The tricks employed to turn a mud-sodden orchard at the back of the Pinewood lot into a bucolic Devonshire summer idyll have become the stuff of industry legend. Barbara Windsor remembered asking if the bad weather was going to be a problem. 'Didn't matter,' she reported. '"Won't show," they used to say.'

Sure enough, once the rain started properly to fall, two days into what was meant to be the tableau of a beautiful blue-skied summer, the props crew really came into their own – climbing up ladders to stick fallen leaves back on the trees, kneeling down to paint the grass beneath everyone's feet, casting great arc lights across the field so it appeared bathed in sunshine. However, even these masters of their craft couldn't warm up the set, with the almost-naked Barbara suffering the worst, complaining her boobs were all goose pimples as she tried to be buoyant in a bikini.

'No, no, Barbara. Tent up first, bunk up later.'

In his memoir, Peter insisted most actors were happy enough, those he called 'professional people' making the best of it, including Sid, Bernard, Terry Scott (who was even having to cycle while suffering from piles, poor man) and Joan, who said of the experience, 'We were a tremendous team and all great buddies, a lot younger, more resilient.'

The combination of the mucky weather, constant midges and usual on-set ribaldry made for testing times for the makeup team as well. Dilys Laye, who played Bernie's girlfriend Anthea, revealed that she and Joan had to have their makeup totally re-done after lunch as the horror of the conditions made them laugh so much. She remembered director Gerald Thomas's beaming smile as he told the cast, 'Think sun!' even while the rains continued to fall, which just made them laugh even more.

Those who remembered it slightly differently included Barbara and Kenneth, who both offered excellent, colourful anecdotes in the decades that followed when asked about the horrors of filming this particular classic.

Kenneth wrote how the field became increasingly water-logged and every step an actor took almost brought his shoe off. He complained to Gerald Thomas about how lousy he found the atmosphere and how difficult it was to create comedy in such surroundings, but the ever-genial director assured him it was all looking wonderful in the edit.

In her memoir, Barbara added how, because the freshly sprayed green grass soon turned to mud as the rain fell, by the time the cast got home each day, 'we had green ankle socks'. On another occasion, she remembered complaining her feet were sinking in the mud, when she was told, 'Barbara, if we were looking at your feet, we wouldn't be employing you.'

Though she laughed long and hard over the following years, so incensed at the time was Barbara that she complained in straight terms to her co-star Kenneth following one particularly shivery scene. The pair recounted their conversation on TV years later, both remembering it word for word. Barbara moaned:

> It's disgraceful making us work in these conditions. Of course it's all right for Peter Rogers. He drives down here in his great Rolls-Royce, gets out in his cashmere coat and wellington boots, sits in the producer's chair calling 'Carry on girls,' then departs to the bar for his glass of vintage champagne. We're treated like a load of rubbish, and he's got his arse in the marmalade.

Of course, this being a Carry On caper, the story wouldn't be complete without the punchline of Kenneth still having his microphone attached, which meant their whole chat was recorded and Peter inevitably got to hear every word. The producer remembered Barbara being suitably horrified when he played the recording back to her at the rushes screening the following day. Barbara was mortified, terrified she was about to lose her job, but Peter said only with a smile, 'Thank you for those few kind words.' In his memoir, Kenneth added that, not long after, Barbara received an anonymous offering from Fortnum and Mason – a giant delivery of Seville Marmalade.

With customary sang froid, years later Peter added only that what Barbara had said couldn't possibly be true – after all, he would never have drunk champagne in the middle of the day!

The truth is, as Peter no doubt well knew, he probably couldn't have sacked Barbara if he'd tried. After the success of the film, there would have been an outcry if his leading lady had lost her job, particularly as the scene she most famously appeared in came to define not just her career, but the Carry On series as a whole and, arguably, a whole era of risqué comedy. I refer, of course, to the outdoor class where Dr Soaper tries in vain to instruct his girls in the benefits of physical exercise. It all starts so well, with his instructions to 'Fling, and in,' until Babs flings a little too wide and … well, everyone knows the rest. I don't know which is more fun, Babs's cheeky grin as Hattie's Matron hastens to cover her up, or Dr Soaper's anguish. The scene lasts less than a minute, it is a completely predictable, uncomplicated banana-skin of a gag but somehow the timing, the performances, even the palpably unglamorous surrounds, all add to the creation of a comedy classic.

'Stop laughing, now that Barbara's fallen out… we will continue!'

Of her most famous moment, Barbara remembered it only belatedly dawning on her that she was going to lose her upstairs undies, saying, 'It didn't read like that in the script at all.'

She also offered up the less than glamorous details of what went on behind the scenes, including the employment of a soon-to-retire props man by the name of Bert Luxford, whose one job it was to stand with a fishing rod and a hook, which he would tug at the appropriate moment. She remembered, 'Every time they did it, the top went straight down in the mud,' often taking Barbara down with it. 'Gerry the director said, "Get her up, dust her down." It went on for about twenty takes. We finally got it, which was terrific. They said, "It's a wrap."'

Of course, the film was customarily delivered on time and within budget, ready to appear on billboards six months later. The film premiered on 29 May 1969 and, as Peter Rogers had hoped, soon pinned the summer audiences to their seats.

Even the stars were surprised at the scale of the film's success. Sid James recounted a trip he'd made to a cinema in Blackpool, following the film's release. 'I'd never heard anything like it. First of all, you couldn't get into the cinema. You just couldn't. I just happened to know the manager and I went and stood at the back. I've never heard such laughter.'

It's not surprising, with some of the jokes that remain wonderful to this day. Matthew Sweet shares with me his belief, 'The citizenship test for Britain should be whether you can memorise the scene from Carry On Camping when they turn up at the gate.'

'Are you the owner of this site?'
'No.'
'Where is he?'
'Gone for a P.'

You know the one – when Sid, Bernie and the girls arrive at the campsite, and spot the noticeboard telling visitors that 'All Asses Must Be Shown'. And where's the owner, they ask? Gone for a 'P', apparently. He soon returns, the letter P in hand, which he promptly nails to its vacant position on the board, naturally. Wonderful stuff.

Carry on Camping may not have enjoyed the same critical acclaim as some of the other titles of the period, but the filmmakers knew their audience, and it became the most successful British film of the year. Its pared-down finances compared with its extraordinary box office success made *Camping* one of the most economical films of the series. *Carry On Nurse* remains the most successful with more than 10 million cinema tickets sold, but *Camping* isn't far behind.

At one point, a director famous for loftier visions, David Lean, had visited the set of *Camping* and asked, 'How can you make these films so quickly?' The answer was easy: everyone knew exactly what was required of them, and they did it very quickly and to a very high standard. By the time those cinema-goers were queuing around the block to watch *Camping* on the big screen, the cast and crew were already back hard at work, filming *Carry on Again Doctor*, due for release six months later.

Of course, the film's success didn't come without Peter and Gerald's customary battle with the censors. The film was given an R rating in the US, restricting audience numbers, and Irish officials refused even to give it a certificate.

A word here about the British Board of Film Censors, kept busy by Carry On's long, colourful run. For many of those years, Peter and Gerald waged a war of wits with John Trevelyan, Secretary of the Board of Censors from 1958 to 1971. Peter later complained that censorship was so tight during that era, it was a wonder anybody could write a comedy at all. With Gerald by his side, the producer generally went into battle in a spirit of what he called 'old-fashioned, traditional bartering'.

These battles started right from the early days of *Sergeant*, when the Censor took issue with the phrase 'Man cannot live by bread rolls alone' (too Biblical, apparently), and Norman Hudis began planting gags deliberately, in order to distract Trevelyan and his cronies from the lines he did want left in. Through such creativity, there was always plenty of wriggle room – as Leslie Phillips discovered on *Nurse* with his careful phrasing of 'Miss Allcock' and Bernard Bresslaw on *Khbyer* in his careful stress of the comma with his line 'Fakir, off'.

While some of both Norman and Talbot's lines had to go, over the years Peter, Gerald and their colleagues delighted in dancing a frequent gavotte around Trevelyan's sensibilities, with Peter explaining in his memoir, 'I may have built the Carry Ons on innuendo, but they were family entertainment all the way. I wanted our business ideals to reflect that.'

But other filmmakers criticised the Censor for being unfair in his determinations of what was acceptable on screen. Director Roy Ward Baker accused him of 'pigeon-holing people', giving more creative licence to those he decided were providing art house cinema, for example Ken Russell with *Women in Love*, while nit-picking and obstructing those projects he deemed commercial.

As well as scrutinising the Carry On films, he made life difficult for the producers of James Bond during the same era, but 007's producers perhaps got their own back. In 1995's *GoldenEye*, the villain was called Alec Trevelyan.

With *Camping*, Trevelyan had more than his usual fun. Charles Hawtrey's saucy early line, 'She's been showing me how to stick my pole up' had to become 'the pole', as though that made it any cleaner. As Valerie Leon points out to me years later, chuckling delightedly, 'It's the same joke!'

While tent talk made double entendre almost effortless for Talbot Rothwell, any dialogue relating to phallic symbols generally was out, as was the line, 'Erection is fairly simple.' The footage of nudist camp scenes at the beginning of the film was considered so rude that it was agreed Sid Boggle would be heard laughing over it, as though Sid James's distinctive chuckle would somehow make it less pervy! To this day, many viewers' experience of the film, on TV at least, is had with those early nudist camp scenes cut from the reel.

Although there were also lots of determined requests from the Censor's office that the filmmakers tone down the innuendo of some of the scenes, it seemed that, when it came to Barbara's boobs, even John Trevelyan knew when he was beaten.

The actress remembered one of the reasons for the multiple takes of the scene was that she kept accidentally exposing herself, and even the final take had Matron accidentally pulling Babs's arm, revealing enough of her décolletage to make the producers nervous for the Censor's reaction. Barbara delighted in Trevelyan's eventual verdict, 'I don't think Miss Windsor's right boob is going to corrupt the nation. I'll pass it.'

Knowing so much more about female exploitation in the entertainment industry, both on screen and off, has made our present-day radars much more attuned to scenes like this, as well as to the story as a whole, and critics have in recent years delighted in the wrongness of it all.

Sid James was clearly far too old for the role of amorous boyfriend, let alone to be lusting after women cast as schoolgirls, so I think it saved the film that Joan Sims was cast as his girlfriend and met him halfway. Of course, Sid's legendary charm customarily rendered his roguishness harmless, while Bernard's deceptive oafishness (this was an actor who taught himself Mandarin between takes, don't forget) served to undercut any intimidating aspect of his enormous size. As a pair, they kind of cancelled each other out, plus of course, their better halves were constantly there to keep them in check. As it transpired, all their schemes and dodgy desires were firmly foiled, and they were ultimately rescued by the love of two good women, and a goat.

Similarly, Barbara at 31 was also too old on paper to be the schoolgirl of her role, but I'm convinced her maturity helped keep the film on the right side of comically acceptable. While delightfully pixie-like and youthful in appearance, in reality she was an actress who knew exactly what she was doing, her boobs were just another part of her comedic weaponry and she was very much in on the joke.

Two other faces necessary in making everything all right were Kenneth Williams and Hattie Jacques. Dr Soaper's hauteur and Matron's fluster created a safe, protective setting for the famous wardrobe malfunction to occur. Babs may have been exposed, but she was never for one moment at risk, and the strength of those actors' real-life personalities was as crucial as their value on-screen in protecting her. We know that Kenneth would have been as horrified as Dr Soaper by an errant female boob. We know that Hattie would have made sure everyone was happy. *Carry On*

Camping gave us true proof of the power of Peter Rogers's ensemble, with every single cast member key to the enormous success of the film. They made all the difference when it was released, and they still do today when so many more risqué things have passed our eyes. Safe in the knowledge of a huge shared joke, we can relax and laugh out loud whenever we watch this scene again, just as we have done for half a century.

The simple tropes of *Carry On Camping* have been often imitated in the decades since its release. The silhouette-in-the-tent device alone has been used over and over again, from *The Rocky Horror Picture Show* to Austin Powers's tireless merry-making.

Why, though, was the original film so successful, and why does its charm endure? Well, for a start it offered an accurate interpretation of our nation's desires for glamorous, sun-kissed holidays and flirtations with the opposite sex, then it just as easily mined all the comedic potential of reality confounding those dreams, much to Brits' secret satisfaction and contentment. Let's face it, when we go on holiday in this country, we don't *really* want the sun to come out, do we? Did Sid Boggle *really* want to disappear into the sunset with glamorous Babs? I don't think so. In this sense, *Camping* summed up the problems men of a certain age were having with what the permissive society offered them in 1969 – such freedoms were unsettling, tempting certainly, but also requiring of actions on their part they felt unsure about taking on. Sid Boggle was the man who had missed out on the permissive society he saw springing up around him, and now, here he was, surrounded by young women, leaving him full of desire, but uncertain and ultimately helpless.

The giveaway is in the film's ending, when the group of hippies turn up and set up camp alongside our favourites. Although the hippies are loud and seductive with some of the young girls running off with them by the end, Sid and Bernie remain behind, saved by the love and good sense of two women a bit nearer their own age.

Matthew Sweet was one of those enthusiastic schoolboys who begged to be allowed to stay up to watch *Camping* when it was first shown on television. 'I was allowed to watch until the first ad break, which was disappointing,' he remembers now. He believes the message of the film is more complicated than it appears, in its blending of old and new desires.

'It was possible for them to create this space in which somehow the middle-aged characters get to partake in the permissive society, but also end up better off than the younger male characters.'

The filmmakers were decidedly on the side of conservative over progressive values – or at least, they were no fools and they knew their audience. It was an audience that didn't welcome the psychedelia, floral tobacco and sexual freedom offered by the ravers, instead it was one that felt comfortable with the boredom of marriage, the repression and thwarting of desire that was so much more familiar.

This film was one of the last in the series to build its great comedy on repression, on suggestion over explicitness, on sharing what we want but can't get, ultimately to our great relief. In that sense, as well as being one of the most popular of the series, *Camping* is also one of the most significant, as it brings down the curtain on Carry On's golden age.

Chapter 13

Star Spotlight – Jim Dale

*'I wouldn't have thought it possible for
one man to create such utter chaos.'*

It's no doubt hackneyed to call someone 'a triple threat' these days. In an era of overnight fame, all it probably means is that you have a TV programme to your name, a radio show *and* a million followers on Instagram. But back when it meant something, Jim Dale was that person – he could sing, dance, act, delight in consummate showmanship plus, most importantly for his Carry On friends and fans, he shared his co-stars' funny bones.

Jim explained in a radio interview in 2015:

> Brought up as a child of British music hall, at that very early age I was given the opportunity of standing on the stage and communicating with an audience. That is something that today's modern young actor never gets an opportunity of doing. So I had vast experience of communicating with an audience and trying to get each of them to relate to me.

Sure enough, while Jim was younger than many of his future Carry On co-stars, he shared with them that magical bridge to the now lost chapter of history in British entertainment and, like them, he earned his stripes on stage facing live audiences.

Raised in Northamptonshire, Jim's first connection to the bright lights was merely the enthusiastic piano playing of his father, who also took his son on his first trip to the theatre. Entranced by the sound of 1,200 people laughing together, Jim decided there and then that was his future. He spent the rest of his youth as a real-life Billy Elliot, the only boy at his local dance school, where he learned ballet, tap, ballroom, judo, even tumbling – ten lessons a week for six years. Seventy years later, he was still grateful for this formidable training, saying in 2015, 'Dance gives you the movement, it gives you everything.' Separately, he added, 'I've spent my life tumbling. You become very physical and you have the confidence.'

By the age of 17, he was ready. He left a job at the local shoe factory when he got on the bill of a teenage music hall tour, where he used his athleticism in physical comedy, plus his talent for voices, to become one of the country's youngest professional stand-ups. He toured Britain for the next two and a half years, playing to a different music hall every week and sharing the bill with the likes of Max Miller. He then spent two years of national service in the RAF, entertaining the troops both in England and Germany. Like Kenneth Williams before him, Jim used this time to hone his performing skills in camp shows.

His return home in the mid-1950s coincided with the end of an era, as the advent of TV in people's livings rooms meant farewell to music hall. Jim has always described his career as a series of happy accidents, but he was clearly nimble on his feet, and able to adapt. Going along to the BBC to warm up the audience for the country's first rock and roll TV show, *Six-Five Special*, he borrowed Tommy Steele's guitar and surprised the audience by carrying a tune. He was invited back as a singer and ended up hosting both this show and another, *Thank Your Lucky Stars*.

In another happy accident, he was spotted by a music producer, one Mr George Martin, who recruited him to be his first recording artist on the Parlophone label. Years before he alchemised The Beatles, the producer's magic touch worked on Jim, bringing him chart hits such as 'Be My Girl' in 1957 and 'Sugartime' a year later.

His pop success and his good looks brought Jim the kind of attention we've come to associate with many a teen idol, but he remembers this time with a shudder.

'Please don't think I'm being egotistical,' he told me when I interviewed him back in 2015 ... as if! ... 'but back in the day, I could stop a car at the traffic light and people were reaching in. It was madness and I hated it. To this day when I go out for a meal, I always face the wall. I never face out.'

He found songwriting far less stressful and later penned the lyrics for the song 'Georgy Girl', the theme for the film of the same name. The still-played tune became a 1966 top ten hit in both the UK and US, where it also collected Oscar and Golden Globe nominations.

Hosting duties on *Six-Five Special* brought Jim his big screen debut in the film spin-off, and he made a handful of other films including, most significantly, a small role as an errant trombone player in a comedy called *Raising the Wind*. The production company was the same as for the Carry Ons, and his leading man was Kenneth Williams as the orchestra's conductor.

Jim recounted years later, 'When they said "Action", Kenneth Williams yelled out, "Where's your music?" I said, "I haven't got it, oh yes, I have, I was sitting on it all the time." Cut. Everyone was laughing, except for one person.'

The reason for the laughter was that Jim had gone rogue with the script – something Kenneth would have secretly endorsed, surely – and delivered his lines in a pitch-perfect impersonation of the star himself. Jim guessed from Kenneth's immediate remonstrations with director Gerald Thomas that he hadn't made a fan. 'He was pointing towards me and making a fist. Then the director came over and told me to hold back on the impression. "You sound more like him than he does," he said.'

A year later, Jim got a call from the same director, asking him for a meeting where he was invited to join the Carry On team.

The actor continued, 'I said, "But Kenneth Williams hates my guts."' Not true, it transpired.

'He'd said, "Use him! If he can take the mickey out of me and make me laugh at the same time, he'll be a godsend." So it was due to Kenneth Williams that I became a member of the Carry On team.'

What did Jim Dale bring to the Carry On films, a series that he joined when it was five years old and already very well established in the hearts of British cinema-goers? Typically self-deprecatingly, Jim explained to it to me like this: 'They needed a young idiot to play Barbara Windsor's boyfriend. With all that going on – Charles Hawtrey wearing glasses whatever the era, Kenneth Williams and his sideways glances – they needed that sort of contemporary innocence, and I was a natural fit.'

I think there was a lot more to his appeal than that. Visually, the series was on the brink of bursting into colour. Narratively, it was broadening its scope beyond the simpler tableaux of their first few years. Original writer Norman Hudis had passed the baton to Talbot Rothwell, who was willing to embrace the changing moralities and attitudes of the era. For the films to continue to succeed, they needed an appealing, relatable protagonist at the centre of them. As well as Jim's own sense of 'contemporary innocence', he brought dashing good looks, charm and the promise of romance, but without any of the roguish arrogance that could easily have come with many another actor. On screen at least, he was handsome but hapless which made him very sympathetic, even before he brought his tumbling skills to the fore with his penchant for physical comedy. Most importantly, his years of stand-up meant he could effortlessly hold his own in the comedic stakes with Sid James, Kenneth Williams and co.

If Jim Dale hadn't existed, the Carry On producers would have had to invent him to secure the future of their beloved franchise. Instead they got lucky because he did exist and proved, as he put it, a natural fit.

Jim's Carry On debut coincided with Talbot Rothwell's first script. Although he had a tiny role as an expectant father, at least he could say he appeared in *Carry On Cabby*, one of the series' finest titles.

Similarly in *Jack*, his role was small and unnamed but gave him a couple of good lines. *Spying* saw his screen time expanded, but it wasn't really until *Cleo* that he came into his own as caveman Horsa, an innocent abroad in Rome, captured by soldiers and somehow interfering with all the goings-on of Cleopatra's court. His chemistry with fellow cave-dweller Kenneth Connor is as warm here as it proves later with Sid James in *Don't Lose Your Head*.

Possibly my favourite title of all, *Cowboy*, gave Jim his first Carry On leading man duties, as English sanitary engineer Marshall P. Knutt who, through a predictable catalogue of misunderstanding (basically being called Marshall) is sent by the powers in Washington to clean up crime in a mid-West town. In this spoof romp where every character is a fully formed triumph, Jim still gets some of the best lines. Marshall tells Sid James's Rumpo Kid, 'Last night Colonel Houston's ranch was raided and they got away with forty cows,' to which Rumpo counters, 'Bullocks.' Marshall's reply? 'I know what I'm talking about.' It's all in the timing, and each had it.

At the time, Jim still had TV duties, filming *Thank Your Lucky Stars* each Sunday in Birmingham, but he was clearly set for stardom. It was after a press screening of *Cowboy* that Sid James's agent wrote to Peter Rogers saying, 'I think you have done miracles for Jim Dale.'

Fellow agent Keith Devon agreed. He wrote to Rogers, 'I wish to thank you for the very great opportunity you have given Jim Dale. I do hope that after his performance in this film, you agree with me that he will be a very big comedy bet indeed.'

Despite being the attractive young male protagonist throughout his Carry On tenure, Jim is never threatening, nor on the make with the beauties who cross his path. His good looks and charm are balanced by his clumsiness and lack of confidence. *Screaming!* is the nearest we get to seeing him trying to take advantage of his young lady, and his efforts are foiled by his own ineptitude as much as by the arrival of a monster called Oddbod. *Follow That Camel* similarly finds him pursuing romance as much as action, but once again his attractiveness is levelled out by his nervousness in dealing with Anita Harris's temptress Corkpit at the Café ZigZig. It is a delicate balancing trick for an actor to play with audiences, but one Jim succeeds in pulling off.

The nearest we get to fully-fledged dashing romantic hero is in the hospital titles of the series. Although he only appeared in two, *Doctor* and *Again Doctor*, it is with his white doctor's coat and stethoscope that I'm sure most people would associate Jim Dale, and I put that down to two enduring images.

> *'Do you feel any fever or giddiness?'*
> *'Yes, I do feel a bit hot.'*
> *'I meant Miss Locks.'*

The first is the era-enabled sight of a white-coated Jim, stethoscope to the ready, tending to a slightly less-dressed Barbara Windsor, her modesty protected only by a trio of strategically placed, sequinned hearts. This film was the immediate successor to *Camping*, where Windsor's bikini had pinged off, and this image was even more exposing. It was the pose for a million publicity shots for the film in a way that would be unthinkable now. At least the good doctor's gaze is firmly fixed on her eyes.

The second is that here is where Jim's talent for physical comedy was given room to shine to the extent it became his hallmark of the films. Long before Michael Crawford entertained us as Frank Spencer on roller skates, audiences watched Jim in action as Doctor Kilmore (see what they did there?) in *Carry On Doctor*, still handsome but hapless, getting his towel caught in the washroom door, but also tottering precariously on the hospital roof, before disappearing into the soap-sudded bath of a unsuspecting nurse.

Two years later, he upped the stakes for *Carry on Again Doctor*, which saw him bouncing down a staircase at high speed on a hospital trolley, before disappearing into a feast-laden buffet table. And this scene comes after he's unwittingly set off a chain of unlikely events and explosions, with his attempts to X-ray Barbara Windsor's insides. One patient speaks for us all, remarking, 'I wouldn't have thought it possible for one man to create such chaos.'

Jim once explained this was all part of his legacy of tumbling in his youth. 'I knew how to fall, so it was quite an adventure for me to say, "Instead of getting a stuntman to fall down the stairs, why don't you let me?"' The actor prided himself on doing all his own stunts, and he had the breaks and bruises to show for it.

'This isn't going to hurt.'

The bumps he received during the scene on the hospital trolley caused his elbow to become infected, and it had to be drained in hospital. The very next day he was due to film a scene where he jumped into a hammock and the walls collapsed on him so, like a trooper, Jim returned to set. He remembered the director telling him, 'Tuck your arm in, and turn your face slightly to camera.'

He once asked the same director why his stunt work was always scheduled on the last day of filming and reported the reply he got. 'For a very good reason, Jim. If you break your neck, it won't ruin anything.'

While his versatility and charm brought a burst of youthful energy to the franchise on screen, Jim slipped seamlessly into place at Pinewood. He told the BBC in 2015, 'It was a period of absolute fun and joy. Three films every two years. It was an opportunity to meet up and be friends again for eight solid weeks with such beautiful talent. Every film was a joy to do, and every film was different.'

For Jim, with his music hall background, he considered the Carry On team to be more than comedians, actually fine actors, forming a true repertory theatre of the cinema. He remembered:

One felt very safe within it. These were professional comedic actors, and the first thing they do is give to each other, knowing we were going to get back. It was a great team feeling, which is what you get no matter what type of group you're in. You give and take, but mostly you give.

No improvisation was ever usually allowed on set, with Jim explaining in 2010, 'The director told me, "If I allow you to suggest a joke, then all of them will want to."'

There was just one exception to this in 1966, on the set of *Don't Lose Your Head*, when Jim worked with Sid James to concoct the perfect line for Charles Hawtrey's character, lying patiently, waiting to be guillotined. Between them the actors came up with a girl arriving with a last-minute message for Charles, who tells her, 'Oh drop it in the basket, I'll read it later.'

Jim remembered, 'That was the only time they allowed it.' You can see why they made the exception.

Because he was a family man by the time he joined the series, the star didn't socialise extensively with his cast and crew beyond general dressing room chat. Despite that, he was befriended by the very discriminating Kenneth Williams.

'There was the Kenneth Williams that you got to see, and the other one,' he told me. He continued:

My background was very shallow as far as education was concerned, because I always had a passion for theatre, and I had no interest in higher education because it wasn't going to help me, and I have no regrets.

But Kenneth taught himself, read the right books, and enlarged his vocabulary so that he could be at the centre of intellectuals, and I was very lucky to have him as a friend because he taught me so much, and I learned a lot about the world.

A lot of actors are scared to trust people because they're so scared it'll end up in print, so if you have a friend you can trust not to gossip, that's a great thing.

Despite his huge stardom and his central role in the franchise, Jim somehow avoided the demons that troubled many of his co-stars. Perhaps it was because for him, as he told me half a century later, 'It's about the work.' More generally, how did he avoid the insecurities and pitfalls that trip so many in showbusiness who reached similar heights? 'It's easy,' he said. 'Sensible friends. Treating it as a career, not as a gimmick to get money and trinkets.'

If Jim Dale had the good luck to appear in lead roles during the golden age of the Carry Ons, he also had the good sense to leave while the going was good, to jump the Carry On ship and leave them wanting more. With his talents beyond doubt, his eyes came to rest on other things. He missed out on roles in both *Khyber* and *Camping* to pursue roles on stage instead – his absence was sorely missed in *Khyber* where replacement Roy Castle brought his own brand of appeal but couldn't bring what Dale could.

The regular's departure was inevitable after he was personally invited to join the National Theatre Company by Sir Laurence Olivier. Jim remembered, 'The theatre always has been my one love. Not a hard decision.'

His time at the National was a triumph. Olivier called Jim 'God's gift to Shakespeare comedies'. In return, Jim told Terry Wogan back in 1986, 'My Bottom was my best part.'

It's fair to say that unlike some of his Carry On co-stars, Jim did not rest on his creative laurels. As a result, his professional postscript makes for longer reading than most. He said in 2015, 'Over the years I realised that the longer I lived the more different Jim Dales there are.'

No Christmas morning in Britain used to be complete without Jim Dale's face appearing on screen in perennial TV re-runs of *Digby: The Biggest Dog in the World*, a film that reunited him with his Carry On teammate Angela Douglas. Other highlights along the way have included playing young Spike Milligan in 1973's *Adolf Hitler: My Part in his Downfall* and signing up for Disney adventure *Pete's Dragon* in 1977. (He also returned to Carry On for the 1992 *Columbus*, but we'll get to that.)

The stage has remained his great love, though, with his singing prowess making for an easy move into musical theatre. Although it was his role of Scapino which made his name in the US theatre, where he has made his home since 1980, it was when he created the role of P.T. Barnum that he properly became 'the toast of Broadway'. Playing the great showman demanded all of Jim's many stage skills, and he even had to learn a new one, climbing up on a high tightrope across the stage and walking across it all the way to a Tony Award. 'Is there anything Jim Dale can't do?' asked Frank Rich in the *New York Times*.

Despite dozens of theatrical triumphs and awards on both sides of the Atlantic, Jim is best known in America for something entirely different, and it's not his Carry On slapstick. There, he's the talented orator who has brought to life around 230 separate voices, all slightly different, for his narration of the Harry Potter audiobooks.

In 2014, he wrote and starred in his own one-man show, looking back on sixty years in showbusiness. He debuted in New York, but emphasised the Carry On material when he brought it to London, where I was fortunate enough to attend his opening night. Looking around from my seat in the stalls, I counted the huge number of entertainment luminaries in the audience, a tribute to Jim's diversity and talent. Not many people in the entertainment industry can draw a crowd from Barbara Windsor to Kenneth Branagh, and be the recipient of air-blown kisses from Derek Jacobi in the stalls.

In 2010 he was inducted into the American Theatre Hall of Fame for lifetime achievement. He'd earned an MBE in Britain seven years before, but by the time I spoke to him in 2015, he was still ambitious, still hungry.

He told me:

I haven't lowered my standards. I have to hit it 100 per cent every night, or it's not going to be me. I just want to get better and keep people entertained for a couple of hours, nothing more than that.

There's no machine, I've been in New York so long, if you want me for a part, just phone me, come round to my apartment for a meal.

I don't have an agent, I don't have a manager, I don't have a publicist, because they wouldn't know what I'm after in terms of challenge.

They say, 'But you've never played a role like that,' and I say, 'Exactly, that's why I want it. Let me fail. Don't turn down anything.'

Jim Dale told the BBC in 2015, 'The joy of being able to be in show business so long is the ability to explore every conceivable branch of that show business tree.'

Bearing in mind the length of his career, and his tirelessness in climbing so many branches of that tree, it's almost bizarre that he should be so closely associated with a franchise that only accounted for six of his seventy years in the industry (not including his return in *Columbus*).

It is a testament to just how special his contribution was to the franchise – with his unique injection of youth, energy, charm and comedic timing. In return, he told Alan Whicker in a 1985 interview in New York:

I look back on those Carry Ons with fondest memories, because you learn your trade all through your life. That particular vehicle taught me to work with the most wonderful talented comedic people and I'm sure a lot of that is what's rubbed off on the stage out here.

When I sat down with him in London 30 years later, he was just as appreciative of the results on screen as he reflected, 'I do think those films were British humour at its best – double entendres, puns, some of the best comic timing I've ever seen.'

Chapter 14

Hot! Cold! Down the Hole!

'I've seen bigger ones in my time'

Joan Sims in *Carry On Dick*

'We never intended to make a series,' Peter explained once. 'It was only when we got to three, I thought we might get to six. We got to six, I thought we might get to ten. When we got to twenty-one, I thought, where are we going?'

The answer was into the shifting sands of a brand new decade, and with it some brand new Carry On faces. As Gerald Thomas explained to the BBC on the set of *Jungle* in 1970:

> We've built up a team of artists, which are almost a repertory team, but they are interchangeable. None of them are really indispensable. I would hate to lose any of them, but we do change them from time to time and occasionally we bring in a newcomer just to give it a bit of a spark for a bit of life.

He and Peter became adept at recruiting names already familiar to audiences from popular TV shows. Sally Geeson was one such popular personality, used to working alongside Sid playing his daughter in *Bless This House*. Sally tells me:

> He was a lovely man and very protective and fond of me … He put a word in for me to join the Carry On team for *Abroad* in 1972. It was such an honour to become part of it, but I don't remember feeling intimidated by the prospect. Call it the courage of youth!

Kenneth Cope was another new arrival, already known to audiences as private detective Marty Hopkirk in the TV series *Randall and Hopkirk (Deceased)*. When he joined the Carry On team for *Convenience* in

1971, he realised it was his small screen success that had appealed to the filmmakers. 'I had a familiar face which they hoped would get more bums on seats.'

Kenneth likened being asked to join the Carry On team for *Convenience* to 'receiving an invitation to a VIP club', and returned the following year for *Matron*.

The changing faces coincided with the films' more open-minded approach to relations between the sexes. Barbara Windsor's top pinging off in *Camping* was a defining moment for Carry On in more than just a visual way. It heralded the series' move into far bawdier territory, with men and women's desires no longer being glimpsed through double entendre. The gags stayed the same but everything else was a lot more ... upfront, I suppose.

One easy comparison is Babs herself. Fresh from her shocking campsite PE session, she turned up in *Carry On Again Doctor* a few months later, wearing even less, well nothing, in fact, unless you count the three strategically placed red sequinned hearts she was sporting. As film star Goldie Locks, she didn't actually feature that much, but the effect, reproduced in a thousand publicity stills, was disproportionate to the small time she spent on screen.

Sid, too, was playing a man far more brazen in his appetites than the patient hankering after 'just one' cigarette of the original *Doctor* film, or even the euphemistic pleasures of 'Tiffin time' in *Khyber*. He didn't actually appear for the first thirty-eight minutes of *Again Doctor*, but when he eventually arrived on screen as Gladstone Screwer, an exiled doctor in a tropical paradise, he made no bones about how he liked to spend his days surrounded by apparently willing young ladies, 'That's Monday, that's Tuesday...'

Despite the shift in tone, *Carry On Again Doctor* retained much of the series' great charm, with much credit due to Jim Dale's talent for physical comedy playing the wronged Doctor Nookey. Let's remember the moment that begins so sweetly with his attempt to take an X-ray of Goldie Locks. This quickly goes haywire setting off a chaotic chain of events – bells pinging, patients spinning, explosions, errant vacuum cleaners, the works – until the scene's crashing finale in which he bounces down the stairs on a hospital trolley before disappearing through the window leaving a Nookey-shaped hole. This remains not just a Carry On staple, but a masterclass in physical comedy, a signifier of all fun on film from that era, and even British comedy in general, I'd argue. This would be Jim's last Carry On appearance for over two decades, and revisiting this scene reminds us just how special he was.

'It's a good skeleton. Did the last doctor leave it here?
'That is the last doctor.'

With Jim's physical antics, a broader plot canvas and bawdier tone than in any of the previous medical titles, *Carry On Again Doctor* succeeded in its efforts to appeal to new fans while including many of the more established appeals of the series. Kenneth Williams hammed away in his distinctive fashion as chief surgeon Doctor Carver while Charles Hawtrey once again assumed drag duties, disguised this time as Lady Puddleton for infiltration of the rival clinic.

With the medical titles proving popular with audiences, as well as a straightforward way of accommodating a large cast, it wasn't long before Pinewood's corridors were again full of nurses, this time for *Carry On Matron* in 1972, set in a maternity hospital, and featuring the highest number of cast regulars of the entire series.

There's an even more risqué screen moment in this one, with Barbara's character Nurse Susan Ball asking a man called Cyril to undo her bra for her. I should add, he's disguised as a female nurse when she makes the request. This time around, it was Kenneth Cope's turn to don a frock.

For Kenneth, this aspect of his role provides a screen-worthy anecdote:

I was walking down the corridor at Pinewood in my nurse's costume and saw four blokes standing there. Well, their backs stiffened as I went straight into the gents, just like in the film. There was a tall gentleman in there, and he nearly fell over when he saw me hoisting up my skirts. He thought he'd got lucky in his lunch hour.

By this point in the series the writers not only invariably knew which regular actor they were writing for when they penned the lines, but they could also make a series of in-jokes. When Hattie's Matron sat down to watch the TV in the film, the drama summary was taken from the actress's own breakthrough film *Green for Danger*. (Similarly, when

Wilfred Brambell had popped up for a cameo in *Again Doctor*, his accompanying music wasn't a million miles away from the *Steptoe* theme. The production team knew how to keep themselves entertained.)

If anybody ever seeks a snapshot of Britain in the early 1970s, they need look no further than the series of contemporary Carry On films that emerged from this period. *Carry On Loving, At Your Convenience, Abroad, Girls* and *Behind* cast the team's unique gaze on the worlds of agency dating, trade unions, package holidays, beauty contests and camping respectively.

Loving was actually set in what was sweetly called back then a marriage bureau, a social enterprise just taking off in real life, its popularity boosted by this film, the fourth most popular box office hit in Britain of 1971.

In similar style to *Regardless* almost a decade before, *Loving* presented a catalogue of separate storylines, those of the clients of the bureau, run by Sid Bliss (guess who?) and his girlfriend Sophie (Hattie). While the franchise's ever-present innuendo was visible in the names of the locations – Much-Snogging-on-the-Green, Rogerham Mansions and so on – the script went for a much more brazen, openly bawdy approach than previously. An advert on the side of a bus promised 'Twice Nightly!' while Terry Scott's character Terry Philpott made no bones about his desires for his 'squeeze' Jenny Grubb – 'Have you had it? Not yet.'

'As far as sex is concerned, I'd like to make my position quite clear.'

This new tone was created by a host of new, younger faces on screen, joining regulars Sid, Hattie, Kenneth, Joan and Charles. Relative newbie Richard O'Callaghan (the son of Patricia Hayes) made his Carry On debut as Bertram Muffet, the earnest, sympathetic lead role previously inhabited by Jim Dale. To my mind, Richard was no Jim, but he earned good reviews and was an unmistakable injection of youth alongside Jacki Piper in her second Carry On appearance after *Jungle*.

All in all, *Loving* was an attempt by Carry On to keep up with the advancing social mores of the time, namely that young people were either constantly at it, or trying to be. As for the older characters, they seemed resigned to being left behind, Sophie describing her partner Sid as having 'the general appearance of an ancient and dissipated walnut' (an assessment with which Sid James would be the first to agree), while Sid blatantly pursued Joan's character, client Esme.

The disappointment for me comes from the final scene, a wedding reception that turns into an orgy of cake-throwing, with no uplifting testimony to true love to warm the hearts of audiences. It seems a cynical and weary message after the more satisfying resolutions of films gone by, but perhaps I'm just old-fashioned.

Despite the film's success, few Carry On fans consider *Loving* one of the treasures of the canon, with critics complaining of the patchy narrative, the sequence of clients' tableaux meaning too little time was spent with the bureau's proprietors Sid and Hattie, or with regular favourites Kenneth and Joan. However, fans remain far more divided on the title that came along next.

Carry On At Your Convenience remains one of the most socially interesting of all the series, and definitely the most political, with its setting in a bathroom ceramics factory, and its narrative thrust in battles between workers and management, often steered by factory floor union rep Vic Spanner (Kenneth Cope in his first of two Carry On outings).

Several of the old guard are on duty here, although some of their characters seem a bit dissatisfied. Foreman Sid Plummer (yes, you know who) confines his pleasures to placing racing bets with the aid of his prophetic budgie and flirting with his brassy co-worker Chloe, played by Joan. Kenneth and Charles play owner W.C. Boggs and designer Charles Coote respectively. It all seems like business as usual, but for the script which contains several lines that traded customary gags for political statements, particularly in the exchanges between union rep Vic and foreman Sid. As Sid's daughter Myrtle debates whether to give her affections to Vic or boss's son Lewis, it seems like a metaphor for the whole class struggle on screen.

> *'Fakes, that's all they are, sitting there staring in their crystal whatsitsnames.'*
> *'Balls.'*
> *'I quite agree.'*

When the discontent is seemingly solved with a workers' outing, only for the hotel caterers to go on strike, it is Vic who gets most upset with them 'for taking bread out of poor workers' mouths', the script pointing to his hypocrisy, and the filmmakers taking a blatant anti-union stance.

For once, the Carry On team lost sight of their audience, with *Convenience* becoming the first box office failure of the entire series. The subject matter undoubtedly surfed the zeitgeist of the new Industrial Relations Act that was passed the same year with the aim of reducing unofficial strikes after tumultuous struggles. However, while repressive institutions such as the army, the police force and NHS had always had their sides poked to harmless effect by the Carry On team, *Convenience*'s lampooning of the trade unions as obsessed with petty rules and regulations didn't land favourably in cinemas, which would have had many a union member paying for a seat. These viewers perhaps didn't take kindly to the film's portrayal of stewards as tyrannical and obstructive, rather than positive and helpful. Myrtle choosing the boss's son over union rep Vic probably didn't help, either.

Or perhaps audiences just wanted the cinema to be a place of escapist fun, particularly when they'd paid to see a Carry On film.

Either way, the film became the first in the series not to recoup its production costs until five years later following sales to television and international distributors – helpfully retitled *Carry On Round the Bend* for overseas viewers.

By contrast, in present times I know many Carry On fans (okay, three) for whom *Convenience* is by far their favourite, most interesting and enduring title, making for stimulating watching to this day. I'll give the last word to Peter Rogers, who said years later, 'I strongly maintain is is a very good film and it did make a profit for the distributor. Someone must have gone to see it.'

'A beautiful wine for a beautiful lady.'
'Was that supposed to be a compliment?'
'Better taste the wine first.'

Equally topical but less controversial was the following year's *Carry On Abroad*. Taking a franchise further afield would become de rigeur for the 1970s (*On the Buses*, *Are You Being Served*), but the Carry Ons did it first with 1972's *Abroad*, channelling British people's new experience of accessible trips to foreign lands, with the flourishing business of package holidays. While the *Buses* team ended up in Prestatyn for their outing and Grace Bros and co made it all the way to 'Costa Plonka' for theirs, Carry

On got as far as the Mediterranean isle of Elsbels on the Costa Bomm – in real life, the car park at Pinewood, with sackloads of sand shipped in. Peter Rogers was nothing if not consistent.

Abroad taps into all sorts of familiar stereotypes of Brits abroad, both then and now – everyone's fear of foreign food, the ritual of losing personal inhibitions from the moment the coach leaves the stop, plus of course the enduring comic potential of 'This hotel doesn't seem to be quite finished' – even more accurate then than today. Against this cosy backdrop, the plot only needs to be wafer-thin – various romps between various guests, Sid's Vic developing X-ray vision (or rather the ability to see through women's clothing, specifically) after sampling the local brew, Barbara Windsor once again being caught in the shower, everyone ending up being arrested and thrown in jail, all the usual goings-on – and *Abroad* I consider a cheerful if unremarkable addition to the series. While the treatment of holiday-goer Nicholas, in demand by the ladies, and his friend Robin, jealous and implicitly gay, is disappointing, sadder still is seeing Charles Hawtrey as bowler-hatted mummy's boy Eustace Tuttle appearing as addicted to drink on screen as we later learned he was in real life. This was the twenty-third and final Carry On outing for Charles, who spent his last days filming the coach sequence on the roads of Bagshot.

> *'Not for me, thank you.'*
> *'Oh, don't drink?'*
> *'No, I tried it once and didn't like it.'*
> *'Smoke?'*
> *'I tried it once and didn't like it.'*
> *'Strange.'*
> *'Not at all, my daughter is just the same.'*
> *'Your only child, I presume.'*

The penultimate scene of *Abroad*, all the guests high on life, rediscovered romance and the magic local lotion of Santa Cecilia's Elixir, even while the hotel around them collapses to the ground, was a reminder of the far finer *Carry On Up the Khyber* and its unforgettable dinner party finale. Similarly, 1975's *Carry On Behind* was really one big tribute act to the epoch-defining *Camping* that had triumphed only six years before. Even the weather paid homage to the challenges faced by its predecessor. *Behind* was filmed in a chilly spring, making the bare trees, muddy fields and even actors' breath clearly visible in what was supposed to be another British summer idyll. A catalogue of new faces – Windsor Davies, George Layton, Sherrie Hewson, Ian Lavender – were all familiar comedy actors at the time, drafted in by Peter to keep the series fresh, while German actress Elke Sommer brought a unique exotic charm to her role of Anna Vrooshka, an unlikely expert in Roman antiquities who even more incredulously seemed drawn to the bare bottom of Professor Roland Crump, played by Kenneth Williams.

Just as the ravers had brought havoc in *Camping*, disruption this time around came in the form of an accidentally-booked stripper, while once again two men's attempts to seduce women other than their wives were inevitably foiled. To anybody thinking of watching *Behind* on a rainy Sunday afternoon, I'd say only, maybe go and watch *Camping* again instead.

Far more satisfying from this period were the films in which the Carry On team still proved to be masters of their craft, namely film genre spoof and period romps.

The biggest joke in *Carry On Up the Jungle* came about purely by accident. When the film was first mooted, it was a blatant parody of everybody who'd ever worn a loincloth on screen, from Hammer Films' *Cavegirl* series to the massive 60s' hit *One Million Years B.C.* and most transparently, Edgar Rice Burrough's *Tarzan* series of books and films. The only problem was, Jim Dale for whom the all-glistening, very physical role of Ug, Jungle Boy, was first written, turned down the part. That meant audiences were treated to the spectacle of Terry Scott, nearly a decade older and a lot rounder, swinging through the trees and beating his chest in a love-call. Once the audience's credulity was sufficiently stretched, the rest of the story pretty much wrote itself. Joan Sims played his mother Lady Bagley, even though in real life she was three years his junior, while Charles Hawtrey, we were led to believe, was King Tonka, king of lovers, master of women, father of countless.

'I'm flabbergasted. My gast has never been so flabbered!'

With all its physical comedy, double entendres and blatant allusions to bonking with confusion over who is in whose tent, *Jungle* is a fully-fledged

Carry On romp very much in the style of *Cowboy*. Ug Boy happily swings on a vine before smashing into a tree and leaving a Tarzan-shaped hole. Returning to the team for the first time in six years, Kenneth Connor spies on Joan Sims from the branch of a tree, innocently sharing his binoculars with a gorilla, all his previous comedic skills intact. Frankie Howerd returned for his second and final outing with the team, reunited with Joan for a scene that the pair famously couldn't get through for corpsing. A BBC documentary filmed the cast and crew at work, and the jovial atmosphere they captured on set was clearly infectious in the results on screen. Even the notoriously critical Kenneth Williams, who didn't appear in the film, noted in a later diary entry that, when he came to watch the film on television, at one point he actually found himself laughing aloud 'staggered to see what they got away with!' No small praise, and reflected in the box office figures, recognising *Jungle* as one of the country's most popular films of 1970.

Carry On Henry and *Carry On Dick* brought up the rear of the team's great period romps, inspired by Henry VIII and Dick Turpin respectively. As Henry, Sid James revelled in donning another of Richard Burton's great costumes (worn by the Welsh star in *Anne of the Thousand Days*) and playing the monarch as a lovable, lusty rogue, surrounded by scheming courtiers and buxom belles.

'Speaking royally, my mint has a hole in it.'

Lots of cracking gags, great scenery, including even the Long Walk at Windsor Castle, plus sterling support from Kenneth Williams as Thomas Cromwell and Terry Scott in, I believe, his finest Carry On hour as Cardinal Wolsey, Joan Sims as a frustrated French queen, and Barbara Windsor as the seductive Bettina – all ensured *Carry On Henry* was as fine a period production as any made during the team's earlier golden age.

'Have you been dallying with the Queen?'
'Certainly not Sire.'
'Your hand on it?'
'Not even a finger on it.'

Carry On Dick was similarly energetic, if a lot fruitier, when it appeared three years later. This was the twentieth and final script to be penned by the extraordinary Talbot Rothwell, before he succumbed to nervous and physical exhaustion and finally put his pen down. It also proved to be the last outing in the series for Sid James and Barbara Windsor, but they went out with a bang, thanks to a script that gave them both plenty to do – Sid revelling in a double role as both the dastardly Big Dick Turpin and his alter ego, the much gentler Reverend Flasher, and Barbara in full flight as his partner in crime Harriet. The film would be Hattie's Carry On swansong, too. Although she was given less to do as the rector's housekeeper, her character Martha Hoggett proved to be a key plot mover. Considering some of the titles that came later in the series, these three huge Carry On stars could always be relieved that with *Dick* they got to take their final bow.

Despite these successful, jolly romps, however, there was a feeling, unspoken on the set at Pinewood but expressed freely by critics further afield, that the quality of the series was starting to fade, or at least that their audiences were after something different. If Peter Rogers boasted that his team kept telling the same joke over and over again, by the mid-1970s this single gag was inevitably starting to wear a bit thin.

At the box office, competition for audience's attention was huge. Bringing a similar sauce to cinemas as the Carry Ons were the *Confessions* films where, only a few short years after Barbara's pinging bra had brought such squeals, it seemed like no woman ever kept her top on. Meanwhile on TV, people were saying the F-word so often, jaws no longer dropped open when it happened. Despite the team's best efforts, Carry On was sadly falling behind in its attempts to modernise and match its rivals for ribaldry, just as its producers were running out of ideas and original stars beginning to drop out. What had previously appealed as saucy in the jolly technicolour of the period spoofs began to feel sleazy in the harsh daylight of more contemporary settings of later films.

'All this talk of Big Dick. I've had enough of it!'

For Matthew Sweet, it was this move, both physically and narratively, from the studio sets of Rome and India to more real-life settings that proved unforgiving on screen:

They spent so much time in these pastiche spaces that when they tried to return to the contemporary world, they suddenly all looked a bit old. *Carry On Loving* was particularly excruciating, and they just looked out of their time. The men looked all wrong wearing their tight nylon shirts, whereas it would have been fine if they'd carried on wearing pith helmets and Roman togas.

A bit like dads being caught trying to look cool dancing at the disco? Sweet shudders. 'Worse than dancing.' Oh dear. The end was nigh.

Chapter 15

Star Spotlight – Barbara Windsor

'What a lovely looking pear!'

The leading ladies of Carry On have always been singular in their style, distinctive and memorable. Shirley Eaton was almost Hitchcockian with her cool, blonde beauty, while Liz Fraser offered a contemporary brunette counterpoint. Joan Sims was the pretty, smiley girl next door before blossoming into a figure of verdant womanhood. And if Hattie Jacques brimmed with burning secret desire, repressed behind an authoritative façade, Barbara Windsor burst onto screen as her liberated opposite, allowing male admirers to dream a little, inviting them in with her big wide smile and, crucially, that conspiratorial giggle. Plus her pint-sized, peroxided appearance lent her a cartoon character quality that only added to her appeal.

Her introductory lines for Carry On, as Trainee Agent Daphne Honeybutt, told us everything. As Kenneth Williams asked her, 'Number?' she replied, '38-22-25.' 'No, your number, not your vital thingummies…' 'Sorry, I forgot where I was for a minute,' she replied. 'Have you had any experience?' he asked. 'Oh yes, a little,' she told him and giggled.

From those very first moments of her 1964 debut, Barbara made it clear that while she knowingly represented the stereotype of the busty blonde, she was very much in on the joke, and willing to play along, with great comedic timing and a huge, tipped wink. It was this jolliness, as well as her physical allure, that ensured she became an integral part of the Carry On team and a crucial part of their legacy, despite only appearing in a surprisingly small number of the films – ten in all. Her arrival also heralded a new dawn of permissiveness within the films, a bridge between two eras as they moved from the golden age of the spoofs and period romps to something far more liberal and unfettered, making her a hugely significant symbol of the series' evolution.

Like her cast-mates Kenneth and Joan, Barbara embraced her Carry On family having experienced a lonely childhood. She was born Barbara Ann Deeks in Shoreditch in London's East End, the only offspring of costermonger John and dressmaker Rose. Her earliest years were lived under the shadow of her parents' tumultuous marriage, culminating in their divorce after a traumatic courtroom appearance, when young Barbara had to describe the nightly arguments and violence she had witnessed. Her father was so disappointed by what he considered her betrayal of him, he disappeared out of her life for many years, a defining moment of abandonment movingly told in Tony Jordan's 2017 biopic drama of her life, *Babs*.

Until then, young Barbara's biggest pleasure in life had been the companionship she enjoyed with her father. In her memoir, she describes how they giggled a lot together, much to her mother's annoyance. 'We had the same raucous laugh and she hated it. She thought it vulgar and, in me, most unladylike.'

Not traditionally ladylike maybe, but it would go on to make her fortune – a delightfully feminine, complicit, mischievous chuckle that got into the bones of her many fans and would define her as much as any physical traits or wiggles in later years.

Her other great consolation was showbusiness. Recognising her flair for performing, her parents enrolled her at theatre school, which meant taking four buses and feeling 'short, fat and loud' compared with her far posher fellow pupils, but right from the start, she stood out. Aged just 13, she went on tour with a production of *Love From Judy*, where her diminutive size kept her in her role long after other girls grew up and left, and got to make her West End debut two years later. During her long run, she became Barbara Windsor, her new surname inspired by two things – the married name of her beloved Auntie Dolly, and also the biggest event of that year, the Coronation.

Some tiny film roles came her way – *The Belles of St Trinians* and also *Too Hot to Handle*, starring Jayne Mansfield. On leaving school, Barbara earned her money for a while like a normal person, including working in a shoe shop, but showbusiness inevitably beckoned. Her *Love from Judy* co-star Johnny Brandon invited her to appear on his TV show *Variety Parade* and from then on, Barbara was seldom out of a gig, whether it was the dawning age of TV, stage roles, cabaret work in Soho or more film roles. A list of the people she met during this period in her life reads like a who's who of post-war British entertainment, with names including June Whitfield, Una Stubbs, Danny La Rue, Ronnie Corbett and Anthony Newley.

On stage she was spotted by Peter Charlesworth, who recognised the 'star quality written all over her' and would become her long-time agent, and also by jazz man Ronnie Scott, who invited her to tour with a new band he had formed. By the late 1950s, Barbara was one of the leading lights of Winston's Revue and it was here she felt her first proper connection with a live audience. 'It was the beginning for me of a lifelong affair with the lovely British public,' is how she described it.

'I don't fancy being a gangster's moll!'
(*Carry On Matron*)

Those years were complicated by another affair of the heart, this one with Ronnie Knight, a charming rogue of crooked connections who was married when they met and soon behind bars to boot. For their long courtship and later marriage, Barbara was as much in the headlines for Ronnie's notorious deeds as for her own professional triumphs. Although they led increasingly separate lives as the years passed and he got into more and deeper trouble, the headlines he created definitely added to Barbara's image as a happy-go-lucky East End woman, standing by her man and overlooking his failings. Not all of it was hyped up. Her memoir also details her friendship with the three Kray brothers, twins Ronnie and Reggie and elder brother Charlie, with two of whom she even shared fleeting romances.

The rising star met somebody very different but equally significant in 1959 when she went for an audition for the musical *Fings Ain't Wot They Used T'Be* at the Wyndham Theatre. Stopping first to have a chat with a lady cleaning the steps of the stage door, Barbara went inside to face composer Lionel Bart and respected, unorthodox director Joan Littlewood – who turned out to be the same woman she'd just met sweeping. Barbara got the job and her theatrical education truly began. Although they clashed at first, Joan saw in Barbara a lot more than her wiggle, saying, 'She's a real actress, give her anything.' Barbara's big challenge was a solo number called 'Where do Little Birds Go?' She gave it an emotional rendition that brought the house down when the show reached the West End.

Like Hattie and Joan, Barbara also got to shine on TV, appearing in the hit sit-com *The Rag Trade*. It's interesting that even then, as far back as the early 1960s, Barbara felt suppressed by what was required of her in the role, basically chewing gum and wiggling, saying she felt 'demeaned to be playing a soppy bimbo in white stilettos'. Experiencing the classic actor's dilemma of quantity versus quality, she felt happier performing to 700 people at the Garrick Theatre than offering a far less substantial version of herself to millions of TV viewers. She knew by then she was a proper comedic theatre actress, even if *Rag Trade* producer Dennis Main Wilson thought she was wrong, telling her, 'You're far too young. And far too pretty.'

Fortunately, she got her chance to shine in the film version of *Sparrows Can't Sing*. The producers didn't want to cast little-known Barbara Windsor, but the director did, and as that was once again Joan Littlewood, nobody argued. The film proved a hit on both sides of the Atlantic, even if US audiences required a glossary for all its Cockney turns of phrase, and Barbara was nominated for a BAFTA Best Actress award. In a sign of her two worlds marrying, the after-premiere party took place in the Kentucky drinking club on the Mile End Road. A-list celebrities who'd attended the screening dined on the food and drink of their hosts, the Krays. The club had even been used for several of the film's scenes.

She may not have realised it at the time, but Barbara couldn't have served up more of an hors d'oeuvre for her future in Carry On if she'd tried, when she accepted a film role in *Crooks in Cloisters*, a comic caper about forgers going on the run and posing as monks to evade justice. Her co-stars included Wilfred Brambell, Ronald Fraser and Bernard Cribbins, and her character's name was, literally, Bikini. The cast had a hoot, and it was to prove even more significant for Barbara later in the year, when her castmate Ronald invited her to lunch with him at Pinewood, where he was filming. Barbara walked into the famous dining room for the first time, tottering on high heels and by her own admission, thoroughly intimidated by such salubrious surroundings and celebrity guests.

As fate would have it, two of the people in the room that day were Peter Rogers and Gerald Thomas, lunching together and chewing on ideas for a replacement for their recently departed Carry On girl Liz Fraser. Now, as pert, peroxided pint-pot Barbara Windsor – veteran of stage and screen but not yet a household name – walked nervously past their table, they had their answer.

Peter Rogers had already spotted Barbara in *The Rag Trade*, and knew she had the perfect combination of cheekiness, comedic timing, plus her performing pedigree that came from working for Joan Littlewood. He said of his new recruit, 'As soon as I saw her, I knew she was right,' and his eye for her talents was vindicated as soon as Barbara joined his team. The actress herself was still hungry to learn. She explained later her simple reasons for accepting the job. 'It was with Bernie Cribbins, who was a friend. I thought, "That'll be rather nice." He said, "You'll learn about filming on that."'

Physically, Barbara brought all the tools of the classic screen figure of the buxom, busty blonde – even if she always chuckled that her embonpoint wasn't actually that large, it was all in the way she carried herself. She gave the impression of great glamour, but it was of the Donald McGill postcard type, completely unthreatening and family-friendly. She underpinned it with comic flair, encouraging her co-stars and audiences to laugh at stereotypes and share the joke of it all. She said herself, 'I don't think of myself as a sexy, a 4'10' little lady. I played at being sexy.' She was just that, a sex symbol without laying on the sexuality, a deceptively difficult balancing act that only her seriously good performing skills could pull off, no doubt helped by her size and, of course, that laugh.

Peter Rogers later gave the actress surely his biggest ever compliment, describing her as 'the most professional artist I've ever come across'. Sure enough, although she was nervous from the beginning of her time on Carry On to be joining such an established team, she always held her own, even against such a perfectionist as Kenneth Williams. Theirs was an inauspicious first encounter, with Barbara fluffing her lines on *Spying*, and Kenneth failing to conceal his impatience with her, even as he stood on set, disguised as a secret agent complete with big dark false beard.

He'd reckoned without Barbara's great spirit, however. As Barbara often related afterwards, she knew that Kenneth had previously fallen out with Fenella Fielding. Now here he stood doing his best to intimidate her, and she was having none of it. 'Don't you yell at me with Fenella Fielding's minge hair stuck round your chops. I won't bloody stand for it.'

And just like that, she made a lifelong friend of the famously snooty Kenneth. In fact, so close did they become that Kenneth even joined Barbara on her 1964 honeymoon with Ronnie Knight (and brought along his mother and sister for good measure). Kenneth's memoir recorded the trip as a disaster beset by terrible weather, saved only by his unlikely but sound new friendship with Ronnie. Like all of Kenneth's favourite people, he discovered Ronnie to be a great listener and appreciator of good jokes and stories.

Back at Pinewood, Barbara soon became a core asset to the team. Anita Harris, who co-starred with Barbara in the first *Doctor* title of the series, backed up Peter Rogers's view, remembering of Barbara, 'She was always on time, always first. You learn from these people. She is a very clever girl, and she started her career with Joan Littlewood so all of that structure came into her work on camera.'

Her charm was more personal than that, though. Tony Jordan, who wrote many lines for Barbara in her later incarnation as *EastEnders'* Peggy Mitchell and also penned the drama *Babs* all about her life, sums it up for me, 'Peter Rogers wasn't a genius for choosing her. That was a no-brainer. He saw what Joan Littlewood saw, and what I saw, within thirty seconds of being in her company. She had a quality about her.'

Tony remembers having dinner with Barbara in restaurants, a place where every actor is used to having fans approach their table, and will often agree to photo and autograph requests only after they've finished eating. According to Tony, this was never the case with Barbara:

Her food was always cold. She'd put cutlery down, do the photographs, go to their table, she'd even leave via their table to say goodnight.

You don't do those extra things if it's put on. She had a real connection with people that you felt instantly when you met her. When she asked, 'How are you?' it was real. She was a little bubble of life that you wanted to follow round, because it made you a better person. Those people who hired her gave her jobs because they wanted her in their world.

Despite such instant success in *Carry On Spying*, Barbara wasn't always that enamoured with the craft of filming, revealing, 'All this hitting your marks and getting your light, it seemed phoney to me, I like the freedom of the stage.' The same year she made her Carry On debut, she was back treading the boards for Joan Littlewood, this time in *Oh What a Lovely War!* a performance that took her to Broadway and earned her a Tony nomination, and she soon followed this up with *Come Spy with Me* on London's West End stage. Such success could have lured Barbara to the stage for good, as it did Jim Dale several years later, but instead she returned to the Carry On fold in 1967, from when she starred as one of their most popular regulars. By then, she had finally given up relying on her errant husband Ronnie Knight and it would seem, like Hattie Jacques before her, that after such personal tribulations, Barbara found the camaraderie of the Carry On team intensely reassuring. She recalled 'the friendliness, the cosiness of it all. It was marvellous, just like going back to school'.

Her return to screen with the team for *Carry On Doctor* was her first chance to play a wiggly nurse, Sandra May. She was delightfully confident of her own appeal, blowing a kiss to a car mechanic, whipping off her nurse's uniform to sunbathe on the hospital roof, a seemingly innocent event that inevitably caused chaos when Jim Dale's Doctor Kilmore valiantly decided she needed rescuing.

Doctor gave Barbara her first ever scene with Sid James. They shared a cracking comedic moment when Barbara's arrival caused his temperature to rise and his medical equipment to explode. From then on, whenever they shared the screen, it was an enduring dance between a chuckle and a giggle. Of their on-screen chemistry, Barbara remembered, 'I learned a lot from Sid.'

The pair grew closer over the course of the series, with their relationship documented by Terry Johnson in his play *Cleo, Camping, Emmanuelle and Dick* (for some reason Johnson went with the original French erotic spelling rather than Carry On's deliberately misspelt version). Barbara said at the time she was surprised anyone was interested, but the play premiered at the National Theatre in 1998, and was later adapted into a film. In real life, she stayed married to Ronnie Knight, finally divorcing him in 1985.

In both Barbara's medical Carry Ons, she was romantically paired with Jim, and he clearly agrees with Tony Jordan's assessment of Barbara, calling her 'a ball of fun. She bounded onto set and was like that all day. It wasn't switched on, it was who she was'.

Happily, filming the *Doctor* scenes in summer 1967 gave the actress the chance to visit another set at Pinewood, where *Chitty Chitty Bang Bang* was being made. This unplanned outing ended up with Barbara being offered a small role in the film, and eventually even taking part in the famous fairground chase scene, not a bad addition to her acting CV.

Barbara's scene in *Doctor* wearing her bikini turned out to be a mere forerunner of what was to come two years later, when, with her flyaway underwear, she sealed her place in the heart of every teenage boy in Britain.

She actually showed a lot less flesh in *Camping* than she did in *Carry On Again Doctor*, filmed later the same year. Many an actress, and actor, would quake at the screen nudity required of Barbara in the role of model Goldie Locks but, ever the professional, Barbara got down to business.

She admitted it was the only time she felt really nervous about her appearance on screen, and she dieted ahead of shooting, turning up on the day with less weight on her than director Gerald Thomas had anticipated, much to his dissatisfaction as it turned out. Never mind how Barbara's curves would look on screen, for Gerald it simply meant one of his favourite gags would now fail to land. The scene where Jim Dale's Doctor Nookey first encounters Goldie includes a calendar on the wall where she is seen modelling Bristol Bouncing Baby Cream. 'That's the gag about Bristols out of the window,' the director complained, although audiences still seemed to get the joke when the film was released.

Barbara's memorable effect in this second *Doctor* outing was actually disproportionate to her relatively fleeting screen time. When she returned in 1971 for *Carry On Henry*, however, her role as the King's mistress Bettina was central. Despite appearing only fifty-three minutes into the film, the character brings the film alive with her energy. For Barbara, this was her favourite film of the series. Not only was the script top-notch, but she enjoyed both the period costumes and the chance to show off her dancing skills in one of the regal court scenes. Her character's full name? Bettina Lady Bristol. Clearly, for the producers, that was a gag-gift that just kept giving.

Another in-joke popped out of her next film, *Carry On Matron*. The filmmakers were prone to referencing the actors' real-life goings-on (as Charles Hawtrey discovered when cast as an alcoholic mummy's boy in *Abroad*), and they had Barbara tell her love interest Cyril, played by Kenneth Cope, 'I don't fancy being a gangster's moll.' Any viewer with half an eye on Barbara's complicated personal life would have spotted the writer's mischief here.

If *Carry On Abroad* did little to stretch her – the storyline demanding her bikini went walkabout once again, plus an inevitable shower scene – *Carry On Girls* in 1973 demanded more of her. Not only did Barbara have to learn to ride a motorbike for the final scene, having assured the producers prior to filming that she already could, her character Hope Springs (!) had to participate in a scantily-clad fight sequence that sorely tested the film censors, demanding cuts before they would give the film a family-friendly certificate.

Like all her fellow Carry On stars, Barbara had a recurring dilemma – enjoying the popularity of the series (plus the job security that came with it) versus the chance to explore other creative avenues. Joan Littlewood, a champion of Barbara's great stage talent, once put it very harshly, telling her protégée, 'You're always playing it safe. I think you're afraid of the challenge. You just want the spotlight on you.' But for Tony Jordan, it's a little more complicated. As well as the ready-made family that came with the Carry On series, he believes Barbara's personality meant she wouldn't have been able to resist the offers to keep on making audiences laugh.

'She loved that people loved it. She loved something that all the people love, and they loved her for it. She was no snob. She loved being popular. She was pure showbiz.'

However, by the time the script for *Carry On Emmannuelle* arrived, even Barbara had had enough. She didn't 'walk out' on the production as the papers had it at the time, but she was clear she wanted no part of it, calling the script 'pathetic' and 'crude' in her memoir.

She was similarly resistant to offers to appear in *Carry On Columbus* in 1992, especially after she spoke to former castmate Bernard Bresslaw. He told her, '*Dick* was a good Carry On, and I loved doing it. I'd rather remember that as my last Carry On film.'

Barbara agreed, which meant that, like Bernard, she bowed out before the films tarnished her legacy. She made her final appearance in *Carry On Dick*, sharing her farewell to the series with Sid James and Hattie Jacques. Far away from her bikini-clutching target of male attention of Carry Ons gone by, Barbara's role of Harriett found her riding horses, holding up coaches and proving just as enthusiastic for a romp as her male counterparts, much to the horrified squeals of one of her targets, Kenneth Williams's Captain Desmond Fancey.

Although Barbara later turned up in *That's Carry On!* alongside Kenneth, her role as Harriett in the Turpin-inspired period romp would prove to be a solid turn on which to say goodbye to the series proper.

Like her fellow co-stars, Barbara was for a long time so strongly associated with her Carry On roles that she found her options for future work severely restricted, particularly as the films found new TV audiences and were constantly repeated on the box.

Peter Rogers admitted himself, 'It does typecast her, which is unfair to any artist, because she's so versatile.'

The offers never stopped coming in, but they didn't stretch. 1979 found her sharing the screen with Jon Pertwee's *Worzel Gummidge* and her old friend Una Stubbs's Aunt Sally. Barbara played Saucy Nancy, a ship's figurehead. From there, she took her own show *Carry On Barbara!* overseas, before appearing in Joe Orton's *Entertaining Mr Sloane*, directed by her great friend Kenneth Williams. There was also some pantomime, some summer seasons, but Barbara could have been forgiven for thinking her best days were behind her.

However, it turned out there was an equally significant second chapter to come. She had, a long time before, expressed her desire to be part of the original cast for *EastEnders*, but the producers at the time had been keen to avoid recruiting well-known actors. That all changed in 1994 after a chance conversation at a party between Barbara and her old friend Mike Reid. Not long after, Barbara made her Albert Square arrival in a role that fitted her like a glove.

As Peggy Mitchell, mother to Grant and Phil, doyenne of the Queen Vic, Barbara became one of the great British TV soap matriarchs. When she bellowed, 'Get out of my pub!' the nation applauded.

She appeared as Peggy from 1994 to 2003, then from 2005 to 2010, before a few more guest appearances and finally a proper farewell in 2016. Intense storylines over those years, including Peggy's breast cancer diagnosis, brought Barbara a whole new fanbase, earned her professional awards and reminded everyone she was far more than a bit of wiggling totty.

For Tony Jordan, Barbara's recognition was long overdue. '*EastEnders* restored the balance,' he tells me. 'People sounded surprised she could actually act, but they shouldn't have been. She always did that. That's who she was. Still, it repaired a lot of the damage, and meant people saw her for what she was, a brilliant actress.'

Despite this success, he considers it a huge shame that someone of Barbara's talents didn't get to enjoy the kind of choices afforded to her contemporary counterparts.

He explains:

Actors these days have a completely different set of options. Barbara's choices would have been reasonably limited, mostly theatre, a movie now and then, but no guarantees. Don't forget she'd had a BAFTA nomination for *Sparrows Can't Sing*. If that happened now, she'd be offered ten films a year. It's a different time.

By the time she departed the Square in 2016, she was long divorced from her second husband Stephen Hollings, and married for the final time to Scott Mitchell. He was by her side that year when she was made a Dame for services to charity and entertainment. By then, sadly, she had been diagnosed with Alzheimer's disease, and she and Scott channelled their efforts into raising funds for associated charities. Barbara remained a tireless campaigner, even turning up in Downing Street for the photographers with her smile as wide as ever.

She once said of her long career, 'I've been in this business since I was 13, and I love it with a passion.'

And she said of herself, 'I'm not a great singer, not a great actor, not a great dancer, I'm not a great-looking bird, but you put it all in a little melting pot and it works for me.'

Tony Jordan, who is clearly an admirer of Barbara the performer as much as Barbara the lady, believes her success was down to a far more heavyweight talent that was often overlooked. Of her appearances in the Carry On films, he reflects:

She grounded them. Everybody else was in a pantomime, doing their usual thing, and in the middle of it, Barbara was acting everybody off the screen. You believed her. She might have been an itsy, bitsy blonde but you believed that performance. When you think about the big characters in these movies, Sid James and Kenneth Williams weren't shrinking violets, but the one you remember is Barbara. She felt real.

Chat show hostess Mrs Merton once told Barbara with her characteristic bluntness, 'You're like a big film star but you're still as common as muck.'

Barbara laughed more loudly than anyone, before agreeing, 'I am. My mother used to get so upset about that. Sent me to the convent, elocution lessons, but still common.'

For Tony Jordan, such everyday charm is key to Barbara's bottomless appeal, and why he concedes that her greatest legacy will remain her contribution to Carry On:

> The warmth they still engender is enduring. She encapsulated our whole country for a period in time. She was all of us, it feels like one of ours was at the top table, one of us managed to make it to that world. We don't begrudge it. We celebrate it.

Barbara Windsor wrote in her memoir, 'I love the public's affection for me and I try very hard never to let them down. No matter how I'm feeling, I'll always bubble and give them the Barbara Windsor they want to see.'

I can personally attest to this. As a child, I went with my parents to see the Christmas pantomime at Richmond Theatre. Barbara was on principal-boy duty as Dick Whittington, and when she came on stage, she didn't just receive cheers from the crowd, but a proper standing ovation. Then later, she seemed to have an emotional wobble during a ballad, and the audience cheered wildly once again. I had no idea if this was normal pantomime behaviour or not. To my young ears, it was confusing but wonderful.

Forty years later, I read Barbara's memoir, which included her memories of that very same night. Ronnie Knight, still her husband then, had just been arrested for murder and arson. Earlier that morning, both her face and his had been splashed across the papers, with Ronnie snapped handcuffed to a copper. As she wrote in her book, she could barely face the public, let alone a pantomime audience, and was fearing boos or even an embarrassed silence when she walked out on stage. Instead, she was greeted by a standing ovation, which to her seemed to go on forever. 'Eventually I held up my hands and said, "Thank you ladies and gentlemen. But my name's Dick Whittington, and I've come to London to seek my fortune.'"

After the show, my family went backstage to meet our friend who was also in the cast. We found him in Barbara's dressing room, dishing out the hankies, doing his best to comfort her as she sat, her curly wig removed, her eyes dripping with tears. With a child's ignorance of any etiquette or the strained circumstances, I stood staring at her for a full minute until eventually, I asked, 'What's happened to your hair? It's different!'

The star of the show, with her errant husband freshly behind bars, her own face on the front of every national tabloid, facing huge pressure to keep going when she probably wanted only to curl up and hide from the world, smiled down at me, wiped her eyes and said, 'It's a wig, love. Nothing's real in this life. It's just a wig. Do you want to try it on?'

Tony Jordan is touched but not remotely surprised when I tell him this story.

'With most stars, the door would have been firmly closed with all of that going on,' he comments. 'But not Barbara. She just loved people.'

He pauses and it is clear he is remembering her fondly. 'How lovely that she did that. That's her to a tee.'

Chapter 16

Women

'*Mischief is a form of self-expression*'

Hattie Jacques in *Carry On Teacher*

The Carry On series has been a regular target for tomatoes thrown by writers and pundits over the years, with the films' treatment of women one of their most frequent topics of criticism. What is their beef?

Well, they claim the women's roles are limited to three types, all of them negative. Back in 2008, on the 50th anniversary of the beginning of the series, journalist Tanya Gold listed these as either stupid and beautiful, bossy and masculine, or ugly and bitter, with your typical Carry On female as depicted by Joan Sims invariably depicted as loveless and forlorn, driven to rage and fury by male indifference. It was no more generous a screen world for men, she wrote, pointing out how seldom they ended up with the women of their dreams, or if they did, only at a high personal cost. If you believed Gold's interpretation, nobody in Carry On was ever happy.

For sure, the comedy of the films demanded that the women, like their male counterparts, be shoehorned into stereotypes, whether they be dreamy sexpots or grim-faced battleaxes, totty or harridans. Ask anyone to describe the films' females, and they'll no doubt answer with mentions of Barbara Windsor's underwear flying off in *Camping*, or Hattie Jacques' sour-faced and sexually frustrated Matron.

Certainly, they and the films' other women have some terrible things happen to them on screen, from Babs being spied on in *Camping*, Joan Sims being all but stalked by Sid's character in *Loving*, to every woman in *Abroad* becoming the victim of Sid's Santa Cecilia Elixir, a local brew which enables him to see through their clothing. For the determinedly offended, Angela Douglas being turned into a mannequin for *Screaming!* only solidifies the sense that the women are on screen purely for the men's desires and kicks. And Joan Sims certainly doesn't always get a fair deal, from losing her husband to 'Tiffin Time' in *Khyber*, to being blasted by her husband Fred for encouraging Sid's attentions in *Convenience*. For my money, two of the worst lines in all the films are thrown at the ever-versatile Joan. In *Camping*, she's told off by her mother for being '33, not married. If that's not looking after yourself, I don't know what is'. Even worse is her treatment at the hands of Phil Silvers in *Follow That Camel*. She is at her alluring best, but has to compete for his affections with a harem, after he patronises and dismisses her in the same breath, 'I can't see, honey, will you get out of the way?' In one film after another, she represents that woman Tanya Gold described, a woman driven to rage by indifference. No wonder the critics aren't impressed.

However, and I'm glad there is one, this broad criticism of the films doesn't stand up to huge scrutiny. If we accept that the period in which the Carry Ons were made was one of great change in British society, as law, economics and attitudes struggled to catch up with women's flourishing sense of freedom, were these films really as bad as those critics would have us believe, or worse than real life around them? Let's go back to the beginning for a fresh appraisal.

For a start, all the female actresses I've spoken to who participated in the Carry On films have only good things to say about their time on set. Joking about money aside, Sally Geeson sums up a common mood of fond nostalgia, describing an atmosphere of 'total respect and equality. No one was starry or more famous'.

Valerie Leon, who appeared in six of the films, affirms this, dismissing any question of the male and female cast members being treated differently, 'I was treated very well. I saw no difference in my experience.'

As in all work places, the tone was set at the top. Director Gerald Thomas had three daughters at home, and a wife he adored. The word feminist wasn't bandied around in those days, but his daughter Deborah is in no doubt, 'He loved and respected women.' If Gerald created the atmosphere, it was an inclusive and charming one throughout.

As for what happened on screen, the good news is that the early titles, relying more on caper and less on bawdy innuendo, were delightfully respectful in their treatment of women, right from the beginning of *Carry On Sergeant*, where Bob Monkhouse's recruit Charlie wasn't lusting after any strange women, desperate only to spend time with his new bride Mary, played with smiling grace by Shirley Eaton. Leslie Phillips's blatant appreciation for Joan Sims in *Teacher* was admiring, harmless rather than lecherous. The bad news is that in those same early films, it was because the women's roles were so much smaller than the men's. I guess that was inevitable with so many of Norman Hudis's scripts focusing on institutions. *Sergeant* gave Hattie Jacques a tiny role as a military doctor, and the only reason a women's band featured in the final reel of the film was because Peter Rogers couldn't find any other military bands on the day.

The better news was that, from the off, Hattie Jacques ruled the show, bringing her unique grace and authority to each of those early roles, her indomitability softened for the first time in *Constable* by a gently blossoming romance with Sid's Watkins. Plus Norman gave her the sharpest put-down of the film, disguised as a question.

'Strange don't you think, that the only efficient rookie is a woman?'

Although everyone's lines got bawdier treatment with the arrival of Talbot Rothwell, he also gave women an agency unprecedented in the series. His first script, *Carry On Jack*, sees Juliet Mills disguise herself as a midshipman to sail away and find her lost love. And his very first Carry On release, *Cabby*, celebrates women as both attractive *and* taking control. Hattie is never finer than in her surprisingly rounded role of Peggy, an upset, devoted wife and equally an aspiring entrepreneur happy to take her husband on at his own game and set up her own taxi company, Glam Cabs. We see women using their brains to outwit their male rivals and send them to the wrong pick-up places, at the same time as teasing their feminine wiles to entice more customers to them. Underneath all the jokes and capers, Talbot Rothwell wrote a clearly feminist script, taking note of society where women were no longer content to be stuck at home, cooking their husbands' dinner. This was the eve of rapid cultural change. Sid's Charlie may have been the remnant of a 1950s man, but Hattie's Sadie was a 1960s woman, and it was Sadie we rooted for throughout.

As the films grew in popularity and the scripts got bawdier under Talbot's pen, so the Carry Ons increasingly met and exceeded fans' expectations. While this formula resulted in the golden age of the spoofs and period romps, it did mean that the women were more often reduced to playing either objects of men's desires, punctuated by Sid James's lecherous chuckle, or that most limiting of personae, the neglected woman. In *Don't Lose Your Head*, Joan Sims may have had the best line in the film, but she was reduced to grappling for the Black Fingernail's affections, just as she experienced in two of the era's greatest titles, *Cleo* and *Khyber*.

By now, the writers realised which actors would be likely saying which lines, and this was Joan's destined place in the firmament. Happily, *Cowboy* gave her a more central role, fabulously glamorous in her sequinned dress, but again she found herself a wronged woman, at one point even slapping Sid's Rumpo Kid for his impertinence. 'Haven't you forgotten, I'm your little ding dong?' He answered, 'I hate to say it, but your little ding has lost its dong.' Ouch!

By now, it was the turn of Angela Douglas to shine, the pretty blonde actress invited by Peter and Gerald to take the dynamic role of Annie Oakley. In our chat, Angela reveals Oakley levels of cool about accepting her first role for Carry On, remembering, 'They asked me, "Can you sing?" Of course, I told them. I couldn't. "Can you ride?" they asked. I'd never even seen a horse. But I'd been working since I was 13 or 14, and because of the arrogance of youth, nothing fazed me.'

This was the first of some great roles for Angela in the series, ones where she got to be glamorous, feisty and perhaps a little disingenuous when it came to how the men around were regarding her. She tells me herself, 'Anything smutty that got said around me would just run off, it didn't seem to register with any of my characters.'

This was most apparent in *Follow That Camel*, where her character Lady Jane Ponsonby upped and followed her lost love Bo West all the way to the Sahara. This involved a bizarre, long journey where a series of strange men 'assisted' this pretty lady travelling alone, much to her apparent surprise. As Lady Jane remembered afterward, 'Everybody was terribly kind. In fact, they couldn't do enough.' This was all a bit strange in the film, with definite hints of consensual capers. Angela laughs now at the idea, reminding me, 'Women of that generation weren't aware of some of the seedier side of life.' And she is certain about her role in the film, 'I was the ingénue. If it was vulgar, it didn't touch me.'

Someone else to get the very best out of Carry On was Valerie Leon. Having starred in Carry On, James Bond *and* Hammer Horror titles, this Glamazon can lay claim to being a one-woman totem of the three tallest pillars of the British film industry, and she appeared in six Carry

On titles in total. Her favourite role in the series was in *Jungle*, where she brought 007 levels of glamour to her role of Leda, the chief of the all-female Lubby-Dubby tribe from the Lost World of Aphrodisia. For a series always castigated as sexist, all too often it was the women who had to take control, here with Valerie and her tribe quite literally saving the skins of the men around them.

Valerie tells me, 'I liked having a part where I could be in charge. My costume was a tribute to Racquel Welch's in *A Million Years B.C.*, although hers might have been skimpier.'

I ask both Valerie and Angela if they ever felt exploited? 'Never,' says Angela. 'I was lucky with my parts.'

Valerie confirms:

I enjoyed the whole thing enormously. It changed my life. On the way to the studios one day, I went to fill my car with petrol but discovered I didn't have my purse when I went to pay, so they somehow took all the petrol back out of the car. The next day, all the newspapers were full of it – 'Val's big bust up at the garage' was one of the headlines, full of wonderful double entendres. I feel very blessed to have been part of it all.

Of her role in *Follow That Camel*, Anita Harris remembered in a BBC retrospective, 'I studied belly dancing from a girl who taught me how to roll my stomach. It was great fun.'

Amanda Barrie's title role in *Cleo* brought her only delight, too, it transpired, as she told an ITV documentary. 'I couldn't believe that I'd been asked to play Cleo,' she said. 'I was even on a stamp. To be expelled from three schools and then to be on a stamp. I am so delighted now.'

'Cleopatra, is she mustered?'
'I have heard a couple of stories.'

Whatever the critics of these films had to say about Carry On's treatment of women on screen, it seems these female stars never worried, only smiled, at the parts they played in what Amanda called 'a bubble of fun'.

The hospital titles in the series have long come in for specific accusations that their portrayals of female staff have done the real-life personnel of those institutions few favours through the decades since they appeared. Peter Rogers may have satisfied himself that nurses found the joke with the daffodil hilarious back in 1959, but many have complained since about his treatment of them on screen, from Barbara Windsor's over-sexualised portrayal in *Doctor*, to Hattie's frequent role of a harridan Matron, with her authority collapsing in the face of her own unreciprocated crush on surgeon Doctor Carver. As the lady famously besieged by patient Sid for a cuddle in *Doctor*, a pose captured in one of the most famous nurse-patient photographs of all time, actress Valerie Van Ost best summed up the typical Carry On nurse persona – 'lots of bright lipstick and a very nipped-in uniform, tucking up Sid in bed and telling him he's a naughty boy because he's smoking.'

This criticism overlooks many aspects of the four medical titles in the series. In *Nurse*, it was clear that Hattie's Matron and her female staff all had the last laugh over an overbearing patient, even if the hilarity of the daffodil remains lost to me. As novice nurse Sandra May, Barbara was a young woman enjoying her own appeal, blowing a kiss to a car mechanic on her way into work and happy to whip off her uniform for a spot of sunbathing. The fact that she was a nurse was kind of incidental, and I'm sure an institution as revered as the NHS can withstand such a character. In *Carry On Again Doctor*, where Barbara appeared wearing even less, she wasn't even playing a nurse, it was just that a bedazzled Jim Dale was standing next to her in his little white coat in all the publicity stills.

Possibly the most disturbing aspect of all the medical titles came with the notorious sexual harasser Dr Prodd, played by Terry Scott, prowling unchecked in the maternity hospital of *Carry On Matron*. This was turned into a comic caper when he unknowingly targeted his attentions on robber Cyril, dragged up as a nurse. While the harassment that followed was designed for laughs, it was clear that our sympathy was with the 'woman' played by Kenneth Cope, never the abuser.

As I've mentioned, Barbara Windsor's association with the whole Carry On series is remarkable considering how relatively few films she appeared in, and her bleached blonde, wiggly charm and promising giggle are all clearly contributory factors, especially when you factor in that keep-fit campsite scene.

She certainly had her share of being ogled, whether it was by Sid, Jim or a roll-call of passers-by, and her bare bottom frequently appeared.

One of the regular tropes of Carry On was that all regular male activity ceased when Barbara wiggled into view, and her giggle promised delights to make Raymond Chandler's bishop start choosing which window to kick. Seldom has a woman on screen been invited to react to so many saucy remarks made about her embonpoint. In *Doctor*, she even got in first, telling the admiring driver, 'What a lovely looking pear.' Of course, he happened to be eating a pear at the time.

As a result of this serial typecasting, fans have long perceived her as the physically sexy and sexual component of Carry On, but Barbara was actually short and pixie-like, miles away from the glacial beauty of Shirley Eaton and the vampish charms of Valerie Leon.

'Barbara's characters were always actually attractive because of her personality, free-spirited and game for anything,' comedy writer Meryl O'Rourke points out to me.

The films find Barbara laughing along to cheeky remarks where so many others may have tutted in disapproval, much like the real-life Barbara Windsor, and that's long been lost on people who just see her through Jim's besotted gaze, and hear Sid's lecherous laugh when she appears. 'She's a lot more than that,' says O'Rourke. 'We often overlook how independent her characters were too, young women who knew their own minds.'

Even as the ringleader of Chayste Place's schoolgirls in *Camping*, she may squirm and wriggle, but she never surrenders. Later, in *Carry On Again Doctor*, Jim Dale's Doctor Nookey discovers this when he tends to her as Goldie Locks with a very non-Hippocratic attitude, until she whacks him over the head and tells him, 'The bone has replaced the boobs.'

Later on in the same film, Goldie Locks refuses to marry the good doctor because she wants to pursue her career. In fact, none of the male characters ever succeeds in controlling her on screen, and, as a result, the actress ultimately evades any sexual stereotypes fans may be tempted to attach to her. Much like her underwear on that cold muddy campsite, Barbara Windsor cannot be pinned down.

If you do come across anybody still not convinced that the films gave their female characters a fair deal, please sit them down and make them watch *Carry On Girls*, the story of a group of women's libbers conspiring to prevent a beauty contest being held in their seaside hometown. As ever,

Peter and Gerald had their noses to the breeze of social change. The all-female publisher Virago had been launched, and the Miss World pageant had been disrupted in 1970 by protestors. As far as the typical Carry On fan would have been concerned, women's lib wasn't necessarily something for good, instead a disruptive force that should probably be frowned upon and contained.

This 1973 title is notable for being the first Carry On to feature neither Kenneth nor Charles, and this made for a palpable lack of campness in the film as a result. Instead, there was a far more risqué treatment of familiar topics than previously, with more nudity and openly sexual jokes than in previous films, and even a fight sequence between bikini-clad characters Barbara and Margaret, blatantly designed to titillate and give the audience what it wanted.

But while critics might view *Girls* as proof that the patriarchy was still flying high in the Carry On world, in fact, there was a lot more going on for those who chose to look. As Meryl O'Rourke takes pains to map out for me, the male characters in this film are struggling for any sense of self, while of an astonishing seven female characters in *Girls*, all conceived as speaking leads, each represents a different notch on the spectrum of feminism. 'At the time, there was a huge movement of sex positivity,' she tells me, 'Erica Jong's *Fear of Flying* was published, and women taking charge of their sexuality was very much 'in'. *Girls* was one of the films blowing the doors off.'

June Whitfield's Augusta Prodworthy is the leader of the protestors, pumping her fist and turning objectification on its end by goosing Peter Butterworth's bumbling Admiral.

The actress herself didn't share her character's hunger for change, with June remembering, 'I felt liberated anyway. I didn't feel I had to go about burning my bra or something.'

Beside her is Patricia Franklin as Rosemary, saying little but standing out as arguably Carry On's only representation of camp-free gender fluidity.

Patsy Rowlands plays Mildred Bumble, who joins the protestors because of her harsh treatment at the hands of her husband, the Mayor. When they set about burning her bra and setting fire to the office, in typical Carry On style, this involves the fire engine being launched by her husband and when it drives off, off too go his trousers. 'How satisfying on a deeper level,' O'Rourke reflects. 'Her joining the group emasculates him, literally de-trousers him.'

In the middle of it all is Joan Sims's Connie Philpotts, not bothered by the contest, just trying to run a hotel and hoping people will come, stay and spend their money, while she keeps a close eye on her partner, Sid Fiddler.

It was Valerie Leon's sixth and final Carry On outing, as Paula Perkins, a plain-Jane secretary whose dramatic makeover makes her feel beautiful for the first time in her life. When I tell Valerie her dowdy bespectacled look during the first half of the film was fooling no one, she laughs. 'They were my glasses from when I worked at Harrods. Model's own.'

Margaret Nolan is the much shallower, vindictive beauty queen Dawn Brakes, happy to steal someone else's bikini, and forcing Augusta's son Larry to photograph her naked against his will.

A year before he became the nation's most notorious window cleaner, Robin Askwith made his only Carry On appearance as Larry, and remembered his experience on set as the chance to work with 'some of the best comic talent in the country'. His role is interesting, though. Just as his caper-crazed window cleaner Timmy Lea has been regarded more recently as a beta male, constantly at the mercy of more assertive females, the same could be said for many a Carry On male , often unsure of self, often reduced to wearing a dress or, like Mayor Bumble, even de-trousered.

Finally, there is Barbara's Hope Springs who, when she isn't tussling in a bikini, is boyish, feisty, riding her own motorbike. When her admirer Sid offers to rig the competition for her, she tells him, 'I'll win this on my own or I won't do it.'

And the film also poses the eternal question: Should the act of women voluntarily taking their clothes off be deemed objectifying, or empowering? As O'Rourke reflects, 'It's an old debate, but one which continues to this day. With *Girls*, the Carry On team was happy to participate in it.'

Of course, with later titles *Carry On England* and *Emmannuelle*, with their brazenness and gratuitous boob-age, all bets were off. Any remaining caution was thrown to the wind, with both films lacking the charm of the saucy giggle behind the hand. By then, of course, the series' treatment of women wasn't a singular challenge, but symptomatic of a wider problem with the films.

Throughout the two decades before, though, they were full of interesting, strong females, constantly smarter than their men-folk and always happy to pull the strings. When they were treated badly, it was often done expressly to show how awful the men were, whether they were being rude, cheeky or duplicitous, and the women invariably came off better. *Camel's* harem scene may have had Phil Silvers pushing Joan Sims out of the way, but he and the other men emerged as ungainly, full of lustful desires but unable to manage themselves, their wishes foiled by their own clumsiness.

When Hattie was made out to be a harridan in her role of Matron, it was quite clear she didn't care, because she was ultimately in charge, and her intrinsic authority made it authentic.

In fact, Hattie, Barbara, June and Joan were all fine actresses who took pride in creating the characters they did, and what a range it was – from young, romance-hungry, chaste and unchaste girls to older women full of sport and smiles, Lady Ruff-Diamond happy to betray the Empire for a turn with the Khasi, Matron protecting her nurses from Doctor Prodd, Augusta Prodworthy asking quite reasonably, 'Why isn't there a female public toilet?' and Nurse Sandra May admiring that lovely looking pear.

As, decades later, Peter Rogers put it bluntly, 'Offensive to women? We make a fuss of them.'

Chapter 17

Bum Notes

'They've sent the wrong film! Turn it off!'

Kenneth Williams in *Carry On England*

By the mid-1970s, nobody could say Peter Rogers hadn't pulled off a most impressive feat in turning a one-off budget big-screen comedy into a globally recognised film franchise lasting almost two decades. During a time of widespread uncertainty for most British independent producers, he succeeded in making one film after another that proved profitable in a market competing against both big screen American blockbusters and small screen offerings.

His coffers were full, not just from repeat fees coming in from all over the world, but from a catalogue of compendium TV programmes and also live stage shows featuring many of the core cast. These familiar faces had all become legends in their own niche universe, but the times were once again a-changing. As early as *Carry On Abroad* in 1972, actor Hugh Futcher remembers the chat among the cast often coming back to each of them pondering the same subject, 'How much longer do you think we've got?'

The faces at Pinewood were changing too. Talbot Rothwell had finally worn himself out of words and left the series in 1974 after *Carry On Dick*, also the swansong of Sid, Barbara and Hattie.

Even without the fuel of Sid's chuckle, Babs' giggle or Hattie's hauteur, the series continued, but it had its work cut out competing with the bigger budgets of American movies like *Jaws* and *Star Wars*, and locally, the more brazen entertainment of the era. By 1970, theatre-goers were pouring into the West End for the sex-filled sketches and total nudity of *Oh! Calcutta!* By 1976, the Sex Pistols had dropped the 'f-word' on live television. On the big screen, up against the likes of *Confessions of a Window Cleaner* and his equally fruity successors, any Carry On film started to feel quaint and outdated in comparison.

For a short while, they did their best to keep up. In the absence of Talbot's bottomless well of clever jokes, the style of the films got broader and far less innocent, as writers Dave Freeman, David Pursall and Jack Seddon, then Lance Peters took up the script baton for *Carry On Behind, England* and finally *Emmannuelle*.

1976's *Carry On England*, a story about a wartime mixed-sex battery unit, a script converted from an episode originally written for TV that became essentially a bawdy reworking of *Carry On Sergeant*, proved a challenge from the start. With the British film industry going through a dip, Carry On's paymasters at Rank were only prepared to put up half the budget for the film, requiring Peter and Gerald to go elsewhere. After various investors put a toe in and then firmly out of the water – the band Pink Floyd among those who decided ultimately not to participate – the filmmakers ended up coming up with the remaining money themselves, while digging deep into their contacts books to borrow props, costumes, even guns, to keep everything as economical as possible.

'Six pence for everyone you shoot down – two bob if it's a German!'

Joan Sims, Peter Butterworth, Kenneth Connor and Jack Douglas were the Carry On regulars who did line up for duty, and Windsor Davies returned for his second appearance (following *Behind*), transparently reprising his Sergeant-Major character from the TV sitcom *It Ain't Half Hot Mum*. Alongside them were a bunch of new faces equally familiar from TV shows, names like Patrick Mower and Melvyn Hayes. George Layton, by then a TV star in the *Doctor* series, reflected on his tiny role, also as a doctor, in *Behind*:

> It was transparently an idea to garner some more fans who already knew me from *Doctor in the House*. They knew I'd look familiar to people in a white coat, so that's what they went for. It was a morning's work for me, but Gerald Thomas was extremely pleasant, I got to be in a Carry On film and they got to say I was in it.

Most memorably, perhaps, after all those teasing displays from Barbara in previous films, *England* was actually the first Carry On to feature topless girls, obeying to the letter the instruction, 'They were to come wearing trousers and that is all.' It was inevitable, really, and at least with their battle with the Censor over the amount of nudity, Peter and Gerald could reassure themselves that some things never changed.

'*That man, he's wearing lipstick.*'
'*Lipstick, sir?*'
'*Yes.*'
'*Where?*'
'*On his face! Where do you think?*'

Despite all this flesh, or perhaps because of it, and despite the jaw-dropping £250,000 production budget that must have brought a tear to Peter's eye, *England* was a commercial dud. Looking back, perhaps the film was doomed from the outset. Poignantly, the very first pre-production meeting took place on the morning of Monday 26 April 1976 and just hours later that evening, the great stalwart of the entire series Sid James died on stage in Sunderland. Everyone on the team was shocked and grief-stricken but pressed on and succeeded in delivering the film as ever, on time and within budget. I wonder, though, if the sadness of Sid's passing didn't somehow make heavier the already weighed-down script, thwart the lightness of touch for which the cast and crew were so celebrated, just as it would certainly have affected England's cinema audiences, watching the latest Carry On film a few months later, still ready to laugh but in the knowledge that their beloved chuckling totem would never be returning.

England is perhaps the Carry On film most notable for what it was not. With its small story, it served as a sort of bookend to the very first *Carry On Sergeant* all those years before, as though the golden age of the films had never happened, but it lacked the pluck, warmth and camaraderie of its predecessor. Made in 1976 but set in the wartime, it wasn't a classic period romp like so many of the series' more successful titles, but nor was it a contemporary portrait of modern society, despite all those bosoms. In fact, against the background of a wartime army barracks, those bosoms just looked incongruous. What it lacked, primarily, was the sweetness of so many of the previous films.

Cultural historian Matthew Sweet goes further, telling me sadly:

Carry On England could qualify as the most depressing film ever made. I remember staying up late to watch it, but all the scatological jokes in it seemed a real error of taste even to my young ears, and I found the presence of Patrick Mower somehow offensive, too confident compared with the likes of Jim Dale.

You felt that a generation was passing, and the next one had none of the charm of the previous one.

One of *England*'s most heartbreaking sights of all is that of Joan Sims properly shoe-horned into a soldier's uniform, relegated to the back row with a few lines, while the buxom beauties bared their breasts out front. Joan was customarily honest about how depressing even she found this spectacle, saying later, 'There was a decline in yours truly. That big face and... bursting out of that uniform. I thought, Go home and put your feet up, love.'

In the latter years of the series, all bets were off when it came to the treatment of women. But although the bare breasts of the female troops are on gratuitous and blatant display in *Carry On England*, they are no more over-egged than the film's repeated humiliations of Kenneth Connor's Captain S. Melly, losing his uniform mid-march, disappearing into the bosom of a well-endowed female private's parts, using a soap that inevitably turned his whole body bright blue and, just when all else is lost, stepping in shit, twice. Subtle, this isn't, and the boobs on show are no gaudier than any other aspect of the story. The most interesting part of the film is the male audience's reaction to an accidentally booked female stripper: by turn confused, disapproving, lecherous but ultimately unable. At least Peter Rogers and his team proved to the end to be a group of equal opportunity lampoonists.

If *England* was the most depressing film ever made, *Carry On Emmannuelle* was possibly the most misjudged, or as film critic Derek Malcolm put it, 'misspelt as well as misconceived'. Again struggling to find a distributor, Peter Rogers should perhaps have heeded the signs that he was fighting a losing battle, both against rival film franchises and also the success of his own cinematic past.

The story of the bored ambassador's wife of the title, played by Suzanne Danielle, intent on pursuing carnal pleasure in the absence of attention from her husband, played inexplicably by a still-shrieking Kenneth Williams, was intended to spoof yet another genre, to lampoon the kind of soft erotica that had been filling cinemas, and also compete with the popular X-rated films of the time, particularly the *Confessions* series that was by now onto its fourth big screen outing.

Kenneth only agreed to take part after he received a pay rise, but his friend Barbara Windsor could not be persuaded. When she received the script for the film, the producers no doubt hoping an appearance by her would entice old fans, she revealed, 'I sat and wept buckets. The opening scene was so vulgar and nasty.'

'You for coffee?'
'No thanks, I'm staying here.'

Barbara wasn't wrong. The film begins with sex-crazed Emmannuelle grabbing the knee of an air steward, before relieving the boredom of her flight on Concorde by seducing another passenger. This is followed by her making a racist joke at the airport that has not aged well, and continues with references to 'Nelson's Column' and even 'the closet queen of Camden Town'.

'It was all an attempt to keep up with the other racist, sexist comedy of the time,' explains Sweet. 'Their humour had always depended on the limitations of what they could say and somehow get away with, while the 1970s allowed everything to be a lot looser, and it didn't play to their strengths.'

The delights of Talbot Rothwell's double entendres had given way to the sordidness of the single entendre, with nothing left for the audience to do. After so many films in the series had danced delightedly between what British people privately desired and what they were publicly allowed to get away with, navigating the gap with sly reference and cheeky innuendo, *Emmannuelle* was brazen and lecherous, and the fact that our heroine was a woman made it no more appealing – appearing in public without her clothes, seducing a fellow passenger on Concorde... it was all a far cry from, 'I dreamt about you last night, nurse.' 'Did you?' 'No, you wouldn't let me.'

Inevitably, through clinging to the old form of the series – recruiting Kenneth, Joan, Peter Butterworth and setting up a catalogue of loosely joined scenes where Emmannuelle and her servants each recounted their most notable erotic encounter – while trying to accommodate the more blatant sexual mores of the decade, the team were left falling between stools and looking, at best, a bit old-fashioned and, at worst, like a bunch of ageing lechers.

'Is it Starsky and Hutch?'
'If you ask me, it's more like Starkers and Crutch!'

As it was, with its London locations and increased production costs, *Emmannuelle* ended up being the most expensive of all the films, but struggled to recoup the budget as critics queued up to condemn it and audiences stayed away. Peter Rogers had always said once the films stopped making money, he'd stop making them, and finally, in 1978, it happened. *Emmannuelle* was the last in the series for over a decade.

If they were honest, the film's lacklustre reception surprised no one, least of all its makers. Gerald Thomas's daughter Deborah remembers his sanguine attitude at the time:

> He saw the writing was on the wall. They had been completely of their time up to that point, and he'd always enjoyed the double entendres that had gone before. I don't think he ever wanted them to get into those realms of crossing the line and being smutty, but comedy was moving on.

So it proved, as *Emmannuelle* went against all the popular tropes of everything that had made Carry On so successful with the vamp of the title failing to protect her spoils in the tradition of every female character who'd gone before her, but instead aggressively foisting them on pretty much any passing male bystander.

While this may have reflected real life at the time, in Carry On's fictional universe, it was an extraordinary switch of sensibilities, summed up by one of the heroine's confused sweethearts asking her, 'Why me, when you could have Tom, Dick or Harry?'

After years of Carry On's cosy, cheeky gags, grounded in music hall familiarity harking back to Victorian days, but brought up to date by Norman Hudis and later Talbot Rothwell's intrinsic understanding of society around them, brought to life by masters of their craft with a light, comedic touch ... Suzanne Danielle's answer was, 'I don't want Tom or Harry.' And with that, the series was done.

This meant that, sadly, *Carry On Emmannuelle* will forever be marked as the final title in the series proper (yes, I know, a mercifully short postscript is still to come). The team really should have signed off with *Carry On Dick*, or arguably earlier. As it was, with this sub-standard romp, they went out with a whimper, not a bang.

Chapter 18

A New World Best Left Undiscovered

'My goodness, you don't think they'll eat me whole?'

Sara Crowe in *Carry On Columbus*

'No one sets out to write a bad script.'

Norman Hudis reported that one of his producers in Hollywood once told me this, and it makes a lot of sense, despite how many dozens of films over the years might lead us to believe the contrary. I do believe it's worth bearing this compassionate comment in mind as we embark on this penultimate chapter, a quick investigation into the making of *Carry On Columbus*.

We won't spend too long on this title, both for its sake and for ours. What I think makes it worthy of a brief inspection at least, is to chart the intentions with which it was made, consider why it failed so miserably and therefore what light it sheds on how its predecessors triumphed so much more spectacularly.

For nearly a decade-and-a-half, Carry On had lain dormant, sleeping in the corner of the British film industry like a giant tabby cat, still bringing in deep buckets of royalties for those lucky few on the receiving end thanks to endless re-runs on TV all over the world, but creatively put out to pasture. Some of the series' biggest stars had died – Sid in 1976, Peter Butterworth in 1979, Hattie in 1980. There had been dozens of ideas for new Carry On titles mooted through the years. The popularity of Australian soap opera *Neighbours* on TV inspired talk of 'Carry On Down Under' but it didn't get off the ground. 'Carry On Dallas' contained the cracking in-joke of the Screwing family at its centre, but that never happened either. In 1988 came the announcement of 'Carry On Again Nurse', its script to be penned by Norman Hudis, but plans came to an abrupt halt with the death of Kenneth Williams in April 1988, and then Charles Hawtrey died six months later. Nothing else happened. But in 1992 came a fresh stirring...

As Peter Rogers described it in his memoir, the Carry On team were simply approached by a bunch of financial people to make *Columbus*, and to him, it seemed like a good idea. The fact was that while Peter had made plenty of money from the TV compilation series and other royalties – continuing to fall in the marmalade as Barbara described it – he remained ever-hungry for a return to the big screen. When comedy producer John Goldstone, a veteran filmmaker with *Monty Python* titles plus *The Rocky Horror Picture Show* to his name, came knocking and offered Peter a fresh pie to put his finger in, he received a warm reception from our man at Pinewood. Peter would be given the title of Executive Producer on the next film in the series, and it would be called *Carry On Columbus*.

Looking back, it is understandable just how attractive this looked on paper to all concerned. Two other far more serious films were being made at the same time to celebrate the 500th anniversary of Christopher Columbus's arrival on American soil, and there appeared a natural gap in the market for a similarly colourful but comedic offering. The anniversary was a big deal in the UK but even more so in the US. With a good wind, the film might have even enjoyed the same trans-Atlantic success as *Carry On Nurse* three decades before.

'I'm off to Italy next week. Michelangelo wants to do me up on the ceiling.'
'Well, you mind you hang on to something while you're up there.'

Accordingly, the wheels were set in motion, with Gerald Thomas signing on once again to direct. His daughter Deborah remembers how he was persuaded:

> They kind of convinced him it would work, and he thought it just might with a new generation. He was very happy about the prospect of working with a set of brand new, younger people, all individual comedians really good at what they did, and he was all for encouraging new talent and giving them a chance. So he said, 'Well, let's give it a go.'

The responsibility for the script went to Carry On regular Dave Freeman, with help from John Antrobus, the same writer who'd almost written *Carry On Sergeant* all those years before. Later on, Dave revealed the pressure he felt to turn the pages in time to meet the proposed release date of 4 July in the USA, and hindsight reflects that the whole process became a bit rushed. With that same benefit of looking back on the past, Norman Hudis recorded his belief that 'Americans would not look tolerantly on foreigners' comedic treatment of their country's hallowed discoverer'. (This was thirty years before statues of Columbus became regularly defaced in 2020, and one even thrown in a nearby lake after anti-slavery protests. Times still do change.)

At the time, however, *Columbus* offered all the potential for everything that had made Carry On great – an epic, colourful romp, a worthy successor to the series' golden age of mock-heroic period drama, built around the central tale of Christopher's odyssey to the Indies by sea with colour guaranteed by his patrons of the Spanish court, his boatsmen and women, and the natives at his landing.

'We've just had a leak in the hold.'
'Well, next time do it over the side.'

The cast, too, offered a comforting mix of old and new faces. While the financiers were keen for up-to-date TV names instead of a roll call of Carry On familiars, this became a list of comedians rather than comedic actors, and Peter Rogers well knew the difference.

The originals who did make the cut included Leslie Phillips, Bernard Cribbins, June Whitfield and Jack Douglas. In the title role was Jim Dale, returning to Carry On after an absence of twenty-three years. He remembered, 'I did it as a favour to Gerry Thomas, but it was also a sort of trip down memory lane, hoping to capture what the old Carry On films had been about.'

Just as distinguished was the number of series veterans who rejected the offer to take part. Kenneth Connor said no, explaining, 'I want to be remembered as a Carry On star, not a Carry On bit-player,' which seems fair enough. Barbara Windsor was more incensed by the script. She later revealed, 'To me, Carry On humour is the celluloid equivalent of a McGill postcard, naughty but nice with rude double entendres. *Columbus*, on the other hand, was just plain obscene.'

She continued. 'It was a bad *Confessions* film, crude, awful. I read it properly and wished I hadn't. I went out and got rat-arsed because I was very, very sad.' She conferred with Bernard Bresslaw and Joan Sims, who both felt the same and said no, preferring to keep their Carry On legacy intact – which, when you consider Joan had appeared in *England*, says quite a lot.

Frankie Howerd was another absence – sadly, he had been scheduled to appear as the King of Spain in the film, but collapsed and died a week before filming began. After Bernard Bresslaw turned it down, the role went to Leslie Phillips who reflected years later, 'I had to come back.'

It was a credit to the enduring power of Carry On just how many top-tier stars of the day agreed to take part. Rik Mayall gave his Sultan Abdul a tone and style redolent of Miranda Richardson's Queenie in *Blackadder*. Richard Wilson, Maureen Lipman, Alexei Sayle, Nigel Planer, Tony Slattery, Martin Clunes and Sara Crowe were among those who came on board. Jon Pertwee, returning for his fourth Carry On film in thirty years, revealed that he'd thought he was being offered a cameo in one of the other Columbus films, starring Gérard Depardieu, an actor he much admired. Only when his script arrived did he realise he was actually booked for another Carry On caper.

Julian Clary was a natural choice to fill the camp gap left by both Kenneth and Charles. For the most part, as Don Juan Diego, prison warden turned shipman, he channelled Charles, offering campness without arrogance or disdain, as well as occasionally delivering Kenneth-like waspishness when the occasion demanded. He even got to say 'Oh hello!' in a clear nod to former Hawtrey glories. I think it's fair to say Julian did a lot of the heavy lifting for this film, and his contribution was rightly one of the few later praised by critics.

'Could do with something hot inside me.'

Shooting took place, at Pinewood naturally, between April and May 1992, with the location work taking Bernard Cribbins back to his old stomping ground of Frensham Ponds, where he'd filmed *Carry On Jack* almost three decades before.

The comedians who took part were from the alternative crowd who flourished during the late 1980s and 1990s, and they performed in a very different style from the Carry On regulars. Jim remembered of his time on the set of *Columbus*, 'They all had their little in-jokes and this time it was members of the Carry On team who felt like outsiders when they joined them.'

One person who was happy to be there was Marc Sinden, who was appearing in a West End play at the same time, but jumped at the chance when he was offered a small role by Peter. Marc tells me:

> The money was pathetic, I earned more doing the play than for the whole film. But it was the honour of being in a Carry On film, and it was a ball. It was a great set to be on, and of course to work for Gerald Thomas was tremendous.

Equally happy was Julian, who said years later, 'I had a lovely time. We'd go to Pinewood. To be in those studios, working with those people. We had such a laugh.'

For Gerald Thomas's daughter Deborah, it was wonderful to see her father swing back into action. 'I was able to bring my own son Tom to the set, and all the young, new talent were very kind and friendly, and they worked very hard too. But I know working with Jim Dale and Bernard Cribbins again, as well as some of the old production team, made my father very happy.'

That happiness lasted all the way through filming, and until the cast and crew were in their seats for a preview screening. Julian remembered that night, 'Everyone was laughing away for the first ten minutes and then the laughter kind of died down. It wasn't terribly good. The first twenty minutes were all right, it was just a bit dated by then. But I'll never regret doing it.'

Sure enough, *Columbus* was panned by critics, and continues to be to this day. Some Carry On purists don't even believe it belongs in the canon and, rights issues aside, it remains a yawning absence in the complete box set of the films. There's no doubt it was a stinker, but it actually didn't flop at the box office quite as terribly as critics like to remember. In fact, it made more money – relatively speaking – than those other two, far more serious, Columbus-themed films that came out that year, due to its customary meagre budget being dwarfed by both of theirs.

Just why did it fare so badly? After all, it looked like a Carry On film, it was directed by Gerald Thomas, written by Dave Freeman, it starred Jim Dale, it was made for a small budget, it wasn't a bad story, the narrative was robust and energetic just like *Follow That Camel*, *Khyber* or its most similar predecessor, *Carry On Jack*. There is even some familiar racial stereotyping, when Columbus and his crew finally encounter the Native Americans on their home soil, bad now but no worse than the mutual misunderstanding enjoyed in so many previous Carry On inter-cultural encounters. It definitely has all the requisite DNA of the bygone series. Had this film been made back in 1972, it may well have slipped under the radar as no classic but a respectable addition to the canon.

Like many of the best films of the series, *Columbus* has a strong real-life narrative on which to hang familiar tropes – switching from the nonsense of royal court to humble shopkeepers then back to the Spanish Inquisition before finally setting sail on the high seas, sending a beautiful woman to infiltrate a bunch of bumbling but ultimately well-meaning men, all business as usual, plus some sneaky satire thrown in about exploitative trading practices and even a cheeky aside about the Second Amendment.

'*Everyone has the right to carry a gun, if he can afford one.*'

Many of the gags are Carry On-worthy. 'We just had a leak in the hold.' 'Well, next time do it over the side…' and so on. In fact, one of the very best lines of the entire series can be heard in idle chat during *Columbus*. Faced with the prospect of sharks, Sara Crowe's Fatima asks, 'You mean, the sharks won't eat me whole?' 'Oh no, I'm told they spit that bit out first,' answers Jack Douglas's Marco the Cereal Killer. Timeless.

Clearly, all of this on paper wasn't enough for the film to earn the fondness still held by so many for its predecessors. For me, watching it again now, it feels like a bad pantomime, with the actors quite enjoying the silly lines, even occasionally smiling at each other as they say them. It all feels like a bit of an in-joke, the opposite of the complete fictional universe that the previous regulars like Joan, Sid and Charles had committed to creating.

The one or two good lines that jump out don't do enough, according to Matthew Sweet at least, to counter the evident lack of warmth on screen:

The people we want to see aren't there. It seemed very strange that all of these people who'd made their careers pushing against this kind of humour, like Rik Mayall and Alexei Sayle, were suddenly there. I don't believe they had a fondness for the material, I just don't buy it.

As for so many critics, Julian Clary is the noble exception for Sweet. 'That was the tradition of humour he worked in, which is why he excels in pantomime. The others were too good in a way, either at being comedians or being proper actors like Maureen Lipman.'

Even for June Whitfield who was in it as the Spanish Queen, the absence of so many familiar faces was also the problem. 'So many of the originals were missing. Maybe you couldn't do the Carry Ons without that particular group,' she said afterwards. 'They were so much a part of it, and associated with it, when none of them were there, they thought, Well, this isn't a Carry On.'

She added, 'There was something a bit strange about it. Maybe it should have been called Carry Off Columbus.'

Jack Douglas, the sole conduit from the previous films to *Columbus*, may have scored the finest line of the whole film, but even that didn't stop him drawing a subconscious veil over the whole exercise, and this from an actor who'd appeared in *Carry On England*! 'I've shut that picture out completely,' he said later. '*Columbus* doesn't exist as far as I'm concerned. If you asked me what was my funniest gag in the picture, I couldn't tell you.' That's a shame, because it was a corker, Jack.

Perhaps the film wasn't the problem. In sensibilities, style and tone, it hadn't changed, but it turned out we had. A glance at the UK box office for 1992 reveals a top ten list that included titles like *Beauty and the Beast*, *Basic Instinct*, *Star Trek VI*, *Patriot Games* and *Wayne's World*. Up against this contemporary fare, *Carry On Columbus* must have felt like an over-convoluted celluloid pantomime.

Ultimately, was *Carry On Columbus* worth doing? Bernard Bresslaw would say not. The thoughtful actor commented at the time, 'It seems to me that to make a Carry On without some of the essential cardinal people was a mistake. It's just to me a mistake to try to recapture that. It's much better to leave us with the memories we have.'

No small thing, though, is the joy making the film brought director Gerald Thomas. Leslie Phillips felt this keenly, reflecting years later on his participation in the beleaguered film, 'I had no idea it was a very important decision because it was the last film Gerry made.'

Sure enough, Gerald died the following year leaving behind a huge and impressive body of work. His daughter Deborah reflects today that he would be amazed that people still continue to enjoy his films. She says sadly, 'You think about the contribution to our nation, our heritage, our comedy. I don't think he ever fully realised what that contribution was, and I'd have loved him to have had the satisfaction of knowing that.'

As far as her father's legacy is concerned, the success or otherwise of his final film is of no consequence. 'I know it got panned, but for the happiness it gave him, I was pleased they did it.'

After all, to the end, he was a man to whom surely a great debt of pleasure was surely owed.

Less personally, the reception for the film was sound proof, if such a thing were needed, that the idea of a reunion is always better than the real thing. If anything, *Columbus* only sealed fans' affection for the original films and it certainly showed how much their success depended on the quality of the script and of the unique cast, those players we will forever associate with the series – Kenneth Williams, Sid James, Barbara Windsor, Joan Sims and all the other integral players. It is them we remember, and it is them we will always want to see.

Chapter 19

Where Are We Now?

'It's not historical, but it's certainly hysterical.'

The trailer for *Carry On Dick*

Pinewood 2004, and Peter Rogers was still holding court as the elder statesman of the studios he had done so much to put on the map. On this particular day, it was only right that he should, as he was marking his 90th birthday with a huge party for friends, family and Carry On alumni great and good. Actor Hugh Futcher remembers sitting down with Jack Douglas that day at one of the many lunch tables laid on for the great occasion. The talk, as ever, was of Carry On, both of pleasures in the past and possibilities in the future. Hugh recounts, 'At that do, Jack asked me, "Has Peter said anything to you?" He told me Peter had given him an assurance that he'd be in the next one. I just said, "Congratulations." But of course it never happened.'

Valerie Leon remembers that same occasion, when all the talk was about a new Carry On film, something she'd been publicly pooh-poohing. It seems, just as Peter had done with Barbara and her marmalade all those years before on the set of *Camping*, even now he was determined to have the last word. 'Peter stood up and told the assembled crowd, "Despite what Valerie Leon thinks, there will be another Carry On film."' She recalled to me, 'Well, of course I just wanted to sink into the floor.'

It's to the credit of Peter's optimistic spirit that he continued to dream of his next Carry On film – despite the fact that, following *Columbus*'s expensive voyage back in 1992, nobody had appeared willing to throw any more money his way, and despite his valiant but futile attempts to produce more scripts, including the ever bandied about title of 'Carry On Again Nurse'.

Norman Hudis, back on scriptwriting duty for the mooted Nurse reboot, reported later that the powers that be had decreed the estimated budget of £1.5m to be too excessive for 'such a parochial subject'. He pointed out that there appeared to be a market for other similarly small topics, such as *Four Weddings and a Funeral*, and *The Long Good Friday*, also what he termed 'introspective movies about intellectuals practising joyless adultery in Hampstead'. That sounds like a perfectly sound setting for yet more Carry On business, but clearly appetites had changed. Nevertheless the chatter of a new film never really went away, nor has it until now.

If, for many Carry On fans, the prospect of a brand new title has long felt like a safe topic for chat on an otherwise slow news day, for at least two people, the prospect of a brand new film is a lot more than an idle pipe dream, in fact it is an actual work in progress.

Brian Baker and his colleague Nigel Gordon-Stewart are two affable gentlemen whose association with Peter Rogers and the Carry On films dates from the early 2000s. Both were based at Pinewood and had previously teamed up with each other when Nigel was working with Gerry Anderson of *Thunderbirds* on a new project in which Brian had successfully invested.

Meanwhile, Peter was long past the age of retirement but, solitary save his beloved dogs after the deaths of business partner Gerald Thomas and wife Betty, continuing to make daily visits to his office at Pinewood before taking his place at his customary table in the lunch restaurant, where he was greeted and feted as the studios' elder statesman that he was.

Aged 94 in 2008, the year before he died, Peter told journalist Helen James that, despite keeping himself busy writing novels, he still came to work every single morning, 'Yes, got nowhere else to go.'

Marc Sinden remembers how much his godfather enjoyed the respect in which he continued to be held at Pinewood, even down to his parking space right by the front door. 'That whole place was his second home. After Betty died it was the nearest he had to a family.'

By Nigel's own description, he and Brian have always been a pair of 'wannabe film moguls, with what we lack in ability and knowledge, we make up for with energy and enthusiasm, charm, flair and derring-do'. When I ask him if this is a case of 'faking it to make it', he agrees. 'Exactly, just as for the entire film industry from top to bottom.' You get the picture – a couple of upbeat cowboys keen to make a buck and have some fun while they're doing it. Back when they met Peter at Pinewood and he saw how hard they worked for Gerry Anderson, he asked them,

'Can you make a film?' They chorused, 'Of course we can,' and that was it. Peter had his new team.

According to Nigel, Peter was never in any doubt that the franchise could be continued. He remembers today:

> He was very funny but also analytical, a good businessman. One day, he made a joke about being egg-bound, and I had to break it to him that no one knew what that meant any more. But he dug in, he wasn't prepared to budge on it. His enthusiasm for the project was as strong as it had ever been.

Marc agrees. 'Peter was constantly believing it would be revived. I don't think he ever gave up. That was still his fun, producing the movies.'

For a while, it looked as though such faith would be rewarded, with plans to make 'Carry On London' being announced in 2003, almost making it to production and drawing in some big names. 'I had a telephone conversation with Burt Reynolds at one point, about an actual film I was making,' Nigel marvels now. 'Just to be able to say that is enough, really.'

At one point, he and Brian even made their way to Cannes Film Festival, thinking that what any self-respecting film mogul needed to do was hire a boat and park it in the port, where they could wave at stars like Andy Garcia and Quentin Tarantino across the water. 'That was when I looked across at Brian and asked him, "What are we actually doing here?" and Brian said, "I thought you knew." We almost fell over laughing, but that was quite an expensive joke on ourselves.'

Despite 'London' falling through, it seems Peter never lost faith in this pair of diehards, and rewarded their loyalty by contracting them the rights to Carry On. 'He was convinced it would one day get off the ground and he wanted to reward our efforts thus far,' remembers Nigel. 'He assigned Brian the rights to Carry On in the hope we'd somehow keep the flag flying.'

And that's exactly what the pair aims to do. Following a legal tussle over the trademark, which is now theirs by law, Brian and Nigel are intent on revisiting some of their original ideas, with one big question remaining - how should they approach the genre?

As Nigel explains:

Peter was adamant that all Carry On meant was the guarantee of a funny movie, not the cast and not the stories. It would do what it said on the tin and offer good comedy. The brand would pre-feed an audience so they were ready to laugh and react positively, which leaves the subject wide open.

Trying to work out how we're going to approach it … are we going to modernise it, make it of the now, or do we just do something that's on the dangerous side of Bernard Manning and see if we can get away with it? Bearing in mind you don't need to theatrically release any more, you can go straight out on a digital platform, so everything becomes much cheaper and less restrictive.

This pair of still-aspiring producers are clearly glass-half-full kind of people. Nigel continues:

We will get it going. Everyone will hate it, because there's no way you could do this and remain politically correct in any way. We've got no chance, hence the reason we have to do it. And besides, it's become part of the vernacular. It's a shorthand for anything British. So it's engrained in us that we carry on with it.

Would Peter approve? 'Absolutely,' smiles Nigel. He reflects:

He totally believed in it, and he knew nothing came easily, that ultimately you just have to commit to something, put your shoulder in and get on with it. That's what he did, he flew by the seat of his pants a lot, so yes, I like to think he'd approve.

50 per cent of people will think we should have left it, and the other 50 per cent might think it's brilliant. The trick is to get it right, otherwise it'll be a one-flop wonder, and we'll be back on that boat in Cannes, rubbing our chins and asking each other, 'What happened there?'

For me, the challenges of making any fresh films under the Carry On banner are two-fold, namely logistics and humour. How would they make them, and what would they make?

The first question is all about money. As playwright Terry Johnson points out to me, both the characters of Carry On films, and for the most part the people who played them, were non-aspirant working-class folk. 'Working-class audiences could relate to them, they could sense the shared origins and roots, and it meant they relaxed in their company.'

As much as those actors may have complained about the low wages Peter dished out over the years, it meant this authenticity on screen never changed. Recruiting such a copious, talented cast in the first place, let alone securing their services over and over again, for such meagre pay would be unthinkable these days. Back during the golden age of Carry On, actors had far fewer choices than are afforded to them now, particularly when it came to moving out of the class where audiences had initially come to know them. As Marc Sinden told us in defence of the actors accepting Peter's salaries, 'None of them had to do it.' But in opting for the professional security of returning to the Carry On fold, together they created a fictional universe that would be very hard to recreate.

And who would be up to the task of taking the baton from the likes of Kenneth, Sid or Hattie, seasoned actors all, who'd honed their craft in the theatre halls, radio and TV studios of the land? The names bandied around for 'Carry On London' back in 2003 included David Jason, Shane Richie, Danniella Westbrook and Vinnie Jones, and of course Nigel's new friend Burt Reynolds.

'I don't think there are the sort of talents around who could do it,' says Matthew Sweet, and I don't disagree with him. Comedic actors good enough to do it tend to have their own big budget projects going on, mostly in America, and definitely with the star so coveted by Charles very visible on the dressing room door. Any new project would definitely need comedic actors, not comedians, and as we saw all too painfully when the latter appeared in Carry On Columbus, there is an almighty difference.

Behind the scenes, too, you'd struggle to get the staff. Even for those times, Peter Rogers was a very unusual film producer in his insistence on keeping things cheap and cheerful. Just as he rejected the idea of attending press shows or turning up on the red carpet for a premiere of a film he had produced as 'narcissistic', equally he delighted in how consistently critics panned his Carry On catalogue. He said it was only what audiences thought that mattered. And how much would you have to pay for the skills of worker bee Gerald Thomas, if you could even find him in this country? The fees would start to look prohibitive.

The second, even bigger question is what passes for funny in this day and age. For a start, many of the targets of Carry On humour were national institutions that could withstand the rubber-ended arrows the team pelted at them. As Gerald Thomas explained of the films' humour, 'It never takes the mickey out of the institutions, but only the people in it. We don't want to make people frightened of hospitals and policemen and firemen, but we don't mind taking the fun out of the actual policemen themselves.'

His daughter Deborah is convinced that kind of humour wouldn't be taken well any more. 'It was meant as harmless humour and it was received harmlessly, but times have changed. We can't laugh at the hardworking staff of the NHS any more. We'd be taken out and burnt at the stake.'

While there's certainly sympathy and support for NHS employees, we feel so let down by other institutions that making them the targets of soft comedy might not feel biting enough. As Toby Young explained in a BBC Archive Hour dedicated to the films, 'They reflected fundamental deference and confidence that government can make things work. You can't make that joke anymore, the fact that things don't really work is the source of volcanic rage.'

Alongside his idea of the comedy not going far enough, Young provides for me the counter-argument, that for a present-day audience, much of vintage Carry On humour would be deemed too offensive. 'The Woke thought police would go bananas. It's not that Britain is no longer obsessed with class and sex, or beset by petty martinets wagging their fingers in our faces telling us what we can't do. It's just that you're not allowed to joke about these things.'

June Whitfield once spoke for many when she realised what little material any modern-day Carry On would have to work with, telling the BBC, 'Most comedy would go out of the window if PC took hold, there'd be nothing you could make fun of and that would never do.'

As for the actual gags themselves, Bernard Cribbins is among those who believe tastes have moved on. 'People are probably more sophisticated now,' he tells me, citing all the imports from America and other countries we're now treated to on the box and the big screen.

The elephant in the room, the thing I'm only finally mentioning, and reluctantly at that because after all I'm British, is sex. The best of Carry On was all about repression, what couldn't be said out loud, but could be suggested in between the bawdy, cheeky lines. They relied on our collective embarrassment at bodily functions, a suppressed list of desires for which innuendo and double entendre provided a comfortable outlet, particularly with the puns beautifully crafted by the tireless Talbot Rothwell, inspired by the seaside postcard humour of Donald McGill. They were saucy but they were gentle and always self-deprecating and diffident, reflecting a social sensibility that has all but disappeared. As Terry Johnson puts it to me, 'The interface between comedy and sex has dissolved almost to the point where it would be very hard to make anything remotely shocking. Without inhibition, where is the peril?'

Comedian and writer Robin Ince agrees, telling me:

A huge part of the Carry On films was the sexuality bursting out of these middle-aged men that couldn't be expressed. By the time you get to *Emmannuelle*, it's all on the screen, it's become available, and that stops the whole thing working so well.

Carry On worked best when it was about what lies in our heads, our secret desires. Once that secret lust was front page news, playing in cinemas and not confined to ropey Soho, it all fell apart. It wasn't their fault, it was the explosion of free love that happened from the late 1960s, or at least reported to happen.

It's similar to Hitchcock, who similarly had to work within the boundaries of what he was allowed to show. Very often, it's not about choice, it's about ingenuity, and when you no longer have to do that, something is lost.

Consider those coy ladies of *Camping*, suggesting their men-folk not go to the bother of putting up another tent, and ... instead sleep in the car. How could that work now? Ince laughs.

'Tastes have changed, and we're living in a post #MeToo world. All the women who wanted to would be sharing those tents, and those who didn't, wouldn't.'

The paradox lies in the fact that, while they couldn't possibly be made in the same way now, the films themselves don't date. In fact, because they are among the few of that era to bear modern-day viewings and they are so distinctive, they've ended up becoming their own genre, surviving long beyond their generation alongside the likes of Laurel and Hardy, Charlie Chaplin and Buster Keaton. As Ince points out, 'You can see just how few films of their era have survived, and celebrate the fact that the Carry Ons have managed it.'

With their perennial re-runs on TV, it appears that the Carry On catalogue has somehow withstood the unforgiving scrutiny applied to the likes of *It Ain't Half Hot Mum* and *Please Sir*, even the much more recent *Little Britain*. How have these films slipped under the door and escaped today's politically correct policemen (and women!)?

Matthew Sweet believes it's the constantly parodic aspect of the films that ensure the best of them survive:

> Because the things they sent up survive, like a Tarzan film or a period or costume drama, the Carry Ons mocking them still make sense. Whereas watching *Carry On Behind* is something that I think would be shocking and totally mystifying for anybody born this century, also a bit alarming.

For Toby Young, the same restrictions that held back the writers when they were made allow the scripts a certain amount of wriggle room now. Even if, as Kenneth Horne delightfully explained once, 'a double entendre has only one meaning', for Young, the sleight of hand required to ensure they got past the censors when the films were made is the same reason they can still get away with it today, just. He explains:

> They belong to a particular era in British post-war history when certain things couldn't be referred to directly, only obliquely. For example, it was okay to allude to anal intercourse, only you couldn't ever say the word 'arse'. So instead you get, 'I was only trying to keep warm' and 'the way the wind whistles up the pass'.

As for the films remaining on our TV screens, though, he isn't so optimistic. 'I expect they'll be verboten for a while, but rediscovered sitting on some dusty shelf by a future, less repressed generation.'

If we're somehow still allowed to watch these films when so many have gone by the wayside, why should we? What do they offer modern audiences? I mean beyond the fact that they offer everything we Brits enjoy the most – jokes about bodily functions, poking fun at those timeless targets of authority, pomposity and the relations between the sexes, women as nymphomaniacs or battleaxes, men as randy or impotent. Are we really as childish as all that? It would appear so. It's not really very complicated, but Peter Rogers never claimed it to be. Is there anything else?

For Matthew Sweet, it is that they contain meat as well as sauce, a huge tapestry of social documentation between all the gags. 'We were in a post-war world, rationing not far in the past, national service and the NHS, relations with institutions, plus periods of history.

'Just because the films are silly, that doesn't mean they don't have a richness. They say much about British feelings and character, plus our loss of prestige in the twentieth century. We lost the empire but we kept the bum joke.'

Those bum jokes are among some of the most finely crafted rude jokes ever made, according to him. 'They teach you a lot about comedic structure and the way language works,' he says. 'There's a lot going on in them, and there's nothing slack, it's all very tightly constructed.'

According to Sweet, the more contemporary titles like *Convenience* and *Loving* paint a portrait of Britain beyond swinging Carnaby Street, real life where women in headscarves pushed prams, and men went off to work and stole a pint on the way home. He says:

> The films were full of middle-aged characters hearing about everything going on in the 1960s, but missing out on it. The characters were expressing emotions of confusion, sexual frustration and other feelings that a lot of the audience would experience themselves.
>
> They offer a very powerful way to engage with the past. They're not totally museum pieces, because we're still shaped by that culture of the NHS, national service and so on, and it is still important in our sense of who we are. They're really sharp on those institutions, so while there are still institutions, the films make sense, plus they offer really good advice on how to survive these systems.

In his *Desert Island Discs* interview, Peter Rogers proudly claimed that he'd made thirty-one films out of one gag, and he likened producing the series to owning a sweet shop, explaining:

> If someone came in every week for liquorice allsorts and I said, 'Don't have those, dear, have these fancy chocolates from France or Belgium' and they took them away, they wouldn't come back again. I give people what they want. They're always true, you know. They're very nice people, the public. Very loyal indeed.

As for the films themselves, he delighted in their down-market appeal, saying, 'Nothing better than being common, I promise you.'

Sure enough, George Layton describes the feeling of watching a Carry On film these days as similar to pulling on 'a comfortable old cardigan from your wardrobe'. He says, 'People are very nostalgic for what they think of as the good old days. There was some dross as well, to be sure, but that's fallen away, and people feel very affectionately towards what is left.' For Hugh Futcher, it's like 'having a day out at the seaside'. For Sally Geeson, watching the films is 'fun, light relief. It's like catching up with your mates'.

Valerie Leon tells me she received a letter recently from a long-time fan who, during the anxiety of lockdown, had turned to his Carry On collection. 'He wanted to tell me how much comfort they'd brought him, how he'd found himself laughing out loud. It was a lovely letter.'

Bernard Cribbins, too, delights in what he calls 'the afterglow' of Carry On. 'I'll get a letter from a middle-aged fan saying, "I remember you in *Carry On Jack*" and I realise they were a teenager when they saw it. I've received lots of very long-term applause.'

What is the secret of all this widespread and enduring devotion to a series of films whose best days passed almost half-a-century ago?

Nigel Gordon-Stewart is convinced that Peter Rogers's superpower was in 'occupying the psyche of every man from a schoolboy to a pensioner, and working out what would make them giggle'.

Sid James's daughter Sue is a successful children's TV producer and she's convinced that the same things that work well for very young children – repetition, humour, being able to anticipate what is coming next – are the same things we delight in Carry On. 'In a way, they offer the same thing.

You know what's coming, especially after you've seen it seventeen times, but still you laugh.'

For Toby Young, the appeal of the films lies in their inclusivity, that they always take the side of the little guy, that there is always a very democratic spirit at play, seeking to redress the balance of unearned superiority. He cites Don Quixote, the high-minded hero of Cervantes' novel but, more importantly, Sancho Panza, the down-to-earth squire who is Quixote's comic foil. Young tells me Cervantes could easily be describing Sid James. 'He is your unofficial self, the voice of the belly protesting against the soul,' he recites from an essay by George Orwell. 'His tastes lie towards safety, soft beds, no work, pots of beer and women with voluptuous figures.' Young adds, 'It is that saturnalian streak in the British character that the Carry On films represent.'

I thank him and quickly reach for a dictionary to check exactly what he means by 'saturnalian'. Ah, there it is: 'Of unrestrained and intemperate jollity. Riotously merry.' Bang on the nose.

Comedy writer Meryl O'Rourke relishes the chance of re-watching a group of actors and actresses 'working at the top of their game, the best actors in the country, making up an ensemble cast that could never be replicated now'.

Robin Ince agrees, and it turns out he was at that same wonderful one-man show by Jim Dale back in 2015 that I attended, the one where I sat transfixed by the sight of Derek Jacobi blowing air-kisses from his seat in front of me. Ince, however, was concentrating on the man on stage. He recalls:

It was a masterclass in how to hold an audience. That charisma and energy stood in total contradiction to his age, and it summarises for me the one thing that all the Carry On stars did, they always played it with utter conviction. It didn't matter that the scripts were sometimes terrible, the same jokes over and over again. It was their performances that elevated the material.

There are so many British comedy films in the style of Carry On that don't have the same level of performer, and you can see instantly they lack these people who were just perfect. The people who gave us pitch perfect performances, they were crucial.

You'd think knowing so much about the stars behind the roles on screen would prevent us being able to lose ourselves in the stories, but, if anything, after all these years, that understanding of their often troubled real lives adds an extra layer of richness. 'It gives us embroidery with enough levels for something to survive beyond the saucy postcard it was originally intended to be,' says Ince.

Matthew Sweet agrees:

> Our knowledge of their hinterlands changes our relationship hugely with the films. As a child, I started watching them for the plots, I actually worried for Bernard Cribbins in *Carry On Jack*, or the spies in *Carry On Spying*. Then it was all about the jokes and the historical detail. Now when I watch them, the knowledge of what the cast went through becomes more important – the laughter and sometimes the agony behind the camera, it does carry an odd sort of charge.

With the writers understanding their cast so well and increasingly creating lines for specific members to say, I wonder where acting stops and something more personal begins. Sweet is convinced it's still acting – 'they're not front of cloth people' – but agrees there's something deeper on display, more revealing of the personalities involved, and this is where I believe the magic really resides in these films, in the chemistry between the members of this extraordinary cast, who committed wholeheartedly to the universe they created together. On screen and off, they stuck together tightly, invariably opting for the comfort of company over the solitude of success.

'It's sheer entertainment, just sit back and giggle.' (Sid James)

While contemporary writers like Noël Coward set plays in aspirational settings on hotel balconies and ocean liners, Carry On's modern-set films concentrated on the challenges but also the pleasures of a more achievable reality, depicting suburban lives well, if mischievously, led. Aspiration is explored but ultimately quashed. We see this from the early days of *Sergeant* where Grimshawe's best men are those right in front of him, and *Teacher*, where school principal Wakefield decides to stay put, through to *Abroad* where every overseas traveller is happy and relieved to head back home and are at their happiest in the local pub. Considering all the fruity eyeballing, there is surprisingly little sexual conquest. From the hills of *Khyber* to the factory floor of *Convenience*, revolutions and rebellions are withstood. The message is clear: strive in whichever direction you like, but true contentment is to be found in the here and now, with everything and everyone in their rightful order.

Sweet calls the films 'a map of our fantasies about the past', while comedian Bob Mills describes the Carry On world as one which never existed in real life, because England was never really that pleasant. But, he adds, 'We like to believe it could have been.'

Obviously, I'm far too young to know if he's right or wrong, but it is a sweet world that Carry On created to be sure – one of foiled capers, misunderstandings and mayhem, pomposity that was pricked, romance that was rescued and, through it all, the twin glories of mockery and affection, or comedy and comradeship.

Watching the catalogue in its entirety reveals men and women all bursting with strong desires but no one ever successfully betraying another, and nor do figures of authority ever get away with any exploitation of power, whether they be Caesar or Matron. Instead, in thirty deceptively simple capers, the films explore institutions – the NHS, the monarchy, the empire, the armed forces, the police and trade unions. They delight in our customs – camping, holidaying abroad, beauty contests, big budget films. They provide us with an intimate social and cultural snapshot of post-war Britain, and they send a timeless message that if we stick together for collective warmth and look on the bright side, we can laugh and survive. It may be a message we need now more than ever.

'Give us the fools and we will finish the job.'
(Kenneth Williams in *That's Carry On!*)

Not bad for a motley cast and crew who turned up on time, learned their lines, hit their marks and seldom knew the luxury of a second take. Many of them may now be gone, but their contribution to Carry On means they remain vibrant and colourful in our memories. As Sue James says of her father, 'I regret my children didn't meet him, but we're very lucky that through his work, we can still share all his warmth and humour. That is the great consolation.'

Now, as I stand in the forecourt of Pinewood Studios, about to make my departure, I look back one final time to doff my cap to Sid and his company, that diverse bunch of actors forming their repertory theatre of the cinema as Jim Dale so aptly described it.

If I squint, I can see Sid, sharing a big smile for newcomers to the set before opening his paper and turning straight to the racing pages, Hattie looking up from her crossword to offer a kind word, Charles tending to his mother with his lemonade bottles clinking in his bag, Barbara and Joan giggling along while Kenneth holds court.

Behind them I can see Peter Rogers and Gerald Thomas, smartly dressed for another day at the office, Peter dreaming of a franchise that could go on forever, Gerald focused only on the day's filming ahead.

It is all these people I'm thinking of, as I head back to my car, return my visitor's pass and drive slowly out through the gates of Pinewood. I am reluctant to leave this wonderful world behind but I am comforted by the sound of their laughter ringing still in my ears.

Research Credits

Books

Bright, Morris and Ross, Robert, *Mr Carry On: The Life and Work of Peter Rogers* 2002

Bright, Morris, *Pinewood Studios: 70 Years of Fabulous Filmmaking* 2007

Davies, Russell (ed.) *The Kenneth Williams Diaries* 1994

Goodwin, Cliff, *Sid James: A Biography* 2011

Lewis, Roger, *Charles Hawtrey, The Man Who Was Private Widdle* 2002

Merriman, Andy, *Hattie: The Authorised Biography* 2011

Ross, Andrew, *Too Happy a Face: The Authorised Biography of Joan Sims* 2015

Ross, Roger, *Carry On Companion* 2002

Ross, Robert, *The Carry On Story* 2005

Williams, Kenneth, *Just Williams: An Autobiography* pub 2009

Windsor, Barbara, *Barbara Windsor: All of Me* 2012

TV Sources

Carry on Forever, Film Night, BBC 1970

Movie Memories, BBC 1984

Joan Sims interview, TV-AM 1987

Wogan: Kenneth Williams interviews Barbara Windsor, BBC 1986

Seriously Seeking Sid, C4 1992

South Bank Show: Kenneth Williams, LWT 1994

Barbara Windsor on the *Mrs Merton Show*, BBC 1995

Best of British: Barbara Windsor BBC 1998

Peter Rogers, interview with Helen Jameson 1998

Carry On Darkly documentary, C4 1998

Heaven and Earth Show, BBC 2000

The Unforgettable Joan Sims, ITV 2001

The Unforgettable Hattie Jacques, ITV 2001

The Unforgettable Kenneth Williams, ITV 2001

Heroes of Comedy: Hattie Jacques, C4 2002

Kenneth Williams Story: A Reputations Special, BBC 2002

Hattie, BBC4 2011

The Many Faces of Sid James, BBC 2012

John Le Mesurier: It's All Been Rather Lovely, BBC 2012

Radio Sources
Radio 4 Extra: *Hancock's Helpers*, BBC 2004
Barbara Windsor in Russell Brand interview, BBC 2008
BBCRadio: *Comediennes Hattie Jacques* 2008
BBCRadio: *Barbara Windsor's Funny Girls* 2011
Radio 4: *Sid James: Not Just a Dirty Laugh*, BBC 2013
BBC Radio: Archive on 4, *Tears of a Clown* 2014

Letters
Gerald Thomas Collection, British Film Institute

Interviews
Dave Ainsworth
Brian Baker
Dave Benson
Tony Bilbow
Stephen Bourne
Gyles Brandreth
Kenneth Cope
Bernard Cribbins
Russell Davies
Angela Douglas
Hugh Futcher
Sally Geeson
Nigel Gordon-Stewart
Sarah Hollywood
Deborah Hunter
Robin Ince
Steve James
Sue James
Terry Johnson
Tony Jordan
George Layton
Valerie Leon
Andy Merriman
Meryl O'Rourke
Jamie Rees
Marc Sinden
Matthew Sweet
Barbara Thomas
Toby Young
Dan Zeff

Index